EAST COKER
A Village Album

Rock Cottage (now The Beeches) at Yew Hill Rocks c.1898. *Caroline Langdon (née Murley, 1851–1937) stands at the door of her cottage with her grand-daughter Violet Sophia Mockeridge in her arms.*

EAST COKER

A Village Album

Compiled by
Abigail Shepherd

Coker Books

Mabel Dodge marries Arthur Mead: a wedding photograph taken on the 13th July 1904 near the bride's home at Redlands.

First published in 1997 for the East Coker Society
by Coker Books, P.O. Box 2305, Bath BA1 5XY

ISBN 0 9531910 0 1

Designed and typeset by Malcolm Preskett
Printed in England by Biddles Ltd, Guildford, Surrey

Contents

Foreword 7
Acknowledgements 8

Peacocks at Coker Court 11
The Boucher Family at Coker Marsh 17
Watching the Soldiers March By 23
A Village Family 37
The Garden Boy 47
Grandmother's Extra-Strongs 57
Cider-Making by Moonlight 67
Apple Crazy 75
A Band of Children 85
Running Errands 95
Darvole Races 107
Count Your Blessings 113
Sulphur in Treacle 115
The Vickery Man 121
The Passing Bell 129
The Cricket Field 135
Hyde Farm in the 1920s 143
From Quilling Boy to Weaver 147
Cooking for Queen Mary 151
Charlie Dances the Twilight Waltz 155
Blue Skies and Spitfires 157
T. S. Eliot 188

Maps of East Coker 189
Sources 192

EAST COKER is a large parish and village, 3 miles south-west from Yeovil station on the Great Western railway and 1 mile north from Sutton Bingham station on the main line of the London and South Western railway, in the Southern division of the county, Houndsborough, Barwick and Coker hundred, Yeovil petty sessional division, union and county court district, rural deanery of Merston, archdeaconry of Wells and diocese of Bath and Wells. The church of St. Michael is a building of stone in the Perpendicular style, consisting of chancel, nave of three bays, aisles, transepts, north porch and an embattled tower on the east side of the north transept with a pierced arcaded parapet and small pinnacles, and an elegant octagonal stair turret at the north-east angle rising above the parapet, and relieved by string courses continued from the tower; it contains a clock with chimes, and 8 bells: the stained west window is a memorial to George Bullock esq. of North Coker House, d. 1885, and the east window to Maria Caroline (Grove), his wife, d. 2nd Feb. 1866: in the north transept is a memorial window to Emily Lucy (Portman), first wife of George Troyte-Chafyn-Grove esq. d. 8th Nov. 1856, aged 19: in the north transept are several mural tablets to the Bullock family, dating from 1753: a brass to George Bullock esq. mentioned above, and memorials to the Skinner family, 1769-1806, and to Thomas Leaves, of Pendomer, d. 1717, and his wife, d. 1724: there are also memorial brasses to the Rev. Rowland Huyshe, a former vicar, and to William Dampier, born at East Coker in 1651, and died in London, 1715: the reredos was presented by the present Mrs. Troyte-Chafyn-Grove, who also partially re-seated the church at her own expense; the remainder of the nave was re-seated and re-floored in 1896, and in 1897 hot water apparatus was laid down at a total cost of £300: there are sittings for 434 persons. The register dates from the year 1560, and there is a list of vicars extending from the 13th century. The living is a vicarage, net yearly value £231, with residence, in the gift of the Dean and Chapter of Exeter, and held since 1877 by the Rev. Charles Powell B.A. of London University. The great tithes, commuted at £335, are administered by the Ecclesiastical Commissioners, £55 thereof being granted to the augmentation of the living. The cemetery, one acre and a half in extent, with two mortuary chapels, was formed in 1877 at a cost of £555, and is under the control of the Parish Council, acting as a burial board. In the parish are almshouses, founded by Archdeacon Helyar about 1640, for eleven women and one man, who receive 3s. 6d. per week each. The ancient manor house, said to have been the birthplace, in 1651, of William Dampier, the circumnavigator, is now a farm house, and retains some interesting portions of the original building, erected in the Perpendicular period, including a spacious porch of two storeys, with a large recessed and moulded entrance arch and a square-headed two-light window above; there is a similar window on one side of the porch, and the main block has two lofty pointed windows, formerly belonging to the hall; these are of two lights each, with transoms and trefoil heads, and in the head of each window is a pentagonal opening; the remainder of the house has been much modernised. In 1753 the foundations of a Roman villa and tesselated pavement were discovered here. Coker Court, the property and residence of Major Godfrey Clement Walker Heneage M.V.O., J.P. and Mrs. Heneage, is a fine structure, situated on the side of a hill close to the church, overlooking a fine expanse of country: the main portion of the building is of the Tudor period, with a Georgian east wing; the west wing was rebuilt in 1900. North Coker House, the seat of George Troyte-Chafyn-Grove esq. D.L., J.P., F.S.A. is a modern mansion of Ham stone. Naish Priory, the property of G. Troyte-Chafyn-Grove esq. is an interesting building of the 14th and 15th centuries, and contains a chapel, with a fine east window, refectory, hall and dormitory; it was restored and added to in 1899, and is now in the occupation of Richard Earle Welby esq. Mrs. G. C. Walker Heneage and George Troyte-Chafyn-Grove esq. are the principal landowners. The soil is sandy loam: the subsoil is clay and sandy loam. The chief crops are wheat, beans, barley, roots and a large portion of land in pasture. The area is 2,185 acres; rateable value, £5,522; the population in 1901 was 798.

North Coker, half a mile north; Burton, 1¼ north-west; Hew Hill, 1½ north-west; and Naish, 1½ north, are hamlets in this parish.

Parish Clerk, Felix Drake esq.

Acting Parish Clerk, Walter Noble.

Post, M. O. & T. Office, North Coker.—Sidney Thorne, sub-postmaster. Letters from Yeovil arrive at 6.45 a.m. & 3.20 p.m.; sundays, 7.20 a.m.; dispatched at 8.20 a.m. & 12.50 & 6.35 p.m.; sundays, 11.50 a.m

Wall Letter Boxes, Up Coker, cleared at 8.15 a.m. & 12.45 & 6 p.m.; sunday, 11.30 a.m.; Hew Hill, cleared at 7.25 a.m. & 5 p.m. week days only; Naish, cleared at 7.45 a.m. & 4.45 p.m.; sunday, 8.10 a.m

County Police Station, George Edward Gould, constable

Public Elementary School (mixed & infants), for East Coker, Pendomer & Sutton Bingham, built in 1851, for 250 children; average attendance, 120; Sydney Edward Webber, master

PRIVATE RESIDENTS.

Dodge Herbert, School house
Drake Felix, Estate cottage, East Coker
Harrison Mrs. The Poplars
Mayo Herbert H. Worsfold, Devonshire cottage
Moore Miss
Powell Rev. Charles B.A. Vicarage
Preston James Guy Houlbrooke, Bubspool house
Troyte-Chafyn-Grove George D.L., J.P., F.S.A. North Coker house
Vere Miss, Mill house
Walker Heneage Major Godfrey Clement M.V.O., J.P. Coker court; & at Compton Basset, Calne, Wilts & 61 Grosvenor street, London W
Welby Richard Earle, Naish priory

COMMERCIAL.

Chalk Charles, gardener to R. E. Welby esq
Cemetery (Sydney Edward Webber, clerk to the burial board)
Cox Mary Ann (Mrs.), grocer
Crumpler Jesse, farm bailiff to George Troyte-Chafyn-Grove esq. Home fm
Derryman Henry, farmer, Paviott's
Dickenson James M. farm bailiff to Major G. C. Walker-Heneage
Drake Felix & Co. webbing & twine manufacturers, North Coker mills; London office, 2 Paternoster buildings, Newgate street E C. Telegrams, "Drake, North Coker"
Gatcombe Albert Charles, farmer
Gilham Thomas Henry, gardener to Major G. C. Walker-Heneage J.P
Granger Charles, farmer, Burton
Greenslade Albert, farmer
Hackwell Charles, carpenter
Helyar Alice (Mrs.), grocer
Helyar Charles, assistant overseer
Hooper Henry, boot maker
Lacey Charles, thatcher
Marsh Thomas, beer retailer
Mitchell Emmanuel, gardener to Geo. Troyte-Chafyn-Grove esq
Moger Robert, farmer, Darvole
Noble Walter, blacksmith, & acting parish clerk
Perry Benjamin, carpenter
Perry Jsph. blacksmith, & saw mills
Perry Sarah (Mrs.), farmer, Burton
Poole William, beer retailer, Hew hill
Pulman Tom, baker
Smart John, farmer, Burton
Somerset Public House Trust Co. Ltd. New inn (Sydney Trout, mgr)
Spinney Rt. Geo. frmr. Skinner's hl
Stagg Henry, boot maker
Stagg Joseph, market gardnr. Burton
Tanner Arthur John, farmer
Thorne Sidney, grocer, Post office
Turner Matthew, farmer
Wall Levi, market gardener

From Kelly's Directory of the County of Somerset, 1910.

Foreword

I cannot begin to say how much joy these pictures and wonderful rambling reminiscences have given me. This is real rural history: without confection or unnecessary grammatical intrusion. Here we have the genuine voice of a village. T.S. Eliot may have written famously about East Coker's beginning and end. This book gives us everything in between – in a warm, accessible way.

I sold my bike (for ten shillings) and left East Coker in 1955 and in moments of contemplation have regretted it ever since. This was where I grew up in a thatched cottage, perfumed by the flowers that my father grew around the door. This was where I went to school – twice caned by Mr Murley – walked up across the Park regularly on my own to the bluebells of Spin Wood, and played in the village cricket team.

It was where my father worked on the estate and my mother was once parlour maid; where, privy to the guest-list at Coker Court, I climbed into a thick yew hedge, lost my balance and tumbled onto the upper lawn within ten yards of Queen Mary and Mrs Walker-Heneage. As an eight year old, I turned and ran. My baseless fear was that my father might get the sack.

This is a book full of love for the village. It is as authentic as the carter's wagon I can still see – and the dry dung on the road that I can still smell. The interviewees are eloquent in their true village tongue. They talk as their parents did before them.

The pages have happily re-acquainted me with cherished names from my childhood: head gardener Tom Gilham and his wife, Minnie, whose consuming interest always seemed to be Yeovil Town Football Club … Gilbie Neville, strong as an ox, ringing the tenor on Sunday morning, false teeth on the table at home … 'Daisy' Langdon and his fiddle … Johnny Hibbs who called for the rags 'n' bones and would at times sleep with loyal wife, Carrie, in a hedgerow just beyond Coker Marsh ….

I had almost forgotten Mr Bath's little bus, on which my mother went to Yeovil for the shopping on a Friday, once a month. But how could I possibly forget the Sunday School outings in the Barlow & Phillips charabancs, so thrilling to children craning their necks for the first glimpse of the sea at Weymouth? What glorious innocence these memories recapture for us.

The book is, in its unassuming way, a piece of social history and a romantic record of ordinary people, rich in their own education. Above all, its pages are laden with affection.

David Foot

Acknowledgements

To begin at the beginning, my love and thanks to my parents Barbara and Clem Shepherd: to mum for her original idea of producing a book about the village, and to dad – I couldn't have started or finished this book without you.

East Coker – A Village Album has taken shape from a series of interviews, taped over a few years, and a growing collection of old photographs. I am deeply grateful to everyone whose name is listed opposite for their contributions, which have made everything possible. Special thanks go to Archie Beales, Joan and Alec Boucher, Mrs Florence Higgins, Dot and Alb Hughes, Doreen and Jim Hunt, Mrs A. Quick, Ralph Stevens and Mrs Hilda Turner, all of whom I visited on many occasions, and whose words tell so much of the story contained in this book.

I am indebted to Gerry Smith and Ralph Stevens for letting me use their photographs and postcards of the village: nearly a third of the photographs in *A Village Album* came from Gerry's own collection which he has been building up over the years, and continues to add to; Ralph Stevens travelled to numerous collectors' fairs and searched out some wonderful old postcards of East Coker which I am proud to be able to include in this book. Thank you to Martin Salzer for making copies of original photographs for Gerry Smith; and to Bryan Evans (W.H. Rendell photographers, Yeovil) who has copied hundreds of old photographs for this project.

For background information I have drawn on the archives of East Coker British Legion, Parish Council, and Women's Institute; East Coker School (Peter Sweetlove, headmaster); and St Michael's church (The Revd David Hunt, vicar of East Coker). Other sources have been Yeovil Library (Robin Ansell, Reference Librarian); Somerset Record Office; Somerset Cricket Museum (G.A. Stedall, Curator); Clare College, Cambridge (Ann Keith, Librarian); English Folk Dance and Song Society (Malcolm Taylor, Librarian); Imperial War Museum (Catherine Moriarty, National Inventory of War Memorials); the Royal Horticultural Society (Miss J. Vine, Assistant Librarian); and the Heather Society (A. Small, Administrator). My thanks to all of the above individuals and organisations, and to everyone who has helped with pieces of information – lending newspaper cuttings and other documents; suggesting books to read or people to contact; or putting names to places on a map.

To Malcolm Preskett – a big thank you for designing *East Coker – A Village Album* so beautifully, for giving me a deadline, and helping me to reach it! Your guidance has been invaluable.

I am grateful to East Coker Village Hall Committee for permission to use the painting of the old post office on the cover of this book, and to Tony Bolton for photographing it. Thank you to Ted Hatch who drew the immaculate maps on pp.189–91; John Horwood for his illustrations; Ros Blackmore for printing the 1918 W.I. plate; John Carter, Lesley Lindsay, Margaret Mainprize, Penny Marpole, Sheilagh Smith, and Bill Williams for providing additional taped interviews; and to Sarah Gould, Chris Hilborne, Teresa Nicholls, Pat Robinson, and Angela Windmill at the Copyshop, Yeovil.

Compiling this book has become a way of life for me over the last four years, and at every stage so many people have willingly given me their time, help and encouragement. This is your book – thank you for giving it to me.

Abigail Shepherd

Trudy Aitken
Mrs Ennyd Andrews
Charlie Axe
Pam Axe
Mary Baker
Daphne Bayley
Archie Beales
Amelia Bennett
Rosemary Best
Anne and Clive Bingley
Joan and Alec Boucher
Maurice Bramwell
Jonathan Cledwyn-Davis
Jean Coleberd
Alan Cornelius
Leo Davis
Miss Joan Daw
Catherine and Peter Denney
Alan Dening
Betty Drake
Flora Duley
Eddie Dunning
John Dunning
Mrs Mary Farrar
David Foot
Percy Francis
Geoff Gilham
Joyce Griffin
Roger Hackwell
Margaret Haward
Doris and Bill Hawkins
Ed Hawkins
Simon Heneage
Timothy Heneage
Mrs Florence Higgins
Ivy and Tom Hodges
Mrs Peggy Horsley (née Cole)
Bill Hughes
Dot and Alb Hughes
Mrs Joan Hughes
Olive Hughes
The Revd David Hunt
Doreen and Jim Hunt
Mabel Johnson (née Dening)
Nesta Kingsmill (née Perry)
Bill Legg
Mrs Margaret Legget (née Mead)
Miss A. Lewis
Mrs S. Lewis
Mary Loarridge
Mrs Bessie Lock
Jenny Lumley
Mrs Lilian Luscombe
Midge and David Matthew
Dorothy May
Wendy and John McCann
Gloria and Bob Mead
Christine and Peter Mead
The Revd Michael Meech
Aubrey Moger
Midge Moores
Elaine Morgan
Jessie Morton
The Revd George Mullard
Don Murley
Mavis and Ray Murley
The Neville girls
Robert Oaksford
Miss Letitia Page
Archie Partridge
B.C. Paull
Muriel and Doug Pilton
Jean Pomeroy
David Pryor
The Revd E.J. Pulman
Mrs A. Quick
Bert Rendell
Dr Kingsley Rendell
Mamie Richard
Miss J. Richards
Gladys and Stan Russell
Betty Samways
Peter Sebag-Montefiore
Pete Shutler
Betty Skinner
Gerry Smith
Mary Snell (née Crumpler)
Mrs Lorna Spearing (née Thorne)
Ron Stagg
Alan Stevens
Molly Stevens
Ralph Stevens
St Michael's bellringers
David Sutcliffe
Joan and Alan Taylor
James Thomson-Bree
Mrs Hilda Turner
Joyce Warren
Nancy White
Mrs G. Winfield

For my mother
Barbara Shepherd
with love

Peacocks at Coker Court

Thomas Gilham (1865–1946) was the Head Gardener for the Coker Court estate from 1902 to 1945. In 1938 he featured in a BBC radio broadcast called 'Coker Court', part of a series of programmes about West Country houses. The programme was a dramatised history of the Court, with Thomas Gilham acting as the guide on a fictional walk around the house. In the first few minutes he shares childhood memories with the Interlocutor and the radio audience.

INTER: Well, I want to learn all there is to know about Coker Court and I'm told you're the best man for the job.
GILHAM: H'm! There must be a lot of history in the old place that even I don't know. It's a good bit older than I am after all. Between six and seven hundred years old, Coker Court. And I'm only 70.
INTER: That makes you sound quite a youngster.
GILHAM: Yes. Still, I've been Head Gardener here since

The circular lawn in front of Coker Court c.1883. *The two children are Weston and Dorothy Helyar, probably accompanied by their mother Gertrude Violet and grandmother Theodora, a French lady known in the village as Madame Helyar.*

1902. And you don't work on a place all that time without learning a bit about it – and caring for it too.
INTER: I can quite understand that, Mr Gilham.
GILHAM: This is the Tudor front we're looking at now. The arch above the door is the oldest part of it – 14th century – same as the pointy windows of the great hall there, on your left.
INTER: I see.
GILHAM: Now this bit of lawn we're standing on – in the middle of this circular drive – this brings back one of my earliest memories. Tea parties we used to have on it when I was a little nipper. Grandmother of Mrs Walker-Heneage, our present lady, old Madame Helyar was ... I can just see the butler coming out under that porch there as if 'twere yesterday, with cake and bread-and-jam in great laundry baskets – and all us village children sitting round the circle on our little stools, with our tin mugs tied round our necks. And he used to say, 'Who shouts cake? And who shouts bread-and-jam?' And then you'd hear something! Then he'd put some food down in the middle of the circle for the peacock, and the peacock would come and peck away at it, and spread his great tail out, right bang in the middle of us all. There's a lot of the older folk in the village can remember those tea-parties still.

The main staircase at Coker Court with portraits of the Helyar family who lived there for over 300 years.

The Paintings Wink at Little Baba

On the 17th March 1884 Horace Augustus Helyar of Coker Court, then serving as a diplomat in The Hague, wrote this letter to his four-year-old daughter Dorothy, and her five-year-old brother Weston.

My dearest little Baba,

Thank you very much for your letter and the pretty sachet, and many times for the lovely lock of hair you have sent me which I shall always value and keep carefully in remembrance of little Baba.

Isn't it nice to be back at Coker again, and see the same old pictures looking down at you when you come downstairs, and don't you think they sometimes wink at you and say 'We see you little Baba, once we were as small as you and walked about and danced in the hall, but we didn't wear such funny clothes as you do'.

Now you look next time and tell me if they don't say that only you must look very hard at them or you won't see them wink.

Much love and a kiss for you and another you must give Weston,

from your loving father,

H.A. Helyar

1881 Snow Memories

Joseph Whetham (1877–1964) farmed at Bryant's Farm, Pendomer, for over 40 years. He then moved to Skinner's Hill Farm, East Coker, and in later life made notes about the history of the village. Here he writes about the great snows of 1881, which made a lasting impression on him as a small boy.

My father took a dairy of 25 shorthorn dairy cows from the late Lionel Harrison Esq, owner of Naish Priory Farm, East Coker. The usual time to take over the cows was the 2nd February. The dairy house being empty we moved in on the 16th January from Hewish, Crewkerne. It began snowing on the 17th and continued more or less for two days and two nights. I remember my father clearing the snow from the kitchen window to let the light in.

The sunken lanes around Naish Priory were filled with drifting snow to the level of the ground and in some places in these lanes it was 12 to 15 feet deep. All cattle were moved to the stock yards and sheltered places. Most of the farmers kept Dorset Horn sheep. They were fortunate to have their lambing season over, as many had to be dug out of snowdrifts and some died from suffocation.

Joseph and Mabel Whetham: Joseph was three years old when his parents moved to East Coker in 1881; the next day it started to snow and the village was snow-bound for three weeks.

Squire Helyar and Squire Bullock organised two gangs of men to clear a cart track from the outskirts to the centre of the village. The farmers supplied them with bread and cheese and cider. The men were kept busy shovelling snow for over a week for the butcher, baker and grocer to deliver food. The average depth of the snow was from five to seven feet.

Severe frost set in on the snow which lasted for nearly three weeks, making travelling very difficult. The sun melted the snow by day, then froze at night. The fields became a sheet of ice. Fortunately the snow kept the root and potato caves from being frosted. The pumps were frozen – people had to draw their water from the wells in those days, there was no piped water in the village. The schools were closed for three weeks as the children living in the isolated parts were unable to get to school.

The blacksmith and his two apprentices were kept busy roughing and frost-nailing shoes for horses. The millponds were frozen, the miller could not grind the corn, the water-wheel being jammed with blocks of ice. Soup was sent around to the old people from the kitchens of North Coker House and Coker Court and farmers gave them wood to burn in their fires to keep them warm.

Fortunately we had a wonderful thaw as the snow gradually melted, leaving some nice luscious grass for the cattle. Snow could be seen in the distance on the Dorset Hills for nearly two months after.

A Handcart Full of Apples

Another of Joseph Whetham's early memories was of George Bullock (1797–1885) of North Coker House (now Coker House). His son, another George, assumed the name of Troyte-Bullock in 1852, and Troyte Chafyn-Grove in 1892. These last initials can be seen on the porch of the old Village Hall (now North Coker Hall).

George Bullock Esq handed over his estate to his son George Troyte-Bullock and moved to the cottage which is now the Village Hall taking with him several old servants including William Hurst his faithful coachman and his single horse brougham. He was well versed in the old Somerset dialect. He was a favourite with the children, him living near the school, addressing them as 'Chills lets zee thee copy book', if the work was good he crossed their hands with a piece of silver. I can well remember a man passing through Coker with a handcart of ripe apples, he bought the lot and gave them to the children.

A Homecoming

Dorothy Helyar celebrated her 21st birthday on the 10th November 1900, and a few days later returned to East Coker with her mother to mark the occasion. They were given a very warm welcome, and Dorothy hinted that she would soon return to Coker Court to live. The day's events were reported in the Western Gazette *of the 16th November.*

Dorothy Helyar in 1892, the same year that her only brother Weston died at Winchester College aged 13. Her father Horace Augustus Helyar died in March 1893. After her mother's remarriage – to Lord Savile – in November 1894, Dorothy's home became Rufford Abbey in Nottinghamshire. Two estate cottages in East Coker, built in 1914, were named after her mother and brother – Violet and Weston.

Coming of Age of Miss Helyar

SATURDAY last was the 21st anniversary of the birthday of Miss Dorothy Helyar, daughter of Lady Savile, and in honour of her coming-of-age the church bells were rung morning and evening, and guns were fired. The young lady now comes into possession of the East Coker estate, which since the death of her father had been held by trustees, and a telegram of congratulation from the tenantry and villagers was sent to her during the day…

Miss Helyar, accompanied by her mother, Lady Savile, arrived at Sutton Bingham railway station on Wednesday evening, and an interesting scene was witnessed, fog signals being let off and the church bells rung in honour of the occasion. The rector (Rev. W.H. Helyar *of Sutton Bingham*) greeted Miss Helyar on behalf of the parishoners, who are all tenants on her estate. In their name and in his own he wished her long life, health, happiness and prosperity in that beautiful Court, which had been the home of the Helyars for 300 years. He then called upon the people who had flocked round the carriage to give three cheers for Miss Helyar, which was heartily responded to. Cheers were given for Lady Savile and Mrs Helyar, senior, who in past years have done so much for the good of those who lived on the estate.

The festivities in honour of the occasion were held yesterday (Thursday), and the village of East Coker and the surrounding neighbourhood was quite *'en fête'*, despite the showery weather which prevailed. The bells of the church were rung merrily at intervals, and parts of the village were gaily decorated with flags etc. Several arches with appropriate mottoes were also erected, and near to the entrance of the field was an arch of evergreens.

At three o'clock the tenant farmers and their wives were entertained to a sumptuous dinner in a spacious marquee erected in a field close to the entrance to the Park. About 60 guests were present, and they were presided over by Colonel J.R.P. Gooden of Compton House. Those present included the vicar (the Rev. C. Powell), and Messrs Witcombe, Sandiford, Marsh (Barwick), Ridout, junior, Vowles, W. Bowles, A. Caplen, O.J. Rowles, Webber, C. Hackwell, J. White etc. The whole of the catering was excellently carried out by Mr C.W. Mead, of the *New Inn*, East Coker, and reflected much credit upon him. A string band from Yeovil played pleasing selections of music during the dinner…

Towards the end of the dinner Miss Helyar, accompanied by Lady Savile, Mrs Phillips (Coker Court), Mrs Arthur Helyar, and Miss Helyar, of Sutton Bingham, arrived, and were greeted with very hearty cheers…

Mr O.J. Rowles proposed 'The health of Miss Helyar'. He congratulated her on attaining her majority, and hoped she would live for many years, and often go about amongst them. He was given to understand she was likely to reside there in the near future, and he trusted this was so. (Loud applause)…

The Rev. C. Powell remarked that it gave him great pleasure, on behalf of many subscribers – first in saying how highly delighted they were to have Miss Helyar amongst them, and then to welcome her to the parish, to congratulate her on attaining her majority, and to wish

ABOVE: *Lt.-Col. Godfrey Walker-Heneage, Grenadier Guards, DSO, MVO, DL, JP (1868–1939). He retired from the army in 1904, but rejoined and served in the 1914–18 war when he was mentioned five times in despatches and awarded the DSO in 1917. Colonel Heneage sold his own estate in Wiltshire a few years after the end of the war; the two cottages in the Park, built around the time of the sale, are named after the Colonel's estate – Compton Bassett.*

LEFT: *Dorothy Walker-Heneage (1879–1947) with her son David. Dorothy, the last of the Helyar line, married Godfrey Walker-Heneage on the 18th January 1902, and their son David was born on the 4th December the same year.*

her a very long life. He was glad she was so old (laughter and applause) – and also that she was so young – old, that she would enter into the enjoyment of her inheritance, and young that she had the full tide of her life before her. He wished her a long and happy life (applause). He knew she had a warm place in her heart for East Coker...

Miss Helyar, who was enthusiastically received, said she thanked them very much for the perfectly beautiful present, and said she would always have the greatest thought and affection for them all. She hoped to live amongst them and to know them very well indeed, and to make that corner of the world one of the happiest and most prosperous (applause). She hoped to see their faces every year for many years to come, and that they would always be great friends...

Subsequently the workmen and the cottagers were provided with dinner in the marquee, between 200 and 300 sitting down.... In the afternoon the children of East Coker, Sutton Bingham, and Pendomer were provided with tea in the school room, and subsequently the women sat down. The children were provided with an entertainment in Mr Squibb's barn, and each received a gift as a memento of the joyous occasion ... In the evening an entertainment took place in the marquee ... Subsequently dancing was kept up with much spirit until the early hours of the morning. The whole of the proceedings, the arrangements for which were in the able hands of Mr A. Caplen, passed off with much 'éclat', and the day was one which will long be remembered in the parish and vicinity.

The 'Ten Houses': cottages at Coker Marsh.

East Cottage (now Walnut Cottage), Coker Marsh.

The Boucher Family at Coker Marsh

Part of an extended family living at Coker Marsh: (ABOVE RIGHT) *Jim and Annie Boucher with three of their children – Doris, Jack, and Charlie – and Annie's father Simeon Stagg;* (ABOVE) *Agnes Neville and Sarah Stagg.*

I WAS born Coker Marsh, April 1909. It was all family up there then. When I was born there was two grandfathers, two aunts – there was only about two families that wasn't related in Coker Marsh in them days. All the Nevilles, they were cousins. Five of they boys and four of us all grew up together there. When Charlie and I grew up, we used to sleep next door in granf's. My two sisters they slept home, and we slept in granf's.

My father never went out of the village to work. Nearly everybody was employed in the village, see. My father had a job in the village all his life, and my mother worked in the webbing factory the biggest part of her life. Mother went back there when we kids grew up, we used to go and have our dinner down there in the warehouse.

Burton Cross c.*1907: in 1891 William and Susan Stevens lived in the middle cottage with the first two of their 12 children – Gertrude aged three, and Lavinia aged one. After the deaths of William and Susan many years later, their youngest son Ralph came to live in the cottage where he was born and stayed there until 1994 – one family's home for over 100 years.*

The Whetham family at Bryant's Farm, Pendomer: (l–r) standing: May, Arthur, Albert, John, Hilda, Austin, Alan; seated: Olive, Joseph and Mabel Whetham, Edith.

could take a farm for a few pounds in they days, you see. They was married near Purtington. The hedges was dragging the sides of the cart as they went down to Pendomer. We were all born at Bryant's Farm. All nine of us. I was born in 1910.

The Stevens Family – a Century at Burton Cross

I'M 88. I was born in 1905 in this same cottage. There was 12 in my family, seven girls and five boys. Mother never worked – well it was 20 years bringing up families. My father, he worked on the Home Farm, which is since called Longlands Farm, where the Crumplers lived. That was the Home Farm for the North Coker House, the Troyte-Bullocks – he was called the Squire – and they used to supply all their dairy products. My father was working there which in the summer-time was the haymaking, harvesting, all hours working hard, and again in the winter-time they had the stables. They were hunting people, them days, and they had to go to Cattistock and places to meets and that, consequently the men was there working in the stables till late, cleaning the horses and whatever they had to do. So anyway he got a bit fed up, no doubt, and chucked it up. Went on down the webbing factory and got a job there. This was coming up to the First World War, I suppose. My father was down there working from early morning till about eight o'clock at night. I was big enough to go down and take his tea for him.

Joseph and Mabel Whetham go to Pendomer

MY husband's people used to go round renting the dairies, and they used to take the cows for a year you see, so much a head, then they used to make butter and cheese, but the farmer had to supply the feed. You'd move into the dairy house, and they used to make the butter and cheese with the milk 'cos there was nobody collecting milk in they days. You had the farmer, and then you had the dairyman, and if they didn't agree on the price of the cow per head, they'd move on somewhere else.

My father and mother, their parents did that as well. Then when they'd done it for so many years, saved enough money, they'd take a farm. When father and mother got married they came to Pendomer. They rented the farm off the Heneage's estate in 1903. You could take a farm for a few pounds in they days, you see.

The Hughes Family Come to Keeper's Lodge

I was born in 1903. My father was a gamekeeper and I was born in the keeper's cottage at a little place called Headley just outside of Newbury. Then we moved to Glastonbury, Marshall's Elm was the name of the place. I was the second eldest and I went to work when I was 12 years old at a poultry farm. In them days the war was on and they was allowed to get you out of school to help on the land. I suppose mother was glad of the wage coming in, if you can call it a wage, and that was three shillings a week. My eldest brother was out of school same as I were. They couldn't get man labour. He was a plough boy. He used to drive these big, heavy horses and the plough. Clay soil it was and they had to have three horses to pull the plough.

The gentleman my father was working for at Marshall's Elm used to lease these shoots and his lease had run out. He didn't want another lease and of course dad was out of a job because he wasn't keeping a gamekeeper no longer. The gentleman that was giving the lease up was a great friend of Colonel Heneage who was in the Army them days. They was looking for a gamekeeper on Coker estate so that's how we came to Coker.

It was a slow journey, very slow journey, and no one knew their way exactly, you see. The driver we hired from Street used to haul the stone along beside the road, and he used to do a lot of quarry work and that so he had these wagons. I was very fond of these little goats on the farm where I worked, and when I left, the toff I was working for gave me this little kid for a present. I used to call her Nan. We all had to make a seat up in the wagon, and I know I used to sit on the shafts of the wagon and nurse my little goat, and every so far used to get out and walk behind the wagon and lead the goat.

I can remember we came in and enquired on the top of Hendford Hill for Coker. Coming up the hill they put

The gamekeeper's cottage on the Sleights: the Hughes family moved here during the First World War.

a trace horse on in front to help pull the wagon on. The one in the shafts would be pulling the wagon, and then they hitch a trace horse on the end to get 'em up over hills. I don't know how many hours the journey took. We started in the morning and it was quite evening when we got here. We came down the Yeovil Road, down to where there used to be a big beech tree in the centre, and I think they went and enquired in Mr Thorne's post office. He directed us to come round by Coker Court, not to go all the way up over Lodge Hill because it was a bit steep. The keeper's cottage was called Sleight Lodge then. My father was always known as Keeper – 'Good morning Keeper' – then of course it come to be called the Keeper's Lodge.

From Hounslow to Naish Barton

I was born in 1912. We came here in 1920. I lived first of all at Camp up on the West Coker Road on the way to Odcombe. Stayed there for a time and then went down to live in Holywell, Yew Hill as they call it. Lived down there for a time, and then we moved to Naish Barton. When I came from Hounslow I was absolutely lost really! I can quite remember it. I soon made friends with the local boys. I had a pedal motor-car – my grandmother's people were pretty well off, 'How do you do' kind of style, they bought me all kinds – I used to go up Primrose Hill and come down in it!

My step-father worked for Crumpler at Longlands Farm. That's how we got to be here I suppose. These houses were all farm cottages. They was all tied cottages. Oh my God, how can you describe them? Today I'd call it a hovel. They were pretty grim really. They'd been standing for hundreds of years and nobody had ever done anything to them. It was really a ramshackle place. All stone flags. The only water supply was the old pump over there for five cottages.

The Andrews Family at Back Lane

My father was a carter at Westfield Farm. He looked after the horses. He had two cart-horses, and a small one to go round with the elevator. Lovely horses. They used to keep them so nice, and shine up the brasses. And the hooves – they had them just so. All cleaned up, and even blackened the hooves and all. He wouldn't beat the horses or anything like that: father was very gentle, he was a lovely man. He'd help with haymaking and things like that. Of course it was horses and wagons then to get the hay in to the elevator, you see. You had to keep the elevator going. You'd have to perhaps go out and get a wagon full and bring that in, and then go and fill up another. They'd be filling up one wagon while another was coming in, right till they finished.

Jack Cox: a Woodman for Coker Wood

He came from Morcombelake near Bridport. He was a carter on a farm, and they used to haul coal

Haymaking at Westfield Farm: George Andrews, a carter, stands in the foreground with his two sons Jack and Dick side by side on the hay wagon. The farmer's name is painted on his wagon: 'James Walbridge. West Field. East Coker'.

from Bridport railway station to different places, and that's how he put his hip out of joint. He was riding on the shafts of the wagon, and when they come to the hill he just jumped off and it was just like he'd twisted his ankle. When they went to the doctor's they found it was his hip, but it was too late to do anything about it and he walked with his hip out of joint all his life.

He saw the woodman's job advertised in the paper, and saw it was at East Coker and 'twas another two and sixpence a week more than what he was earning down there. They wanted someone that could make spars and hurdles and he could do this on the farm, see. He had no means of getting up here, he didn't have no bicycle, so he walked. He got the job, and they said 'Well, how did you get here?' and they admired him for walking all that way. So they said did he know that if he got to Sutton Bingham station he could get a train back to Axminster which was half-way home. I think they gave him the fare to Axminster.

The family travelled up here in a horse and cart with the furniture. When the grandmother was taken ill, and she lived still at Morcombelake, someone from down there came up to Coker Wood in the night with a horse and cart all the way from there to get Mrs Cox. She took her youngest child with her. Going on the cart of course it was pitch dark, and somebody said to her 'I dunno what's up with this youngster, he won't stop crying' and when they looked he had the baby upside-down!

Jack James Comes to Slade's Farm

DAD was so fond of horses. He was a carter on the railway. They had their own horses down the bottom of Hendford. They used to take the beer and that round. Big wagons. They'd drop the drink off, you see, at the pubs. Mr Newman had Slade's Farm, and he was down Great Western Railway. He went round the stables and saw my dad doing his horses and he asked him 'Are you fond of horses?' Dad said 'They're my family', and Mr Newman said 'Well, I'm looking for somebody to help with these horses'. It must have been the beginning of the 1914 war, see – there were these horses that they did bring back from the front, and put them up to recuperate. That's how he came to Coker. He had to do the farm work as well, but dad was the horse man mostly, you see. I know he used to sleep over in the stables, in case the horses wanted help in the night and that. Then there was bitter tears when they did come and collect them, to take them on back to the front. Had to go on again, and then a fresh lot would come in.

Workers at Drake's webbing factory in 1914: Felix Drake (1845–1914) stands at the front, fourth from the right, in a light waistcoat and hat. Standing behind Mr Drake, to the left, in a stiff white collar, is Bert Rendell who left school at 12 to go and work in the webbing factory.

Bert Rendell at Hardington Mandeville

I was born on the 11th January 1902 in Hardington Mandeville. I was more or less a mistake because my mother had finished her family some nine years before, and she'd even sold her pram. That meant to say they'd finished having children, you see. But anyway they couldn't bring the pram out when I was born so what they did, they had a fish box and they put a pillow in it and put me in this until they could afford to get another pram.

I started school when I was three, and was there until I was 12. When I was 12 an Inspector of the schools walked in, and after greeting the school mistress, doing what business they had to do, he asked if the large boys could stand up. So all the large boys stood up and then he said 'How would you like to do something to help win the war?' Of course we all did, and so 'You, you and you stand up, all the rest sit down'. And then he said 'I've just come from East Coker factory, and they want two boys to work two looms which is being sent from Switzerland'. Well, these looms would weave a circular hose, and when these looms came and were fitted up, there was two boys chosen by the factory to work them – and I was one.

Watching the Soldiers March By

ALONG Halves Lane one morning came a battalion of Gloucesters, they were going for a route march. We knew they was coming all the way round, and the word got in to the factory and everybody downed tools, stopped the looms and went out to see them 'cos there was hundreds you see, they seemed unending. They were all billeted in Yeovil, and every now and again there was a bugler went round to every corner of more or less every street and blew some call so that the fellas billeted there would know what to do and where to meet.

The village had a guard out there on Sleight Hill. According to what was said then, Sleight Hill had a kind of reservoir there. Well there was a yarn that German spies had been seen up there poisoning the water, so there was so many people detailed off to be there day and night to see that it didn't happen.

12 THE WESTERN GAZETTE, FRIDAY, AUGUST 7, 1914. [Guaranteed Circulation: Upwards of 59,000 Weekly.

"England Expects That Every Man This Day Will Do His Duty.

METEOROLOGICAL OBSERVATIONS.

Weather Forecast.

MILITARY PRECAUTIONS ALONG THE COAST.

Necessary precautions are being taken to defend the towns and harbours along the coast, and the railway tunnels and bridges are being strictly guarded. For reasons which are obvious, details of these defensive measures it is not permissible to publish, but we may speak generally by saying that at Portland and Weymouth, as well as at Bridport and other points along the coast, precautionary steps are being taken in the event of surprise attacks occurring. That is all we feel justified in stating.

The Royal Family.

SEVEN NATIONS AT WAR.

GERMAN CHALLENGE ACCEPTED.

ENGLAND TO FIGHT

ARMY AND NAVY READY

KING'S MESSAGE TO FLEET.

FOREIGN BATTLESHIPS COMMANDEERED.

LORD KITCHENER AT WAR OFFICE.

STATE TAKES OVER RAILWAYS

JOIN THE ARMY TO-DAY!

Your King and Country need you.

WILL you answer your Country's Call? Each day is fraught with the gravest possibilities, and at this very moment the Empire is on the brink of the greatest War in the history of the World.

In this crisis your Country calls on all her young unmarried men to rally round the Flag and enlist in the ranks of her Army.

If every patriotic young man answers her call, England and her Empire will emerge stronger and more united than ever.

If you are unmarried and between 18 and 30 years old will you answer your Country's Call? and go to the nearest Recruiter—whose address you can get at any Post Office.

FINANCE OF THE WAR

100 MILLIONS TO BE VOTED.

KING GEORGE'S MESSAGE TO THE NAVY.

BRITISH ULTIMATUM TO GERMANY.

NO VIOLATION OF BELGIUM NEUTRALITY.

GERMAN EVASIONS.

PREMIER'S STATEMENT IN THE COMMONS.

Mr. Asquith announced in the House of Commons on Tuesday afternoon that an ultimatum had been sent to Germany on the question of the neutrality of Belgium. The chief points in the Prime Minister's momentous speech were as follows:—

GERMAN ATTACK ON BELGIUM.

HEROIC DEFENCE.

DESPERATE FIGHTING.

GERMANS REPULSED WITH GREAT LOSS.

Official news received at Brussels states that a fierce fight occurred at Liege on Wednesday. The present situation is very favourable for the Belgians, who have victoriously repulsed all the German attacks.

The Germans, who endeavoured to pass through the intervals between the forts, were driven back with heavy losses by a mixed brigade.

"NOT ONE RETURNED."

It is said that not a single one who passed the intervals returned.

The German shells were unable to pierce the defences.

German aeroplanes showed themselves much inferior to the Belgian.

None of the Belgian aeroplanes sustained any accident, but several of the German did so.

It is confirmed that the Germans behaved disgracefully on Tuesday at Visé. They shot many civilians, expelling the remainder of the inhabitants, and giving the town to the flames.

BRUSSELS, Wednesday, 5.30 p.m.

Heavy fighting is going on near Fleron. The Germans have been completely repulsed, and have not been able to renew the attack on Liege.

NAVAL OPERATIONS COMMENCED.

GERMAN MINE-LAYER SUNK.

ALGERIAN TOWNS DESTROYED BY IRONCLADS.

EARLY DESPATCH OF THE EXPEDITIONARY FORCE

MEDIATION OFFER ... STATES.

Births, Marriages, & Deaths

The Western Gazette *for Friday the 7th August 1914: a formal declaration of war had been made on the previous Wednesday.*

Guarding the Burton Spring

SOUTH of Kingstream Lane there's a small reservoir there, and during the First World War my father and a lot more men used to take it in turns to go up and keep guard in case it was poisoned. Our water came from there, right down through.

Hugh Stevens Volunteers

I had a brother who went to Coker Court from his leaving school age till he joined the army in the First World War. It was Hugh Stevens – his name is on the memorial in the church. He was only 18 when he was killed in 1915. At Coker Court they used to call him the odd-job man, go and do everything: see to the fires, run to the post office taking letters, cleaning boots, cleaning cutlery and things like that. I know my mother kept on at him not to think about volunteering yet, like until he was called, but he insisted on it so of course I suppose she give way to him.

Fred Sandford my mother took in from a baby more or less, from her sister that died living here in the village: she and her husband died at the time of the consumption, they both died within a few weeks of one another and left this boy. My mother brought him up until he went. Fred was working in the Court garden I think at that time, and he went in the Army, called up, and then he was killed.

I don't know where we knew much about the war. If anything desperate happened we didn't know about it till a month or so afterwards quite often, you know. Big losses or whatever, was kept secret. I know I remember when my mother had the letter from the War Office saying her son were killed.

'Tis well sometimes to recollect,
How fast our moments fly,
And never, while we live, forget
How soon we too may die.

We loved him, Oh, no tongue can tell,
How much we loved him, or how well;
The Lord loved him too, and thought it best,
To take him home with Him to rest.

In Loving Memory
OF
HUGH,
The dearly beloved son of William and Susan Stevens,
(Burton Cross, East Coker, Yeovil),
Who died at No. 17 C. C. Station, France,
On Wednesday, October, 19th, 1915.
AGED 18 YEARS.

Deeply Mourned by his sorrowing Parents.

One of many village men and boys who volunteered for the Army: Hugh Stevens joined the Gordon Highlanders in June 1915 and died in France on the 19th October 1915, aged 18.

Brothers and Cousins Killed in the War

I can remember I used to go home from school and if my mother had a parcel for one of the boys, I used to have to go back down the post office and post it. I always remember I was playing at Buntham with some other girls, we were all friends you know. There was four of us: there was May, Ivy, Ella and myself. Ivy had a brother in the Army, and we were there playing round the back of the houses and Ivy's sister came out and said that Arthur had been killed. That was their only brother. And I can remember that as plain as anything. We were all upset.

My brother Hugh worked at Coker Court, and when he used to have a day off he'd go home and clean my mother's bedrooms. He'd do anything for my mother. Hugh was in the Gordon Highlanders, my other brother Stanley was in the Navy. Stanley was born in what they call a veil [*a caul*], and they say they would never get drowned and he went right through the war, you see. I had a cousin Charlie in the Army, and another cousin, Fred, he was in the Army too. Charlie was killed, and Fred was reported missing – well, he must have been killed, we never heard any more.

The only time I can remember Hugh was we'd come out of school and we'd got to the shop, and he walked up the road in his Scots uniform with his kilt on, and he picked up my younger sister and carried her home on his shoulders. That's all I can remember of him. He was ever so tall, great big strapping fellow.

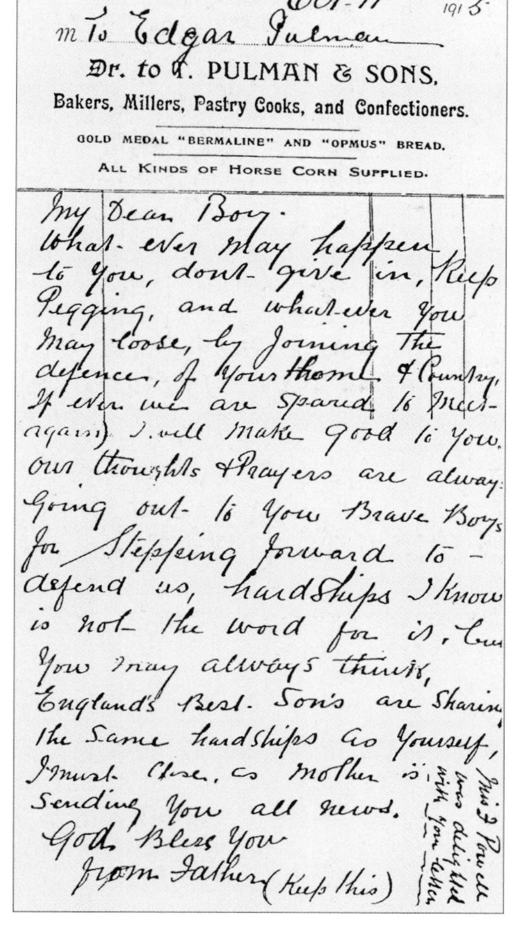

Oct-11 1915

Mr To Edgar Pulman

Dr. to T. PULMAN & SONS.

Bakers, Millers, Pastry Cooks, and Confectioners.

GOLD MEDAL "BERMALINE" AND "OPMUS" BREAD.

ALL KINDS OF HORSE CORN SUPPLIED.

My Dear Boy.
What-ever may happen to you, dont give in, Keep Pegging, and what-ever you may loose, by Joining the defence, of Your Home & Country, If ever we are Spared to meet again) I will make good to you. Our thoughts & Prayers are always Going out to You Brave Boys for Stepping forward to defend us, hardships I know is not the word for it, but You may always think, England's Best Son's are Sharing the Same hardships as Yourself, I must Close, as Mother is Sending You all news.
God Bless You
from Father (Keep this)

Miss J Powell was delighted with your letter

A letter to Private Edgar Pulman, 1st Middlesex Regiment, from his father Thomas Pulman, the village baker. Edgar (shown above) joined the Army in 1915 and was mentioned for distinguished conduct in the field in October 1916. As a Company Orderly he took messages from the front line to Headquarters through the German barrage. He died of his wounds on the 17th April 1917.

Sending Eggs for the Soldiers

In 1915 the schoolchildren responded to an appeal for eggs for wounded soldiers, collecting 264 in the first week alone. They took the eggs to Bridge Farm (now Hymerford House) where Miss A. Newman forwarded them to a central depot.

I were four year old when the war broke out. There was shortages of things, and one thing and another, and mother sent some eggs to Netley Hospital near Southampton. Perhaps they'd give 'em a couple dozen eggs when they were collecting to go to the hospitals, and mother put our names on the eggs. I still have a thank-you letter for my egg from a nurse there. The soldier died before he could write.

Shutting Out the Zeppelins

We used to shut the shutters outside the cottage night times in case the zeppelins came over. We went on natural, had what we could have, and that was that. The war didn't affect us at all because dad wasn't in it.

East Coker School Goes Blackberry Picking

As part of the war effort, village boys collected horse chestnuts in the Park (to make oil for munitions); the girls knitted for the troops; and in September 1918, when the fruit harvest failed, large groups of schoolchildren went blackberry picking – over eight days they picked 492lb.

I remember going out during the war – we used to go blackberry picking for making jam for the troops. I can remember going all up round Pendomer and Coker Wood. All the school teachers and all went to have a day out. Take a picnic lunch. We all picked a lot of blackberries.

Private H. J. Farnham (5th Dorset), East Coker, Yeovil. Missing.

Henry Farnham of Wraxhill Farm as he appeared in the Western Gazette's *Roll of Honour on the 21st January 1916. Henry was posted missing the previous August following an engagement in Gallipoli, and was reported as dead on the 26th June 1916.*

Bert and Jack Start Work at the Webbing Factory

We were going to start work and have seven shillings a week. Now that was twice as much as the soldiers was getting, because what they was being paid there was a song about: 'All for a tanner a day'. Two tanners were a shilling. The circular looms hadn't arrived yet, so we had to learn the way to thread the harness which went up and down in the loom, and to be what they called 'drawing boys'. The drawing boy had to sit inside the loom when the loom was stationary and join on new warp to go through the harness onto the loom. So we

Local Defence Volunteers: (l–r) Arthur Mead, Sydney Webber, Mr Thorpe, Mr Albutt. In 1921 Mr Webber, the headmaster of the village school, was killed in a motorbike-and-sidecar accident at White Post.

No
TELEGRAMS (COUNTING AS TWO WORDS) "DRAKE NORTH-COKER."
Dr. To
CONTRACTORS TO THE WAR OFFICE & ADMIRALTY.
F. DRAKE & Co
F. DRAKE & Co
REGISTERED TRADE MARK.
ESTABLISHED 1872.
MANUFACTURERS & MERCHANTS OF
LONDON WAREHOUSE, 2, PATERNOSTER BLDGS, E.C.
MANCHESTER, 4, CHAPEL SQUARE, BIRCHIN LANE.
BIRMINGHAM, 61, ST PAUL'S SQUARE.
NORWICH, 110, EADE ROAD.
DUBLIN, 12-13, EUSTACE ST
BROOMS & BRUSHES OF ALL KINDS.
WEBS OF EVERY DESCRIPTION FOR THE SADDLERY & UPHOLSTERY TRADES
TWINES, LINES, CORDS, ROPES, MATTINGS, RUGS, &c. &c.
ORDER No
TERMS
NO DEDUCTIONS FOR WRAPPERS CASKS OR HAMPERS UNLESS RETURNED IN GOOD CONDITION CARRIAGE PAID.
NORTH COKER MILLS, SOMERSET
190

Drake's webbing factory, 'Contractors to the War Office and Admiralty': during the 1914–18 war the factory was kept busy supplying, among other things, belts, putties, rifle slings, and machine-gun ammunition belts. In 1915 the factory was working overtime on Army orders and, in 1917, 90% of the output was for the government.

learned the way to do that, and it was not always the best of jobs because it was awfully dusty and sometimes the weavers who were paid piece-work – the more work they did, the more money they got – so when the drawing boys were a bit slow, they used to try and hurry them up by catching their fingers in the loom.

Going to work the two of us used to meet up some way or the other. Just outside the boundary of Hardington there was two field gates on the right, and across those fields was the footpath which led towards the factory. So we would go across these footpaths and out onto the road, and down through a field called Long Mead. When the grass was very long, we used to play tricks on one another: when we got to high grass we would bend some grass from each side and tie it in a knot, then the one that came on second if he didn't see the grass tied in a knot he would trip and fall down.

When the two new looms came they discovered that one boy could work the two circular looms, you see, and Jack Guppy didn't care much for the job and he went on the buildings. So I was the boy that was chosen to work the two looms, and I went on weaving the circular hose. What they wanted this circular hose for was to chop up in pieces and thread on to the chains used in the ammunition trucks that went from the bases up the lines to the fighting people in the night. As the chains was inside this web they didn't rattle, you see, and it wasn't giving away the position of the supply trucks to the enemy.

The Steam Tractor Arrives

THEY had to grow beans during the war, they'd give you orders and you had to grow 'em: they wanted the beans to make feed for the horses. We had two horses from the front down at Bryant's Farm, one of them died the next day. I don't know who used to bring them, 'twas somebody that supplied 'em, you see, after they were shell-shocked. They were in a terrible state, poor things. They used to be sent round for you to have something to get on and work for the fields. One field at Pendomer I can remember the War Agricultural Committee come and ploughed it with a steam tractor: a tractor each end, with a long wire rope between them and a plough share attached to it. They supplied it 'cos father didn't have the equipment to plough the field.

Mrs Heneage Shakes Hands with Jack James

DAD used to work Sundays and all during the war. He came home one Sunday, and you know they must have been up Coker Marsh in one of the fields ploughing or something, and he said that Mrs Heneage had been up and shook him by the hand for working on a Sunday. The village didn't half kick up, mind, 'cos they worked Sundays for the war effort, see.

The Flax-Pullers' Camp

In the years leading up to the First World War only 50 acres of flax was grown in Somerset, but after 1914 this increased to 3,500 acres to meet the demands of the aeroplane-building industry. There was a flax-pullers' camp in Barwick Park, and young women recruited from universities and teacher training colleges camped there for six weeks in the summer to help harvest flax in the Yeovil area.

Finding a Skylark's Nest

I'LL tell you another thing, during the 1914–18 war I used to go out with my mum in the fields flax-pulling. Used to go pull it up, and then put it in bundles and tie it up. Then they'd take it down Preston somewhere to the flax works. Nearly all the farmers had fields of flax. And then I can remember once I went up Burton way somewhere with my mother and we found a skylark's nest in the flax. My mum'd take her babies, see, and I'd have to go with her to look after the babies when she was flax-pulling. It was hard work. In the end, if they were in a

Land girls helping with the flax harvest at Longlands Farm. The farmer, Jesse Crumpler, was managing director of Wessex Flax Factories Ltd: its two nearest factories were at Bunford and Preston in Yeovil. The land girls – pictured here in their farm breeches and smocks – worked a nine-hour day and were paid piecework, with a minimum wage of seven shillings a week. Aeroplane production depended upon a successful flax harvest.

East Coker scout troop in front of Coker Court, 1913: the Heneages were instrumental in founding the scout troop which was inaugurated in 1910 as 'Major Heneage's East Coker Troop'. (l–r) back row: Jack Stagg, E. Stagg (scoutmaster), S. Webber, F. Jarvis (assistant scoutmaster), Fred Beater; middle row: Percy Harwood, Harold Gilham, Percy Williams, Gideon Pomeroy, H. Hacker, E. Thorne, Leslie Rendell, Percy Crumpler, - Caplin, Stanley Stevens, Cecil Hacker, Reginald Giles; seated by drum: H. Cox, Jack Pomeroy, F. Thorne. On the outbreak of war in 1914 five members of the troop volunteered, and two of them became buglers in the 6th Somersets.

hurry and the flax had to come in – well, evenings children were put to bed and mum would be getting supper – I would be out, see, and I would be doing as much as I could. You couldn't do it heavy like women and that 'cos I was only a girl. Your poor hands would get sore as anything. You had to go on so long, and that's that.

Ralph the 'Head Gardener'

BEFORE I left school, when I was 13, the bigger boys in the First World War was detailed or allocated to go on different things – agriculture, on the farm or whatever is beneficial to the war. Like Archie Neville and Bill Begwell, Vin James and Ern Lacey. They were all for it, of course. I was asked, or told, to go to the vicarage at the time of Reverend Powell for so many half-days a week. I tell people that I was Head Gardener – I was the only one! – sweeping up leaves and things like that. I used to have to go in with coal; clean the knives; pump water up to the roof for about an hour every morning from the well underneath outside, gravity-fed then, see.

Poor old Parson Powell. I know I used to lead him a bit of a life because I used to be off and about so much. He were always around Coker looking, saying 'Have you seen my boy?' Of course he were getting up along I suppose, and I know I used to scarper off sometimes. Fox and hounds met up *Helyar Arms* or something another, I were away then after 'em, up on the top, you know. He'd be out with the bell at the front door of the vicarage calling me in! I gradually cottoned on that there was no control over me, I suppose, with the war on and one thing and another.

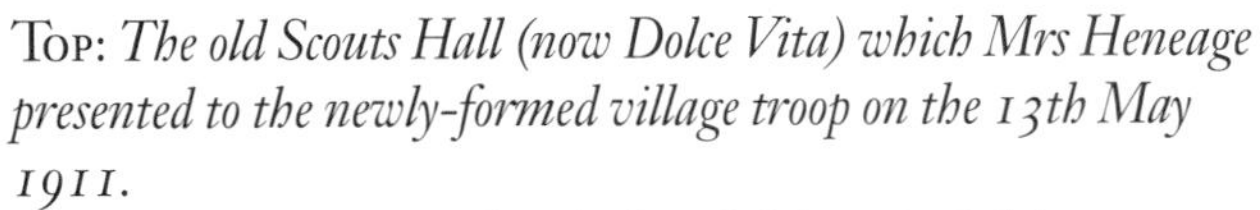

Top: *The old Scouts Hall (now Dolce Vita) which Mrs Heneage presented to the newly-formed village troop on the 13th May 1911.*

Above: *The Mÿseman family from Malines in Belgium were refugees who lived in the Scouts Hall during the war. The scouts used the cricket pavilion as an alternative meeting place.*

Right: *Jack Stagg of Box Cottage who won the national Scout Cycling Cup in 1913. A few years later Jack was riding motor-bikes as a despatch rider in the First World War. The East Coker scout troop saw its older boys leave to fight in the war, and it soon disbanded. When the scouts restarted for a second time in 1963, Jack Stagg was a strong supporter and frequently attended meetings.*

East Coker Scout Troop

When I was in the scouts they had a bugle band, seven or eight bugles, a big drum, and two side drums. Nights, we used to march all around the village. The blacksmith's son used to play the big drum. In fact there used to be a story that going under Sutton Bingham railway bridge he could throw the stick up in the air and he'd catch him when he come round the other side when they were marching under! We used to go around, especially of a moonlight night, all up around some or another of the roads. That was a drill for the scouts more or less, you know, and exercise, and give the band a practice because people used to crib, I suppose, what lived around the Scouts Hall if they were in there practising too long every evening! Give 'em all a treat! We'd go on up round Sutton Bingham, and Darvole, and down around Yew Hill.

There used to be a flagpole outside the Scouts Hall. 'Twas during the First World War there was some Belgiques, refugees, come there to live. 'Twas being disbanded more or less when Mr Webber was running the scouts – all the older ones had gone in the Army or were working. There were wounded soldiers in Yeovil – a lot of 'em were billeted in the Newnam Memorial Hall. We went to Coker Court to this do in the great hall, I think we marched up and these soldiers come. We had to entertain 'em whatever way we wanted to. Some of 'em were in wheelchairs. There were games, a lot of card games, ludo. I know we had a good feast, tea and that.

Jack Stagg with his sister Nell after his return from the war. The motor cycle was Arthur Mead's Bat Jap with carbide lamps on the front.

The School is Closed

We had an old postman used to walk from East Coker, he was crippled, and he used to go all round Pendomer and right out to Hardington Marsh. He had to go across the fields out to there. He used to torment us kids! If you were near him he'd put that stick about anybody that could get near him. Course he was as bad as we were really, and he told us once when the very bad 'flu was in the First World War – 'cos people were dying like flies – he said 'You haven't got to go to school today' and we said 'Why?' 'Oh,' he said 'They got the bird "flu" out the window'. We said 'Get on you old liar! You be only trying to keep us from going to school!' And course we got up to Keeper's house where Mrs Hughes come out and she said 'Well you haven't got to go to school today – didn't the postman tell you?' 'Oh, we don't never believe him.' So we had to turn around and go back. They closed the school for about six weeks: the soldiers were coming back from the World War, you see, and brought this 'flu back.

The Men Come Home

Some of 'em were gassed weren't they. I know one in particular was queer in the head. I don't know if 'twas the gas, or if he was shell-shocked. I forget who that was. There was one that used to walk about and kids used to call after him and all. My mother said 'If I hear you go after him, you'll get a lacing – I'm telling you that'.

Jack Boucher is Buried

Private John Boucher of the Grenadier Guards died in an English hospital on the 13th April 1918, aged 24, from wounds received in the battle of Flanders. The only one of the 22 village men killed in the 1914–18 war to be buried in East Coker cemetery, his headstone was provided by the Commonwealth War Graves Commission.

I was only nine year old when the war finished. I remember my uncle Jack Boucher. I can remember when he went in the Army – he was a Guardsman. The last time he went back off leave he had to go back to the front where he got mortally wounded. They brought him back to a hospital in Sidcup – he'd had half his head blown off – and my father went to see him. He lived a week and when he died they brought him back on the train to Sutton Bingham. I can remember seeing the coffin draped with the Union Jack coming out here to Coker Marsh, they took him and laid him in the church and they buried him the next day up the cemetery.

Alb's Keepsake

Mr Gilham, being the Head Gardener for Coker Court, his privilege was he had to be kept in vegetables, and I had that job as well, to go and take down Mrs Gilham's order. I always remember one morning I had to go down with a few potatoes and a spring cabbage for dinner and peace had just been proclaimed. Of course we didn't know it, and Mr Wild the estate agent he'd just got the news that peace was proclaimed and signed and he'd called in on his way to tell Mrs Gilham. She was that delighted, when I got down there she come to the door and told me all about it, and she put a half-crown in my hand and shook my hand upon it, 'Here now my child, you keep that one. See how long you can keep it'. And I've still got it over 70 years later!

Minnie Gilham (née Hardman, 1863–1957) standing in front of her home at West Wells c.*1908. She came to East Coker from Southampton in 1887 to work as a housemaid at North Coker House, and married Thomas Gilham in 1895.*

Listening to the Bells at Gunville

I can remember my grandmother taking me up the lane to the Plot to hear East Coker church bells ringing because the peace was signed.

Armistice Day 1919

118 men from East Coker served in the forces between 1914 and 1918. Only three years before the outbreak of war, the total number of males in the village, of all ages, was 361.

WE'D see the men come back one or two at a time. Used to come back to Yeovil, train I suppose, and walk the rest of the way.

They had a real peace day afterwards, 12 months after the armistice was signed. I was working up Court gardens then and Mr Gilham he said 'Here sonny, you know you've got to leave off. We're all closing the gardens'. 11 o'clock. I remember the hooter down the factory blowing as we were coming on down the road by the cemetery. I remember that plainly.

On the 5th October 1920 the war memorial in St Michael's church was dedicated to the memory of the 22 men from East Coker who gave their lives in the First World War. The two panels on the base of the memorial read 'Who dies if England live' and 'Their name liveth for evermore': 27 years later these words were replaced with the names of nine village men who lost their lives during the Second World War.

ABOVE: *St Michael's church.*
BELOW: *The Reverend Charles Powell (1843–1923), vicar of East Coker from 1877 until his retirement in 1921. With Mr Powell and two of his daughters, Lucy and Frances, is Stanley Stevens, home from the war. In his final illness Charles Powell asked to return to East Coker where he died a week later, at the home of his old churchwarden Charles Hackwell.*

NOTES
About East Coker.

CHIEFLY GLEANED FROM
OLD PARISH BOOKS AND PAPERS,
WITH
GLIMPSES OF VILLAGE LIFE IN THE
18th CENTURY.

BY
Rev. C POWELL, EAST COKER VICARAGE,
YEOVIL.

Charles Powell was a keen historian, publishing a booklet Notes About East Coker *in 1910* (ABOVE) *as well as articles and an essay on William Dampier, the buccaneer and circumnavigator who was born in East Coker in 1651.*

RIGHT: *An early photograph of East Coker Women's Institute which was founded in June 1918: its President was Mrs S. Kennard, Vice President Mrs Hardy, and the Secretary/ Treasurer was Miss A. Newman.*

The W.I. motto
'Do all the good that you can,
To all the people you can,
In all the ways you can'.

The illustrated border used to frame the first Women's Institute programme of events in 1918: that year there were talks on local history, care of children, prevention of disease, and local government; a demonstration of hat-trimming; and subjects for discussion included 'What can I do for my country?' and 'How can I bring down the cost of living?' Annual membership was two shillings, and visitors could attend for sixpence a meeting. The W.I. set up the first monthly refuse collection scheme in the village in 1927 at a cost to households of 2/5 per month.

ABOVE: *Verandah Cottage on the left with the walled garden, St Michael's church tower, and the roof of Coker Court in the background.*

LEFT: *North Lodge in 1905: the three girls, sitting in a field on the other side of Longlands Lane, are Katie Dawe, whose father was the butler at North Coker House, and Brenda and Ethel Crumpler who lived at Longlands Farm.*

A Village Family

For Mrs Heneage, her village people were like her family. David Heneage used to come on with his two nurses. As he grew older he used to ride with his gun and that, and if ever he passed you he always said hello. Always. Mr Powell the vicar, he used to be a toff too, mind. We used to go to the vicarage for Sunday School once a year and have a party.

Curtsying to Mrs Heneage

If Mrs Heneage passed, the schoolchildren always had to curtsy. And if she came to the school she always had her white gloves on, she'd just have a few words to say and was gone again. The Squire used to stand out in the road, and when the boys came on they'd lift their caps.

The Georgian wing, Coker Court, built in 1766.

Colonel Heneage

HE used to call you by your Christian name. None of this high-up business. We didn't know what his Christian name was, otherwise we'd have called him that. We just used to call him Colonel.

First Pair of Long Trousers

OLD Colonel Heneage used to give me clothes. He give me the first pair of long trousers, Colonel did. A pair of cricket flannels. My mother had 'em dyed brown – I never wore 'em out, I grew out of 'em. I had 'em when I was in the choir. My mother had these trousers ready for me on the Sunday morning, all creased up these flannels, I tell 'ee what, I was like Lord Caernarvon they days. Went up to the choir, you know, dressed up in the first long trousers ever I had, 14 or 15 years old. Course most of the other kids were in short trousers. The Colonel was always asking people how they were and did they want anything if he was out for a stroll.

Coker Court staff photographed near the servants' entrance to the South Wing.

Sending Food from Thorne's Shop

MRS Heneage was a marvellous lady. She would come down and walk in Coker and if anybody was in trouble she'd see that they had a parcel of groceries. After dad left the farm, she got to hear my dad was bad and that they were in difficulties, so she sent to Thorne's and she paid them so much a week for a big

The last meet of the season: the Cattistock Fox Hounds in front of Coker Court, 1906.

North Coker House, built by the Bullock family in the 19th century. George Bullock (1797–1885) was a sailcloth manufacturer whose rising fortunes made him a prominent landowner in Somerset and Dorset; in 1886 he was sheriff of Somerset.

parcel of groceries for us. And then we had to fetch it every week. She didn't forget us, see.

Tickets for Yeovil Hospital

I can remember when my brother was about six he had St Vitus dance. My mother had to go up and get a ticket from Colonel Heneage to get him admitted to the hospital. He was President of the hospital at the time. Cyril Maudslay was the same. Certain people, they'd donate so much to the hospital and they had a list of tickets they could give out to their friends, like. You go and ask for it and they'd give you a ticket to go to hospital, otherwise you had to pay to go in there.

Daisy Dade (right) one of the housemaids at Coker Court.

The Squire

SQUIRE Troyte-Bullock used to stand out in the road, and when the girls came on they'd curtsy, and when the boys came on they'd lift their caps, going to school.

Knowing Your Place

MY mother was very strict. We were brought up to know our manners, and you didn't have to step out of place, mind. You wouldn't have to answer back, and you wouldn't say 'old Bill Somebody' or something like that, else you'd get your knuckles rapped – 'That's Mr So-and-So'. And of course if you met Mrs Heneage, or Mr Preston from Bubspool, or anything, you had to bow. Mrs Heneage

ABOVE: *The Squire's bridge across the main road into the village linked North Coker Park with land on the other side of the road where Tellis Cross is today. The bridge had a wooden structure raised high on stone piers so that loaded hay wagons could pass underneath. The bridge was demolished in the mid-1920s just before the first 12 houses were built at Tellis Cross.*

LEFT: *George Troyte Chafyn-Grove (1829–1913) of North Coker House, with his wife Alice and members of their family. A landowner with over 10,000 acres in Somerset, Dorset and Wiltshire, George Troyte Chafyn-Grove was a deputy-lieutenant and JP for Somerset and Dorset, a JP for Wiltshire, and in 1888 sheriff of Dorset.*

The East Coker Band: founded by George Troyte Chafyn-Grove in 1897, its first engagement was to play at local celebrations for Queen Victoria's Diamond Jubilee. During the Boer War the band joined with the Crewkerne Military Band to raise money for widows and orphans, and on the return of Cecil Drake from the war, workers from the webbing factory pulled his carriage from Sutton Bingham station through the village and the band marched in front playing 'See the Conquering Hero Comes'. (l–r) back row: P. Francis, J. Boucher, S. Hooper, R. Rendell, G. Rendell, A. Rendell, E. Baker, N. Pitcher; seated: T. Neville, E. Gilham, T. Sibly (conductor, bandmaster of the Crewkerne Band), H. Rendell, F. Rendell, T. Lawrence.

would often come down and walk in the village, you know, up round the village and she'd have a talk. They owned it you see, and everything you did was, well, would she approve more or less. Oh yes, we had to be very aware of that. Especially them that worked for them, mind, they had to be very precise.

Hiding From the Squire and Madame Helyar

You had to curtsy to the Squire when you saw him. When she was a girl, my mother and her sister saw him coming up the road prancing on his horse, and she and her young sister ran into a field that was allotments then, and the old man ran in after them and told them to come out and pass his horse. Madame Helyar was the same, that's Mrs Heneage's grandmother. She used to drive down the village after church and go into anybody's cottage and see if they had anything for dinner. Old Mrs Neville told us that they used to hide their food not for her to see it.

Parish's Food

Our mother used to get Parish's food – she used to go to Mrs Maudslay as other mothers did, and you had her signature on a piece of paper and that entitled you to free blooming Parish's food, and cod-liver oil and malt.

A Temporary Eviction from Burton Cross

My father, he'd been working at Home Farm – long hours, hard work – then he went down the factory to work, got a job down there instead. That's when Troyte-Bullock sent the bailiff and the policeman up here and turned everything out. Old Harry Stevens used to tell me all the story, my father had never mentioned it, and he said the policeman were up there throwing bedclothes and stuff out of the bedroom window. My father was honestly so gentle with anybody and anything, he was a real gentle man, and he went up there and he said 'If you throw anything more out there, I'll throw you out'. The family's belongings were stored over there in a barn for three months, and they had a one-up, one-down at Holywell in the drainway by the pub. It could have been four children, and there was one expected, that was in 1896 I think 'twas. And then Troyte-Bullock sent a note to my father and told him he could go back to the cottage at Burton Cross.

The Bed Gets a Hiding

If the boys didn't salute the Squire, raise their caps to him, or open a gate for him because he'd be on his horse, there'd be trouble. I remember our next-door neighbour telling my husband and I that he met the Squire whilst going home from school to his home at Redlands. The Squire was on his horse and he didn't lift his cap to him, and he said 'You go on, I'll take you down and tell your father of you'. And he went down and the Squire followed him on. When he got down there, the Squire told the boy's father that he hadn't lifted his cap to him and he said 'You give him a hiding'. So his father took him upstairs and said 'Now son, you get right under the bed and when I hit the bed, you shout'. So the bed had the hiding, and the boy went free.

Off for a Ride on the Steam Lorry

I remember when Compton Cottage and Bassett Cottage were built. I was up there working at the vicarage when it was all on, after the First World War.

The Coker Court 'fire brigade' c.1907*: estate workers pose with hand-pump, hose, and buckets. This pump would be the first to arrive whenever a thatched cottage or hayrick in the village caught fire.*

The Colonel had them built by F.R. Bartlett's of Yeovil, and they had to employ ex-servicemen, that was the stipulation. And mind, the old stonemason he used to drive a donkey and cart. He lived at Hardington, old John Hawkins. And of course every chance I could get when I was at the vicarage I was up there just looking on. They had a steam lorry, Wort & Way from Salisbury, working away, hauling the stone that was drawn up the top of Lyatt's, out on the Pen Lane. F.R. Bartlett, the boss, he used to come out to see what was going on periodically, you know, on horseback. The bloke on the steam lorry said to me one day 'Here, want a trip?' Of course I were all for it! The funnel was just above the cab roof – of course I were up there on top of the cab. I was just thinking 'Oh my God, I won't be home for two or three days!' you know, when a spark come out of the funnel and into my eye. I've never had such pain in my life I don't think.

LEFT: *Jack Bush, a woodman on the Coker Court estate, who later worked at Lyatt's Farm.*

BELOW: *Martha Trim was the cook at Coker Court when this photograph was taken in 1917.*

Visiting the Estate Yard in Moor Lane

I was fascinated to go in and watch the carpenters work. They didn't tell you to go away or anything like that, and you'd get to know the men who were working there. I used to watch them cramp the 'H' in the gates for the Coker Court estate. It was part of the structure, because it was a straight letter, but you couldn't help noticing it when the gate was painted white and the 'H' was painted black. The 'H' was for 'Heneage'.

The Laundry at Coker Court

My mother worked at the laundry at the back of the stables for a long time. When we were children she worked up at the laundry washing everything for the Court. I expect the sheets were changed every day, and the towels and everything. There were two or three women working there.

Turning the Mangle

There were tubs all along the wall in the laundry, you had to use scrubbing boards and brushes and things, and all along there were the wooden tubs. They used to draw the water as they wanted it, see, out of the tap. Of course that's why the boiler had to be lit early, for to get the water hot. Then I used to have to go in sometimes and turn the mangle. I've never seen a mangle like it. It was a great thing – I forget how many tons it weighed. The weight of it as it rolled along would press every bit of moisture out. There was a flat-top stove, red-hot all the time, and the irons used to stand around the stove on little legs. They used to have to wash everything, even the sacking aprons they used to wear. They had a little green outside on the end of the stable, proper airing clothes across it. Down the bottom of the laundry room they also had a drying room with hot pipes round.

Mrs Andrews' Washing Lines

We used to have a wood-house at the back of the cottage at the top of Back Lane. We'd go up there and play when it was wet. We used to keep things in there, tools, the wood, and the coal, and father used to have a barrel of cider in there. Then we had the wash house next to it where mother used to do her washing. Mother had to have her clothes-lines put out in Little Down, the field behind the cottage, because otherwise when anyone walked along the Beech Tree Walk at Coker Court, there was a clear view of everything over here, and Mrs Heneage didn't like to see the washing. So mother had to have her lines over the other side!

Estate Workers Collect Their Pay

Jack Cox was a woodman from Coker Wood and Pen Wood, and he and his family lived with the animals and the trees. He never went nowhere. All he had to do was when he used to come down Friday evenings for his pay. When Mr Wild the bailiff had an office on the end of Honeysuckle Cottage, I've seen the blokes down there, all the masons and carpenters, and woodmen and whatever, they're stood out waiting to get paid, and he had to come all the way from Pendomer to get about 30 bob a week pay.

Jack and Nellie Cox with their youngest child, Joan, outside the garden of their cottage on the edge of Coker Wood. Jack Cox was the last woodman for the Coker Court estate to live there.

John Humphries, who worked as a groom in the stables at Coker Court.

brush was made into faggots for people to light fires. He would make hurdles in the woods from hazel wood, and then they were sold to the farmers. When it was wet, he used to make spars in one of our outhouses. He would be foreverlasting chopping, making these spars for thatching. I used to like watching my father coppicing and the smell of the wood being cut.

Sundays we'd walk out through the woods. You had to be kept quiet and still to see the deer – the most I've seen in Coker Wood was eight. You could stand motionless and so would the deer if he saw you – you'd be standing there staring at each other, but if you made one move, he was off. My mum always said a deer stamped its foot at her once when she walked out in the wood. She thought it might have had young there, you know, and she said that was the only time she felt a bit nervous.

Every I don't know how often Mrs Heneage used to like to come up and walk with us in Coker Wood, so we had a postcard saying that she was about to come and mother used to walk with her through the woods, and I had to keep back behind!

Crossing the Field to Coker Wood

My dad always had to go down to East Coker to get his wages. Then he used to have a drink in the pub, and my mum would be worried because he hadn't come home, knowing that he had to come across the field at Wicket's Beer, where there was always a bull in the field and he was walking across in the dark. My mum used to wonder if the bull would have him.

Jack Cox and his Family in Coker Wood

He did a full day's work. He used to clean the ditches, and he was always coppicing different parts of the wood. As he cut it down, so he'd faggot it up. Perhaps they'd cut out say ten acres of hazel – because Coker Wood alone was over 100 acres – and when they cut it they'd go back through and do it in spars, pea-sticks, bean-sticks, and then there was firewood and all the small

The Woodman's Children

Coker Wood was oak mainly, and ash. There were a few sweet-chestnut trees and we used to like going out and picking the chestnuts. The drives that went through the wood used to be fairly wide and covered in bluebells. Especially they used to be more noticeable when a whole patch was cut, the bluebells would spring up. And primroses, I used to be always picking primroses because there was so many, you know. Mrs Thorne at the post office used to want primroses, so I used to pick her bunches and she would give me a few pence. There were butterfly orchids. Bee orchids was in a field nearby but not actually in the wood. My brothers used to pick moss by the bagful which Lock's, the seed merchant people, used to have to make wreaths. They used to get about sixpence a sack.

Keeper Hughes Gathering Pheasant Eggs

It used to be a job because when the pheasants started laying dad had to go round and pick up the eggs. If they were going to rear so many hundred, dad had to go round and get the eggs first. He'd be out from the morning right round, and I've known him gather the eggs and bring them home careful, and then when he had enough to put under a broody hen he used to go to the farms and buy the hens, make up the nest boxes and hatch 'em. And perhaps sometimes when a farmer is cutting the grass and he what they call 'cut out' a pheasant – a pheasant flies off of a nest of eggs just in time – if they can save those eggs, and bring them straight to dad before they get cold a workman was allotted two shillings. And then if anyone should cut out a 'hot' nest – where the eggs are still hot – I've known dad come home many a time with his shirt all tied round with the eggs in it, on the heat of his body to keep them warm.

Frank Foot Walking to the Woods

When my father was working on the estate as a woodman with Jim Hughes, they quite often were doing a job four miles away from Verandah Cottage, in Pen Wood or Coker Wood, and they would have to carry a ladder on their shoulder all those four miles in the morning.

There was Jim Wild who was the steward, well he would have been theoretically the man to give the jobs, but the Colonel every two or three days would check progress, and Frank would look at Jim, or Jim would look at Frank, and say 'The old man's coming' 'cos (a) they would hear the car; and (b) they would see his dogs – he had two retrievers, Lion and Tiger – and then they affected added interest in the work they were doing!

There was a wonderful Daffodil Walk at the Court, and during the daffodil season two boys from the school were nominated on a Saturday morning to knock off the heads of the daffodils, so there were no dying daffodils around, and we were paid sixpence. I think we started at nine o'clock and finished about half past three in the afternoon, but the big bonus was that we would go into the servants' hall for lunch. So there was never a faded daffodil.

Sutton Bingham,
Yeovil.

To Preserve Pears

Take off the rind & core
your pears – to each put
four cloves – to 6 lbs of
pears put 3 lbs loaf sugar,
powdered – the juice of
2 lemons & the rind of 1 –

A recipe for preserving pears, written on notepaper headed Sutton Bingham: the Heneages lived in the manor house there from 1924 to 1928. The crest from the Helyar coat of arms – a cross and cockerel – stands beneath the family motto 'in labore quies' ('in work is peace of mind') given to Archdeacon Helyar in 1607.

the whole to be put in a
stewpan & set on the fire
to simmer, slowly 6 or 8
hours.

A wine glass of cider
improves the colour of the
pears.

The Garden Boy

AFTER we came to the keeper's cottage I had to stay on with dad for a fortnight to help feed the chickens and clean out the houses, then I had to come down the laundry at the Court and start work – milk four cows, light the laundry fires and things like that. It was all arranged with father before I got there. I didn't have no say in it those days. I was shifted then into the Court as a hall boy, and had to live in. I were there for a little while and they wanted someone in the gardens so they asked me. I always were a bit fond of gardening. I stayed there six or seven years along with Mr Gilham; there were six or seven men working on the garden.

I was just the garden boy, see, do all these little jobs. I know I used to have to come up the Court every morning and see what vegetables they want. I used to take up a basket of potatoes first, and perhaps a couple of cabbages because they always wanted them, and go to the kitchen or the scullery. I always had a cup of cocoa or coffee, perhaps a bit of cake as kiddies used to them days, that were wonderful, then find out what other vegetables they want and go down the garden to get it and bring it back there.

Alb Hughes who started work in the gardens at Coker Court as a garden boy, and continued working there for seven years.

Inside the Walled Garden

THEY grew everything – they had a lovely old mulberry tree, quince trees, medlar trees, and old-fashioned apple trees. The whole thing was intersected by paths all edged with box – well the pears, cherries and plums were against the wall and the apple trees were all cordons with their branches trained out sideways which went behind the box hedges. Everything was trained – plums, pears, cherries against the wall, and then further down they had a patch where the medlars and quinces and things grew. They had a huge cage which ran from the centre gate down to the far end, and that's where all the soft fruit was, and they had the most extraordinary underground greenhouses. You went down steps into it – it was a pit and glass was over

Thomas Gilham, Head Gardener on the Coker Court estate. For most of his life he was a member of the church choir, and served for many years on the parish council.

the top. I think you grew cucumbers and melons and things like that in them. I don't think I've ever seen them anywhere else! I can remember being sent up to the walled garden as a child. It was beautiful. Immaculate little box hedges around each section of garden. It was the most beautifully kept garden with all these paths running across it. They had the big greenhouse nearly from the gate right up to the corner of the almshouses. There was a great long greenhouse all along that wall and there was a lovely vine in it. Underneath the vine there was a water tank, so that they never ran short of water, and a pump.

Fred Foot Mows the Lawn at Coker Court

FRED FOOT worked in the gardens. Of course he was in the first war, and he was wounded I think. He had a plate put in his shoulder, something like that, so he couldn't do big, hard or heavy work, but he could do ordinary trimming, and cleaning, and lawn-mowing. He used to lead the pony for mowing the lawns. They used to go down and get the pony, and put the boots on the pony – leather boots not for the pony to mark the lawn. Great thick-soled boots with little straps round them.

Mr Kidley's Bougainvillea

In 1894 the Royal Horticultural Society gave an award of merit to a Bougainvillea glabra *'Coker Court', a free-flowering variety of bougainvillea with deep-red flower bracts. The blooms were sent to the RHS by Samuel Kidley, the Head Gardener for W.E. Hall Esq, then living at Coker Court.*

Wrapping the Pears in the Slip

THERE used to be fruit trees all the way round the outside of the walled garden facing the church. The Slip they used to call that. All that wall right down through there used to be apples, plums, pears, and you used to see these white paper bags around a pear to keep the birds from pecking 'em. That were old Tom Gilham's idea I suppose.

Mr Gilham and the Walled Garden

I'VE nailed those fruit trees in a good many times all around the walled garden. It used to be my job to nail them in. Mr Gilham used to go on and prune them out, and I'd come on and train them. The Court used to have a good strip of ground adjoining the walled garden, with holly trees in the hedge every so far down. There used to be a little iron gate at the top in the hedge, nothing could get in there. That's where we used to keep the bees and right down round the bottom I helped plant a lot of

The Paddock. In springtime, nurses from the Yeovil District Hospital could come and pick bunches of daffodils to take back to the wards. Colonel Heneage had been president of the old hospital since 1921 when he laid the foundation-stone of the building.

nut-bushes. Some red leafed ones there, all filbert nuts, a good class nut.

They grew a lot of flowers as well in the walled garden, because Gilham used to go up every morning with a basket to do the Court vases. Artichokes – everything you can think of, we had it. Marrows, cucumbers, tomatoes. Down in the pit there was two big stoves, we used to burn a lot of coke in the winter. It was like big frames down three or four steps, as you go down there – well I were a nipper and the ground just come to eye-level. The cucumbers used to be on that bed, and of course there was trellis work above and the cucumbers grew up it and they'd run and tangle there overhead. It was a picture to see them, all lovely green cucumbers hanging on. That was my job as much as anything, to scrub that out every week.

We had a peach house, lovely peaches and nectarines we used to grow down there. That was my job as soon as I got there in the morning, to turn on the tap and wash the peach trees with a big hose-pipe. Then we had a great vine run right through that one. Gilham used to sit on a box thinning the grapes out so you get a lovely bunch of big grapes. He used to sit there with a little twig of a stick, turning the grapes and snipping out all the tiny grapes with a little pair of scissors. Underneath there we had carnations growing all under the grapes, and then the peach trees come up over that again.

There was another big boiler in the potting shed, proper stokehole. It was put to heat four greenhouses all in a row, and all the big hot-water pipes used to run through them and in under the ground in places to heat the ground.

The Colonel's Paddock

Colonel Heneage had an extensive knowledge and love of trees, shrubs and flowers, and took a personal interest in their care. He had a collection of over 200 varieties of lilacs in the garden at Coker Court and in the Paddock.

HE used to keep that Paddock beautiful the old man did. He was always in that Paddock trimming the lilacs and that. He had some beautiful lilacs in there and round the back of the Court. Best lilacs in the world up the Paddock. Old man always done the pruning hisself, he didn't pick up nothing, mind! He only cut it and somebody else had to come and clear it up! There were two notices there 'Please keep to the path'. You could walk through it but you had to keep to the path. He had 'EAST COKER' spelled out in daffodils there. He used to give the kids a shilling to go up and pick off the dead heads. They used to have nurses out from Yeovil Hospital picking bunches of daffodils when they were in full bloom, carry back a big bunch.

Trees on the Estate

Mrs Heneage had planted trees on the estate as a young girl, and hated to see trees cut down for any reason.

MRS Heneage wouldn't have a tree cut down. We had an ash tree up in the allotment at Coker Marsh, overhanging the allotment. Father wanted to get rid of him so I tell you what he did. He asked several times if they'd have him down, and Mr Wild, the bailiff, said 'You can't. She won't have a tree down'. And my father drilled and put some quicksilver in and killed the tree. But do you know what, he kept on to Wild about having this tree down that was dead, and he said 'The only way you're going to have that tree down is if you get up early one morning, early before anybody's up, cut that tree down, and clear it up'.

Spin Wood

Colonel Heneage's nickname was Spin – from his schooldays, it was short for Spinach! – and the Sleights Plantation where he spent so much time is known locally as Spin Wood.

WE used to play in the Rookery a lot because we wasn't never allowed in Spin Wood when we were kids. We used to go in there but you had to keep out of the way of the keeper! If I saw him I'd climb a tree. They used to rear all their pheasants in there in them days, see. All the drives through Spin Wood were beautiful, there was flowers, box bushes and flowering shrubs and all through. The paths was kept like Court gardens, like Daffodil Walk. Two or three woodmen there working all the time, keeping the paths and that clear. You never knew when you were going to see the old lady. Mrs Heneage used to stroll up there with her parasol. We'd hide behind a tree if we saw her about. Colonel used to spend a lot of time in Spin Wood with his secateurs, trimming the bushes and that. You could always tell when he was about because he had his dogs. If you seen his dogs, you knew the old man was about.

Odd Jobs for the Almshouses

OLD people generally moved into the almshouse after they got so old they wasn't able to work any longer. Sometimes they'd perhaps do a couple of hours work somewhere near, or if it was only to just brush a few leaves or something, just to occupy their time, you see. The Colonel was always employing some old chap

The Almshouses, founded by Archdeacon Helyar c.1640.

in the village to come and help in the gardens. There was one there called Alfie Langdon, he was always jobbing around and often the Colonel would get him to come up the gardens. I know on one occasion there was a lot of celandines all down the borders and he said 'I must get Langdon to come' and he'd get him to come and fork these celandines out, see.

Garden Party at Coker Court

In August 1929, over 500 guests attended a garden party to celebrate the wedding in two weeks' time of David Heneage to Joan Cely-Trevilian. Tenants of the estate and their families, estate employees, members of the Ex-Servicemen's Association, and the Women's Institute, together with over 100 schoolchildren were among the guests. The day's events were recalled in the Parish News.

The garden party given by Colonel and Mrs Walker-Heneage to celebrate the approaching marriage of their son and Miss Cely-Trevilian will long be remembered by all who had the privilege of an invitation.

The glorious summer afternoon in the grounds of Coker Court with the generous hospitality and the first-rate entertainments were enjoyed by a gathering of between four and five hundred adults and children; and everything, so splendidly arranged, went with a happy swing from first to last.

In an interval, Major Batten on behalf of subscribers presented Mr David Walker-Heneage with a very handsome silver salver, a lovely silver tea-pot and mustard pots, and Mr David Walker-Heneage expressed his thanks in a very happy little speech.

Miss Troyte-Bullock, President of the Women's Institute, gave him from the members a silver canister, with which the recipient was evidently surprised and delighted.

Amusement for the children was provided by way of races, with splendid prizes, which were handed to them by Miss Cely-Trevilian. Dancing on the lawn by the young people to the accompaniment of the Yeovil Town Band brought one of the happiest days in our village life to a most successful end, and everyone went away, saying: 'God Bless Colonel and Mrs Walker-Heneage and their son and his future bride'.

MISS CELY TREVILIAN'S WEDDING

BRILLIANT CEREMONIAL AT DRAYTON.

TWO WELL-KNOWN SOMERSET FAMILIES UNITED.

MIDELNEY MANOR BRIDE.

FIRST FOR 260 YEARS.

HOST OF DISTINGUISHED GUESTS.

...id popular rejoicing among the villagers ...n the presence of many friends of both ...s, the marriage took place at St. ...ine's Church, Drayton, near Langport, ...turday, of Mr. John David William ... Walker Heneage, only son of Colonel ...

... not fall." In the course of his exposition, he said it might seem an anti-climax for the words to be put in that order, but really one proceeded from the easiest thing to the more difficult. It was very easy to soar with wings and easy to mount up as eagles on love's young wings. It was easy to begin a new life's course but far harder to walk the trivial round of the ...

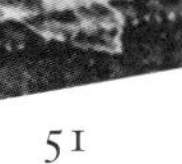

On Saturday the 10th August 1929 David Heneage, son of Colonel and Mrs Heneage, married Joan Cely-Trevilian at St Catherine's church, Drayton.

EAST COKER, SOMERSET,

Lying between YEOVIL and THE COKERS, within easy distance of STATIONS on the Great Western and the London and South-Western Railways.

Particulars, Conditions of Sale, & Plan

OF AN

IMPORTANT & VALUABLE FREEHOLD

Agricultural Property

BEING THE REMAINING AND GREATER PORTION OF

"The North Coker Estate,"

COMPRISING :

Two Well-known Excellent SHEEP and DAIRY FARMS,

"LONGLANDS" & "PAVIOTTS,"

FIVE SMALL HOLDINGS,

Several Lots ACCOMMODATION LAND,

BUILDING FRONTAGES, 3¾ Acres TIMBER,

FACTORY PREMISES, known as "EAST COKER MILL,"

With "DEVONSHIRE COTTAGE,"

PAVIOTTS HOUSE, BUSINESS PREMISES, and a

NUMBER OF COTTAGES.

THE WHOLE COMPRISING A TOTAL AREA OF ABOUT

550 ACRES.

TO BE OFFERED FOR SALE BY AUCTION, IN LOTS, BY

Messrs. R. B. TAYLOR & SONS,

AT THE "THREE CHOUGHS" HOTEL, YEOVIL,

On Saturday, 17th July, 1920,

The sale of the North Coker estate in 1920, and outlying portions of the Coker Court estate in 1926, gave tenants the opportunity to buy their farms, cottages, and other premises.

SOMERSETSHIRE

IN THE PARISHES OF

EAST COKER, SUTTON BINGHAM, PENDOMER, AND HARDINGTON MANDEVILLE.

About 1 mile from Yeovil (G.W.R. & S.R.), and 8 miles from Crewkerne (S.R.), and 1 mile from Sutton Bingham (S.R.)

Particulars, Plan and Conditions of Sale

OF A VERY ATTRACTIVE AND PRODUCTIVE

Freehold, Agricultural and Sporting Property

Known as the OUTLYING PORTIONS of the

COKER COURT ESTATE

COMPRISING

9 GOOD DAIRY FARMS

with Suitable Houses and Ample Buildings,

2 ATTRACTIVE SMALL HOLDINGS

One with a Charming Old World Residence.

VILLAGE SHOP, SCHOOL AND SMITHY

FORD FLOUR MILLS

SEVERAL SMALL RESIDENCES

WOODLANDS, BUILDING SITES, COTTAGES

and Numerous Lots of Valuable

ACCOMMODATION LAND

the whole extending to an Area of about

1,750 ACRES

FOR SALE BY AUCTION (unless previously sold to the tenants), by

R. B. TAYLOR & SONS

IN CONJUNCTION WITH

W. PALMER & CO

at the TOWN HALL, YEOVIL,

On MONDAY, 20th DECEMBER, 1926

The total amount of the 1926 sale, both on the day and by private treaty, was £58,497. 0s. 10d.

ABOVE: *North Coker Hall, built in 1895 by George Troyte Chafyn-Grove, was originally intended for family entertainments but increasingly came to be used as a Village Hall. It was sold in 1985. Standing in front of The Tree – a beech tree that was blown down in 1960 – is Henry Pulman, one of the village baker's sons. The present tree, an acer Crimson King, was planted by Mrs Hilda Turner in 1995, in memory of her husband Wilfrid Turner of Primrose Hill Farm.*

RIGHT: *'The Bingos': a photograph of members of a concert party, taken at Bridge Farm. The concert was held in North Coker Hall to raise money for the East Coker and District Nursing Association. The village nurse was supported by subscriptions, donations, and grants. Mrs Heneage provided her with an almshouse to live in, and a bicycle. In 1925 Nurse Davis made 1,918 visits in the village.*

Above: *Bridge Farm (now Hymerford House). Home of the Hambridge and Hymerford families in the 16th and 17th centuries, it took its name from Jonathan Bridges, a yeoman farmer who came to live there in 1661.*

Right: *Douglas and Reverdy, two of Jesse Crumpler's sons; they are pictured again* (below) *sitting on the gate at Longland's Farm.*

ABOVE: *Naish Priory, as it appears in an engraving from 1853. Thought to be all that remains of a larger building, in the 16th century Naish Priory was owned by the Courtenay family who were lords of the manor of East Coker and owned Coker Court.*

LEFT: *The main entrance at Naish Priory showing the small doorway in the centre of a much larger one.*

Grandmother's Extra-Strongs

I can only remember my old grandmother, my father's mother. She used to live up these what we call New Buildings, she used to wear her little old bonnet, I can see her now, and her white apron. And she used to always have these white, hot mints. Extra-strongs they used to call them. And she said 'Have a mint, chiel?' Chiel – that's for child, see.

The Candle Blows Out

In 1895 a man living at Naish Priory died after falling downstairs. Ellen Stevens, his housekeeper, would tell the story of that night.

My grandmother and another lady used to look after this man, and he was always getting drunk. It happened that my grandmother was there this particular week and this dog kept going to the big staircase and looking up and barking. Well it seems the dog must have had a premonition that something was going to happen. This man was very drunk and he went up the staircase, and when you get so far you turn to go up and he got too close to the bannister and fell down in the hall and broke his neck. Well, the wind from his fall put the candle out, that my grandmother was lighting him up the stairs with. The dog of course they had shut out in the other room, it started going mad. She had to go through the house in the dark, and across the drive to the other houses to wake someone up to tell them what had happened. My mother used to tell us all sorts of what used to happen years ago. I can't remember it all but often my sister and I were afraid to go to bed the things she used to tell us!

Another of these stories was about Suki Cook who lived at the hamlet of Sheepslake (which was demolished early this century). People disapproved of her selling coal on Sundays, and when one day they found her dead under her bed, it was said that the devil had dragged her there.

Recuperating with Aunt Mary Perry

This account of visiting an elderly aunt in the almshouses at East Coker c.1907 *is taken from* In my End is my Beginning, *by Nora E. Davies.*

As children we naturally caught the infectious illnesses common to children. But allowing for the incubation period, if we did not catch the infection at the same time, from the same source, it meant that mother was sick-nursing often for months, before the last to succumb had recovered. Fortunately, we had a maiden aunt at East Coker who had been a village nurse and had now retired to one of the almshouses near the Court and the church.

It was at the lovely little village of East Coker that I first became aware, dimly, perhaps, of awards given for service, of the loneliness of old age or the scope for friendship. It was the place where our family roots, on mother's side, went deep. Here with aunt Mary Perry, living in one of the almshouses … I first went to visit an

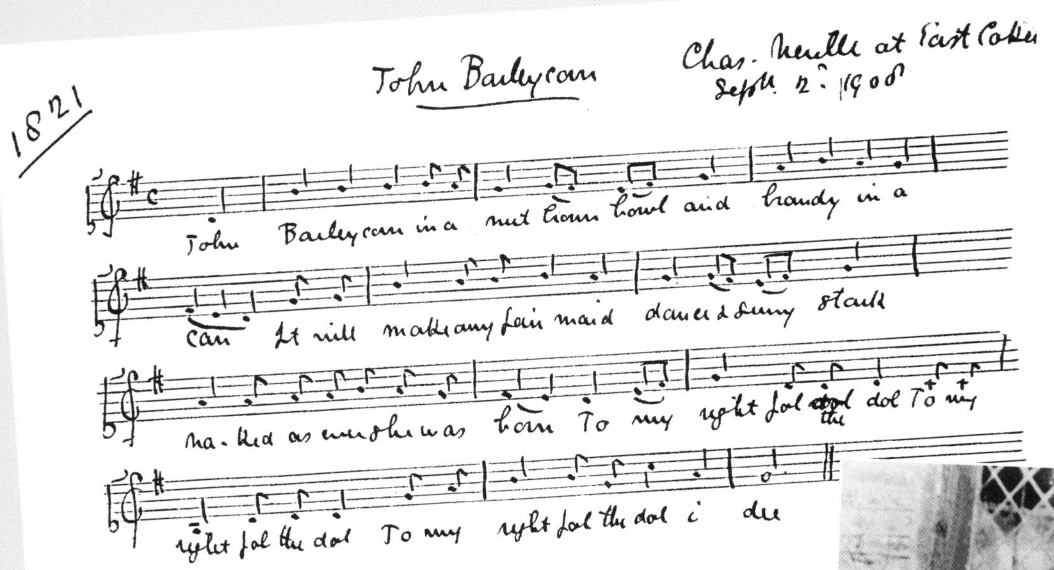

In 1908, three adults living in East Coker sang for Cecil Sharp, the English folk-music collector and editor. Charles Neville, a woodman, and his son Alfred, sang 18 songs for him; and Ann Abbott, a 79-year-old woman, sang a song called 'William and Harriet'. Sharp's first publication was Folk Songs from Somerset *issued in five parts between 1904 and 1909.*

RIGHT: *Ann Abbott (1829–1918) sits in front of her almshouse to have her photograph taken.*

Sweet Kitty

Charles Neville. at East Coker. Sept. 2: 1908

1820

As I was a-ri-ding a-ri-ding one day I met with Miss
Kitty all on the high way and sing fal the diddle le-ro sing
fal the diddle le-ro sing le-ro i day

Sharp's notation on this page and p.60 reproduced by permission of the Master, Fellows and Scholars of Clare College, Cambridge.

Jack Foot and family in front of the keeper's cottage on the Sleights: Jack was the sexton at St Michael's church, as was his eldest son Fred who took over from him in 1924. When Fred died in 1927 aged 32 – as a result of injuries suffered during the war – his younger brother Frank took over as sexton, and for 60 years continued in that role, for 50 of those years climbing the church tower every day to wind up the clock and carillon.

old lady and read to her from the Bible. It was at Auntie's suggestion, and I was not very old – six perhaps. And we spent long hours picking up the beech nuts fallen from the lovely old trees, outside, washing and shelling them and packing them down tightly into clean jam jars. I did not realise then the full meaning of 'alms', but I knew that mother's aunt was highly respected in the village. There were no old-age pensions in those days, and wages had never been large…

It was not so much what our parents and grandparents taught us in words but what they taught us by their example. It was the way they lived, what they were, rather than what they said. They were honest, upright, God-fearing folk, who would not compromise with evil. I do not claim that they were perfect men and women, but they were people whom we could respect and remember with pride.

Drink for a Poacher

MY grandfather Fred Neville emigrated from East Coker to South Wales where he found work as a miner in Pontypridd. There was a story that he left Somerset in rather a hurry because he had been caught poaching, and the local policeman was so pleased to hear he was leaving that he stood him a drink on his last night in the village! I can believe the bit about the poaching, because later, in the Depression and during the long strike when there was no work to be had, he used to set snares and catch rabbits on the mountains.

Jack Foot

In his book A Country Reporter *David Foot writes affectionately about his grandfather Jack Foot, a former gamekeeper on the Coker Court estate.*

HE'D long been one of my heroes: a one-time gamekeeper with a thirst so indiscreet that whenever he was given a gold half-sovereign for 'beating' at a Boxing Day or bank-holiday shoot, he had spent it all by the time he was led home by his faithful spaniel. He could read with great difficulty but had the big family Bible out on the table every evening. He claimed that he had read the Good Book from cover to cover three times and I believed him. I was transfixed as I watched him slowly run his engrained fingernail along each line. It was for him a laborious but rewarding process. Sarah, his sweet-natured wife, would sit in silence at the side of the hearth, bravely bearing the constant pain of acute rheumatism she had suffered for 30 years. My grandfather would fetch her long, lethal-looking bunches of stinging nettles, the stems and leaves bristling with toxic needles. She would rub the nettles up and down her frail arms and around the warped knuckles of her hands, in an effort to offset the pain.

As a young man he was a fine athlete and ran the 18 miles from his home near Dorchester to Sherborne Castle where Sarah was in service. Then, after a night's innocent courting below stairs, he would run home again. He had to be up at six o'clock next morning. I heard him often described as the best gamekeeper in Dorset.... My grandfather's accuracy with a gun was legendary. Such precision of aim was still evident in later life as he sat at the table, leaned to his left and spat into the fire – always to my astonishment missing the bars and reaching the blackened hunk of apple wood with a triumphant hiss.

Walking to Crewkerne

YOU used to walk everywhere then. T'wan't everybody that had cars then, and my great-grandmother'd walk for miles and miles and think nothing of it. I remember once, when she was in her 80s, she walked along Stony Lane to catch the train at Sutton Bingham station. She missed the train, she decided she wouldn't walk home, she'd walk up top road to catch a bus; she'd missed a bus and she walked all the way into Crewkerne. What my great-grandmother used to say, you knew everybody in the village, and if they saw anybody new they'd say 'Oh, they've come over'. Anywhere outside, you know, or if they were passing through – 'They've come over'.

Sunday Best

THEY were allotments in they days, mind. We kids weren't allowed to go down anybody else's path, these old chaps at the allotments, you weren't allowed to go down their path! They were beautifully kept then. Mill Close, Brown's Island, Kingstream, Brimble Hill. We used to have those allotments up there for eight bob a year. We had to pay it half-yearly in the pub – go down and pay four bob and have a bottle of stout for paying it. Never played football Sunday in our day. No one played football or cricket Sundays. They were wicked but they wouldn't never do it Sunday, see! My father wouldn't cut a cabbage Sunday. Never went to church but he wouldn't do anything in the garden Sunday. I suppose they worked so bloody hard in the week they were glad to have a day off! Always put their best clothes on Sundays. I remember my old granfy coming up the house every Sunday after dinner. He always had one of them big stiff collars. He had half a dozen studs in. The old man used to have to put they studs in. We used to laugh – the old man crumpled his face trying to put them in. Always dressed up Sundays – didn't go anywhere! The old men used to walk around the allotment Sunday afternoons, up Coker Marsh here, with gold watch chains on, walked around the allotment with their best clothes on.

On the 2nd September 1908, children at the village school sang six singing games for Cecil Sharp, and danced the East Coker Ribbon Dance for him.

Out for a Stroll

SUNDAY was a sacred day in those times. You'd only go to church, chapel whichever. A couple of services you'd go to perhaps, Sunday school and church, and you had to make your own fun whatever you done then. You might go for walks with your parents Sunday nights, used to visit other aunts and uncles perhaps. Every time you see anybody – 'Hello cuz!' Well cousin I suppose it would be, 'twas all round about the family.

There was a dear old chap, George Pullen, he was a little old fella, he was dairying down Bridge Farm, and the cottage for that farm was one of them up here at Burton Cross. And you see he'd come down here of a Sunday afternoon, half past two or three o'clock, and he had on his clean corduroy outfit, and he looked smart, you know. And that was every week you could bet your life on seeing him out for a stroll!

'Eternity'

Mr Wellman used to live with the Dunning family at Slade's Farm. Here Eddie Dunning writes about his old friend.

MR Wellman, dubbed by the villagers as 'Eternity', became a member of our family in 1924 when he was in his early 60s. During his boyhood he started on a farm and delighted to recall his 'bird-scaring' days, running from one end of the field to the other as the rooks settled, rattling his cocoa tin filled with small stones and shouting:

> Yo, hallo, hallo Blackie Cap
> If I sit down and have a nap
> And perchance the Master come
> You must fly and I must run.

Later he was apprenticed to a wheelwright and carpenter. His bench still stands at Slade's Farm. His vocabulary was – linseed oil, turps, yellow ochre, burnt sienna, and red lead, putty, glue and graining combs, making his own paint on a large slate slab. I watched him as a small boy with fascination.

His mode of transport was his beloved 'trike'. He fitted a large box at the rear, 'ETERNITY' was fixed above the front light bracket with another text above, another hung down from the cross bar, with a text on both sides, and then on special occasions another larger board fitted to the side of the box was raised displaying texts again on both sides.

As his somewhat reluctant 'curate' we used to visit various spots in the village. His aim was to evangelise, especially among the children. A favourite site was Tellis Cross. Our 'tools of office' were Mr Wellman's concertina in a cloth bag, and chorus books, text cards and bag of chocolates. These chocolates were given out to all who gathered round for a simple service, and in my case he fed them to me after pushing up the hills. Downhill was a glorious relief, hopping on the box behind Mr Wellman who – since the trike had no free-wheel mechanism – put his feet up on the two cross pieces he had fixed! To the village perhaps he was 'Eternity' but to me a faithful servant of Jesus Christ and a very dear friend.

Mr Wellman – 'Eternity' – on his trike at Slade's Farm in the 1920s.

When the Horse Bolted

OLD Charlie Neal lived in Cross Cottages, he used to do the dying down at the factory, because when we were kids we always used to say 'Cor, Charlie Neal's dying again today!' Old man Lawrence, Joe Lawrence who used to drive the horse, lived a few doors down.

He'd take the yarn, the webbing and all that in to the station down the bottom of Hendford Hill. I shall never forget him, when he used to drive that cart. He had a big black horse. Blasted great thing it was! And he was loaded-up down the factory one day, he used to go from the factory, come up through – there's a gateway half-way between – and then come past Cross Cottages out on the road. And do you know he was all ready to go, and he went in and got his horse, and the horse took off – he bolted! You never seen anything like it! This blasted great thing cleared a five-bar gate, he went and he run right down to Hendford station and he stopped right exactly where he had to stop waiting for Joe to get there!

The old line cottages that once stood by the railway bridge on the road to Coker Wood: people who lived in these cottages usually worked for the L&SWR (London & South Western Railway) and would pay their rent by leaving it in a can by the side of the railway line to be collected. The couple in this photograph is believed to be Mr and Mrs Spragg; Mr Spragg was a ganger, the head of the linesmen.

Sutton Bingham railway station c.*1908*.
Stanley Norman, who had been a signalman there for over 30 years when the station closed in 1962, remembered when the Devon Belle was derailed just outside the station, and the 'cowslip specials' that ran from Yeovil for the benefit of flower pickers.

Granfy Boucher the Lengthman

My father's father was a railwayman. He worked as a lengthman. In them days there was three or four men working on the railway repairing the line and that. My grandfather's length used to be Yeovil Junction to Sutton Bingham. In them days they wouldn't have a father and son to work on the same length. My grandfather got my father a job on the railway and he had to move to Bradford Abbas, to go the other side of the Junction. But my mother wouldn't leave East Coker and that's why father left the railway. And when he got my uncle a job, he had to work the other length from Sutton Bingham to Hardington Marsh.

In them days all the railway embankments and all they were mowed by hand, see. My granfer would cut his hair with his scythe! I heard a story that they had a bet in the pub here once said he'd cut his hair with a scythe, brought the scythe in and cut his hair! They old railwaymen they could sharpen, see. All them banks from Sutton Bingham to Hardington Marsh won the first prize for the South Western Railway from Waterloo to Exeter for years. Four old men – there was Bert Patten, he was the ganger, my uncle Gilbie Neville, there was Purchase, and a bloke called Donnington lived up Kit Hill. They kept all those hedges and banks beautiful.

They say he was on Sutton Bingham platform when a train driver's mate got killed under the train. My grandfather always wore a beard, it was black – they reckon my grandfather turned white in a second. He saw him fall under the train and his hair went white with fright.

I can remember my grandfather retired on the railway on one and sixpence a week. He had to walk to Sutton Bingham every week to get it.

We kids wasn't allowed on the line. We were always dared by our parents never to go on the line. We used to watch the trains, especially when there was a new one coming on. I can remember the 'King George V' come through. We used to go up to Sutton Bingham to see 'em come through.

Sutton Bingham was a busy station when I was a kid, mind. I've seen 12 or 14 horses and carts up there at eight o'clock in the morning with milk to be put on the train to go to London. They had milk floats in them days, carry about four or six churns. There was a station master, two porters and two signalmen at Sutton Bingham when I was a kid.

Sarah Dodge with one of her grandsons outside the family's house at Gunville Lane. Sarah's husband William had been the steward for the North Coker House estate.

Granfy Stagg gets Alec at the Grindstone

Here Alec Boucher writes about his grandfather Simeon Stagg.

As a schoolboy I recall spending many winter Saturday afternoons turning the grindstone for him to grind his scythe and hooks. He had a habit of coming to our house at dinner-time – usually rabbit stew, the rabbit having been given to father by Sid Giles who was an expert at knocking them from a tuft of grass with a knobbed stick – and he'd say to father 'I want the boy for a couple of hours'. They did not ask you in those days, they told you and you went. The grindstone was outside the cellar door at Slade's Farm, the farmer being Bert

Newman who had plenty of cider which all the local men could help themselves to as they always helped in the summer with the haymaking and harvest. So I turned the stone and he ground the tools between drinks. I remember the old farm cock bird crowing and granf used to swear he was saying 'Lock the cellar door!' After a few more jugs and a few more grinds and getting a bit fed up with the crowing he'd cuss to the cock bird. He never got those tools sharp until it was too dark to see the tap on the barrel! Then he'd wrap them in a sack, take out his purse and give me a halfpenny, and tell me to run up Mrs Helyar's shop and get some bull's-eyes or my mother would wonder where I had got to. Then off we went to Coker Marsh – granf drunk, and me frozen.

Granfy Stagg goes Haymaking

HE was a character he was, mind. I've heard my mother tell he used to go out on the booze and at this time of the year they'd leave their work down the factory and go up Pendomer haymaking for weeks on end, and never had no money for it, they'd just go up for cider and bread and cheese! Never come home, he used to sleep in a barn. They never had no money, lost their wages, they'd have a fortnight's holiday up Pendomer haymaking for Joe Whetham! Well, a lot of 'em did go to work for farmers, these old men that worked in the factory, it's a monotonous job in the factory for country people, isn't it? Our granny had a hard life. She used to do a lot of laundry then – she'd be at the wash-tub or ironing all day long.

Cheese for Grandmother Bowles

GREAT-GRANDMOTHER lived at Bridge Farm for a time. I always remember her birthday was the 11th May. In those days they all knew how to make cheese. Grandmother Bowles loved cheese and mother used to

Sarah Newman and Mary Hardy with their mother Rachael Bowles at Key Farm.

make her a truckle cheese for her birthday every year. They used to make cheese at Key, and my mother made cheese at Pavyott's and before that at Bridge Farm. We had a dairy, perhaps up to 50 cows. All the milk was brought in from the two milkings and you had the night milk and the morning milk and that was all brought into the dairy, put into the big round cheese tub and made into cheese. The cheese was all stored in the old cheese rooms and had to be turned every day.

In the year of the General Strike, which was 1926, all our milk from Pavyott's and Key Farm milk in those days used to go to London. They'd stopped cheese-making by then. Any case there were no trains so what happens? They return the milk home to Pavyott's Farm and luckily my mother stored all her cheese-making equipment up in the cheese room. What does she do? She turns around and she gets it all out, the milk is tipped into it, and she makes cheese all the night. She made some good cheese apparently. On the odd occasion in the winter if they hadn't the demand for milk in London, my mother would make Caerphilly cheese. My mother was a great buttermaker as well. She used to show at shows and that's where she met my father. He used to be a cheesemaker. She met my father somewhere in the Chewton Mendip area – she was showing butter, and he was showing cheese. He borrowed my mother's scotch hands but that was only an excuse to meet her. Mother was married from Key, it was the first of March and it snowed. They snowballed on the lawn in front of the house and filled her umbrella with confetti.

Jim Baker who in 1947 retired from twine-making at Drake's factory aged 85, having worked there since he was ten. He remembered the days when children would run up to the West Coker Road to see the coach go by, and the severe winter of 1881 when cottages were half-buried by snow. For over 13 years Jim was caretaker of the cemetery and when digging a grave knew he had reached the right depth when the ground was at eye-level – he was 6' 4" tall.

Jack Foot and Jack Neville

My grandfather knew so much about nature, as all village people did. The garden was the creative force, it was the one thing they could always be creative and artistic about. I always remember he had very long nails – usually dirty – and he would spend hours walking up and down the back path taking off the tops of the dandelions before they went to seed. He was quite a good-looking man, a slightly intimidating moustache, and a weary face, like most old village people. A face of an old man who'd never really had much, and had worked very, very hard for it.

My grandfather had his weekly groceries from Mrs Ray's shop, and always included extra-strongs, I remember, and Quaker oats. He lived on Quaker oats virtually, and extra-strongs, and humbugs.

Jack Neville, who lived opposite, was an old countryman and he was always standing at his gate, looking across as everyone went by so he didn't miss anything.

George Rendell of Hunt's House

My grandfather was a market gardener. He owned a plot of ground called Hunt's Ground. He had been a gardener to the famous firm of Brutton's the brewers in Yeovil, and he was well respected as a gardener in the whole of the district.

Grandfather grew cabbages of various kinds, he grew turnips, spinach, he had quite a number of apple trees, different kinds of apples, and he had plums. He grew a lot of curly kale. He rented the land at the back of Hunt's House which was called Half Acre. He refused to have anything mechanical such as a plough – he dug everything by hand, and he dug it most meticulously. The produce was picked by my grandmother.

Grandfather was a quiet man. He liked his drink of cider, and the *Foresters Arms* down in Holywell was a place where he usually obtained it. He was a keen Forester. It was a friendly society and that was its base, the *Foresters Arms*. It was down there that he used to pay in the contributions that would lead ultimately to a small pension.

Grandfather had three barrels of cider which we kept in an outhouse. I remember that the barrels had to be attended to, and if it was too sour they used to add quantities of figs to it to sweeten the cider. One of my last memories of my grandfather shortly before he died, when he had pneumonia developing, was of him sitting in the kitchen with his feet on the old kitchen range, supping a mug of hot cider and ginger, and singing his old favourite hymns.

George Rendell of Hunt's House, Holywell. A keen market gardener, a variety of heather was named after him: Erica x darleyensis *'George Rendell'. One of his maxims: 'Every man eats a pound of earth before he dies'.*

Hunt's House, Holywell.

Cider-Making by Moonlight

LOTS of times they used to make cider at Sid Giles's in the moonlight, they only had hurricane lanterns. My father, Jim Boucher, used to go there for hours and hours making cider with Sid Giles. I can remember Granny Giles because when I used to come home from school I would go and pick up her apples for her in the orchard there. Freezing cold, pair of old gloves on, picking up these apples as it gets dark. She had a hearth fire, and used to always make crock cake in the crock on the fire. I can remember going in there cold, I'd been picking up apples, and sitting in the chimney corner warming my hands, and the old lady giving me this crock cake.

Sid Giles with daughter Lottie and granddaughter Nancy at the back of his cottage in Up Coker (now Bwythn Bach). Sid was a thatcher by trade but also made cider for local pubs. It is said that Sid Giles did most of the thatching for the Coker Court estate, and Robert Lacey of Naish Barton the thatching for the North Coker House estate.

Sid Giles and his Mobile Cider Press

SID GILES spent a lot of time making cider. He had a mobile cider-press, pulled with a pony, and people like Bill Poole down the *Foresters Arms* used to sell cider in them days – they drunk more cider than they did beer. I can remember once a year Bill Poole used to have a day out up at the *Helyar Arms* and buy all the apples around, all the different orchards. All these old boys like my grandfather used to know when Bill Poole was coming up here and they'd all be there. He had to spend a pound or two buying them drinks. They used to buy the apples in the orchard. Say the

Mrs Giles bringing the cows in for milking c.1949.

farmer had an orchard, he'd give them so much for it and the farmer had to pick 'em up and deliver 'em. And Sid Giles used to go round to the *Foresters* with his press and his pony and spend two or three days making the cider, see. He used to go round to the *Foresters*, the *Castle*, the *Mandeville*. I never knew the *Helyar Arms* make cider, there was never much cider sold at the *Helyar*, mind.

I've helped Sid Giles make tons of cider when I were a kid. I used to grind the apples up with a hand grinder. I used to go down there and suck the cider coming down the press through a straw. What you did, you lay a layer of straw, then you ground your apples into pommy – you know, soft like you make a tart with – and put a layer of apples. The straw was a bundle like you thatch with that was laid out. When they'd put the first layer of apples on they'd turn the straw back in, then they'd put on another layer of apples, then they'd turn the straw in again. Do about three lots of that. Then they'd put some more straw on then. It was all knitted in – it was a neat job, mind, all done nicely. And they used to go round with the old shears and snip off the end of the straw. A cider cheese – that's what they called it, when it was built up like a block about four foot high. Then they wound the press down. They had long poles on the top of the press what wound down on the spiral: they put the poles in there and walk around and pull it down so far and then leave it. Then when it stopped running, you'd press it again see.

Making Cider at Burton Farm

My father used to keep a barrel of cider up here in the garden – nine-gallon barrel. He used to go over Burton Farm making it, see. Used to always have nice cider over there. Used to be an orchard all down the back and all different sorts of cider apples. You had to have the right apples for cider: *Bloody Butchers*, they were red all the way through nearly, and little *Yellow Horners*, and mix 'em up. They used to have a long pole – they used to cut 'em out of the woods – and they'd rattle it all around the trees, shake the apples down, and pick 'em up. Then they'd wait for the apples to 'come' – get softer. If you used them straight away they'd be firm and you wouldn't get the amount of juice out of 'em like they

Cider-making at Isles Farm in 1966: (l–r) Bob Richards, George Ford, and Bill Richards. The press is now over 100 years old, and is still in use in a nearby parish.

would by waiting. Well, they didn't used to like those what used to go black, they didn't mind any just going rotten, that didn't matter, they'd all go in together and they'd have 'em in the wagon perhaps, leave the wagon in the orchard and then come the time they'd have 'em whenever they were going to make the cider. They'd shovel the apples out then in baskets, carry 'em in.

At the back of the stables at Burton Farm there used to be the cider-press. I used to go over there then. That was up my alley, you know, go up there, three or four old blokes been to work down the factory, see, go in there and making the cider. Father, and Tom Clothier, old Jimmy Baker used to go in there and give to on the grinder, grind the apples from the loft up over. That were my job to go up in this loft and shovel the apples through a hole in the floor, with sack round to guide it over to the top of the grinder. The cider were their pin-money for haymaking and all that. Father used to have his barrel filled over there. Cider-making was always done at night, see, after their daily work down the factory. Maybe weekend as well perhaps, but mostly at night 'twas. The old lantern hung up to the ceiling, like.

Cider for Longlands Farm and Pommy for the Cows

My step-father Fred Charles he'd cut the hedges, they was wonderful hedges in those days, and dig the ditches. Then when the mangels and sugar-beet come along, he'd do the hoeing and all that kind of stuff, and then go and pull the mangels up. They all used to be pulled by hand. They'd pull 'em up, chop the leaves off very often, and lay them in a long row as they pulled them, and then they'd come along with a horse and cart and pick the mangels up. That was another trade – picking them up! We kids used to help, lend a hand – we used to get a couple of coppers, sometimes a glass of cider maybe. Haymaking time when they used to build the ricks there was always cider there. Nobody would go to work without they'd drunk the cider!

Another thing that my step-father used to do – make the cider. We used to put the apples through the grinder, the apples was all like pulp, then you'd have a layer of straw, a layer of apples, a layer of straw and a layer of apples till it was all what they used to call a cheese, a cider-cheese. Then you had this great big press, a big screw at each end, and you'd turn it down. When it was all pressed out and practically dry they'd take it down and they'd chop it up and feed it to the cattle. They like it, you'd see them rolling around drunk, a herd of cows! I'm not kidding you! They're foolish, cows, they'll eat apples and get drunk. And they also used to get stuff from the brewery, farmers would buy the mash. You'd see the cows get drunk on that, they wouldn't know where they were going.

Meeting Old Shep

Crumpler always had a flock of sheep. He always kept a shepherd. Old bachelor bloke he was, lived up at Crumpler's. He always had a shepherd's crook, old Shep did. Shep used to go down the *Foresters*. Crumpler met him at the lane one evening when he went to go across and get a bottle of port or sherry down the pub. Of course he went home late through they lanes, Kingstream Lane. Shep fell down in the lane. 'Coo,' he said 'Shep that cider's strong' – 'It isn't bloody strong enough to hold I up!'

A Bucketful of Cider at the Foresters Arms

That was a right place down there, mind. In those days they used to make their own cider, see. 'Twas all cider down there at one time. The landlady – Crying Mary they used to call her, she always looked as though she were crying so old Harry Stevens up here told me – she'd say to my father 'Will you go get a drop of cider, we're nearly out'. They used to keep it in wooden buckets, see, for the evening. He

The back of the Foresters Arms *in Holywell seen from the footpath that crosses to Skinner's Hill. Mrs Blanche Blackaller's little shop is on the right-hand side of the footpath.*

The New Inn c.*1908. The pub was renamed the* Helyar Arms *in 1948, partly in memory of Dorothy Heneage, the last of the Helyar line, who died in 1947; but also because of the number of inns in the area with the same name. An old granary was converted into a recreation room for the East Coker branch of the British Legion in 1934, and its members converted the stables below into a skittle alley, still popular today.*

used to go out with these two wooden buckets across a field to a tin shed where they used to store it. He'd come back and go in the taproom door. 'Twas a longish room in them days, and narrow, and the blokes each side were sat up, see, and they'd each dip their cup in as he were going on! Time he got there the buckets were only about half full!

Drinking at the New Inn

THAT was more sedate up there always, you know, well it used to belong to the Coker Court estate the pub did until recent years. I mean the estate workers were shy to go in there, I think, to drink, bar old Albie Dunham used to live down the lane. He'd go in there, he were bold, he didn't bother. But others they'd creep round the back with a bottle, for the bottle-and-jug department for to get a bottle filled up or whatever. That was only a little trapdoor out round the back of the pub, see. 'Twas outside and they'd come there and tap and put the bottle in, they'd fill the bottle up and pull the trapdoor on again. They were scared to go in the pub. Couldn't let Mrs Heneage know they was in the pub!

Albie Dunham's Brushes

YEARS ago you'd very seldom see anybody in the *New Inn*. It was never used. I think the people working on the estate, which most of them did up there, were afraid to go in there because of their neighbours! The only time they used it, they'd go to the taproom for their bottle and come out with it hidden underneath their coat. One old chap, he was a labourer, Albie Dunham. He lived down Moor Lane and he wasn't a bit worried about anybody. He was a hard-working bloke. He used to go around chimney-sweeping after he'd finished the day's work. He carried his brushes on his shoulder all down through the village, like a soldier with a rifle. He'd gone on back one night, we were up here we kids and Albie come down the road, he'd been off chimney-sweeping then, see. He goes off to have his pint or two and he'd left his brushes outside the porch there under the arch, you know. One of us hided his brushes, of course we all congregated round the corner somewhere there, waited till he come out. Cor, you never heard nothing like it! He found 'em I suppose, but he frightened us at the finish I think. He frightened us serious!

Above: *The original Devonshire Cottage, demolished c.1938 when the new building was completed. Part of this façade survives as a garden wall, and the shapes of former windows and the front door can still be seen in the stonework. In the mid-19th century Edward Taylor, sailcloth manufacturer and owner of the powerloom sailcloth factory on Halves Lane, lived here.*

Left: *Cross Cottages, 1937: Mrs Annie Boucher stands at her door, with two of her children, Jack and Doris.*

ABOVE: *Jane Groves stands in front of her cottage in Back Lane. For many years she ran a private school with her mother and sister at Bubspool House. The school closed c.1902.*

RIGHT: *Gran Cooper (Mary Giles, born 1837) in the garden of her cottage on Moor Lane (now St Roch Cottage). One room of the cottage, with a door opening onto the lane, was used as a Methodist chapel from 1841 until it closed in 1977.*

ABOVE: *Key Farm, which stands on the main Yeovil to Dorchester road: the little boy is Frederick James Newman (1926–94) who lived at Key all his life and was to farm there as his parents had done before him. The dog, Neville, was a present to Fred's mother on her wedding day.*

RIGHT: *Townsend Farm, with four of Hannah and Levi Vowles' children – Sydney, Harry, Matilda and William.*

Apple Crazy

When I was a girl we used to go pinching apples from the orchard at Townsend Farm, crawling across the Park from the church path. Get in that kissing-gate and go across. There was a *Sweet Acreman*. My step-mother used to more or less send me up there to get those apples. She said to me 'You go up there and you can bring home a few apples'. I think she was carrying one of her babies or something – she was apple crazy – and I used to go up through the hedge and pinch 'em there. Sometimes I'd put the apples in my knicker legs 'cos 'twas elastic round the bottom!

The Coker Seedling

Many different varieties of apple trees could be found growing in the gardens and orchards of East Coker and village children knew where all the best trees were! One very local variety is the Coker Seedling: *its apples are good for both cooking and eating, and it is said to be very easy to propagate – some trees in the village started life as pea-sticks or flower stakes, took root, and grew into trees. The* Coker Seedling *is said to have been 'found' by Charles Neville, a woodman on the Coker Court estate. It was first exhibited in* 1934.

Children playing in a hayfield near Redlands.

Scrumping at Longlands Farm

ALL the kids used to go scrumping! Old man used to catch us a time or two – you'd hear him coming down across the field, all cutting the thistles off 'cos he had a knife on the edge of his stick. 'Jesse Crumpler's coming!' – over the hedge and away! He knew we were there alright.

Chestnuts and Walnuts

USED to be sweet-chestnut trees in a corner of the Park behind Townsend Farm. Three or four or five trees there and another one up in the corner by the churchyard. We used to nip up there after them, mind! When they got really ripe they used to fall out of the prickly shell, you could eat them raw or roast them. Used to be walnut trees there too – we used to know where all they was in the Sleights.

'Daisy' Langdon's Pocket of String

THE people were going on into the factory to work as we were going on to school. A lot of them worked out there on the webbing. Then there was this old chap at the bottom of Primrose Hill called 'Daisy' Langdon and he used to always carry some string in his pocket for us, for our spin-tops. He used to be out in the twine walk seeing to the twine as it was drying. 'Have you got any string, Mr Langdon?'. Well there was nearly always some there.

Skipping in the Road

WE would play hopscotch and skipping – one stand one side of the road and someone stand the other, holding the rope and twisting it. Because

Bob and Margaret Mead of Gunville Lane who shared their father's passion for motor cycles at an early age! As a young woman Margaret went on to compete in many motor-cycle trials, including the London to Land's End.

East Coker School children, c.1920, with headmaster Sydney Webber: (l–r) back row: Jack Andrews, Bert Hellyar, Stan Ostler, Bert Whetham, Johnny James; third row: Les Symes, Sid Neville, Alec Boucher, Jack Lacey, ?Bond; second row: Lilian Harris, Margaret Mead, Amy Dunster, Dolly Purchase, T. Cox, Louise Helyar, Orpah Woolmington, - Thorn, - Thorn, Ada Stevens; front row: Norman Lacey, Len Farnham, Harry Hardy.

father worked at the twine factory he would bring home a bit of rope, and we had hoops, iron hoops, wooden hoops, and you'd have a stick and hit them and follow them all down the road. Spinning-tops, you had a stick with a bit of string on it and you would flick the top and it would spin and, if you keep hitting it, it went on up and down the road. We loved that in those days. Holiday time a little party or gang of us, we'd go down across the field pinching apples from Mr Crumpler's orchard, then we'd go nutting, picking the nuts off the hedges.

'One Arm Samuel' and Others

Nicknames were a common feature of village life, perhaps because so many people shared the same surnames. Some nick-names heard during an East Coker childhood: Royal Blood, One Arm Samuel, Long Jimmy, Long Roser, Silk Britches, Crying Mary. There is a rhyme that starts 'Hardington partridge and Coker hounds' so even villages had nicknames!

Archie Helps the Blacksmith

I'D always go to the blacksmith. He used to make hoops for us, iron hoops, and if one broke he'd weld it and he used to forge it. You'd go down there and ask for them, there was plenty of them about. You could go in the forge and watch – keep well out of the way of those horses' hooves. I used to go in there and blow the bellows for him. I felt very proud of that, helping the blacksmith. They used to have the same kind of bellows on the church organ – same thing. Sometimes I had to go and do that. When the guy was sick that used to work

East Coker School children, c.1920, with teacher Ella Hayward: (l–r) back row: Ken Gillingham, Jim Hunt, Ben Woolmington, Archie Beales, Arthur Whetham, Len Lacey, - , George Woolmington, - , Stan Ascott; third row: - , Dolly Bull, Lorna Thorn, Orpah Woolmington, Alice James, Dorothy Ascott, - Woolmington, Yvonne Lacey, Gwen Pitcher, Margey Patten, - Bright; second row: Ralph Ridout, Billy Dunham, - Haines, Reg Griffin, Sam Walbridge, Kathy Stagg, Dora Doddington, ?Stagg, Monty Ridout, Gordon Watkins, Teddy Woolmington, Eddie Hawkins; front row: Ivan Lacey, - , Harry Hughes, - Woolmington, Bill Andrews, Jack Neville, - , - , Len Parsons.

the bellows, they used to pick on a choirboy. I tell you, when Mrs Hackwell got on that organ, she started hitting those high notes, you had to blow like hell otherwise the bloody organ'd stop!

Fox and Hounds

And we used to play fox and hounds – one'd be the fox and hide and you had to find one another going on. Each side of the road there was bushes and trees and you could get in behind and hide in they places. Sometimes we'd play going on to school, but we didn't have to dawdle about too long! Course you see you were never bored – there wasn't enough time in the day for to do what you wanted to do.

Swimming in Slaford Bottom

Down in Slaffits where the river goes through from West Coker, we used to bathe down there when we were kids. Never had no bathing costumes on or nothing like that! I've been down there many a time.

My mate Herbie Cox, his father was the miller down there for years at the mill. He used to take his father's lunch down. Course we had to watch us all the time, you didn't get into no mischief, you know, 'cos the old stones were going round, grinding down the wheat or barley. Very heavy. They rolled round and round and round – 'Round goes the wheel, and troubles I have few' he used to sing! They call them dusty miller: he used to come out looking like a flour bag! All his eyebrows was white!

East Coker School children, c.1920:
(l–r) back row: Howard Hayward, Austin Whetham, Stan Ostler, Charles Rowles, – ;
third row: Dot James, Margery Cheney, Eva Stockley, Lily Hutchins, Margery Lacey, May Rendell; second row: Miss Stacey, Annie Walbridge, Harold Baker, Stella Lacey, Violet Ostler, Lily Grey, John Cox, Bill Hutchins, Doll Gray, Elsie Hughes, Gladys Tewkesbury; front row: Jack Helyar, Dave Watkins, Ed Dollington, Mervyn Lacey, Vera Harris.

Watching the Water-Wheel

WHEN we were kids we used to go and open the trapdoor, and watch the wheel going round. Big wheel mind, big wheel. They say the mills of God grind slowly, but they grind exceeding fine, don't 'em!

Swimming at Sheep-Dip Time

WE used to go down Pavyott's Mill and swim. Jump in. It was quite big when the water was dammed up. But then it was dangerous really because they used to dig out a place in the stream, and dip the sheep there. They used to use that arsenic stuff that they put in sheep-dip and they'd dip the sheep in there, in the same bit of water you'd been swimming in at sheep-dip time! Us boys, we used to go all over the place. We'd have paper-chases, we'd probably end up the other side of Sutton Bingham or Closworth or somewhere like that. It was our own sport, you know. Well there wasn't nothing else to do. Cowboys and Indians and anything. Oh yes, it used to be quite a lot of fun.

Bogged Down in Coker Moor

WE used to get into trouble if we went down the Moor when we were small. We had to go down there on the quiet. My young brother and nephew and some other boys went down there one night and got bogged in coming through one of the gateways. They'd been told not to go down there, it used to be wet down there in the winter, mind. Jack got out and come on home and never told anybody because they'd been dared not to go down there. The old man questioned him where they boys were to and he told him then. Father and two or three of the men up Coker Marsh went down and dragged them out. They were up to their waists!

Skating in Quarry Ground

There's a stone quarry there next to Tellis Cross. It's not a deep one, it's very shallow. The stone used to come up something like crazy paving, in layers, like. They used a lot of it around here in the old days they tell me for different jobs. You'd get flat stone slabs out of it if you didn't break it before you got it – it was very brittle stuff. I used to go skating in the quarry. It used to get filled with water see, always flooded. We never had skates – we'd calmly call it skating – you'd take a run and slide across it. I got a split lip as a result!

The Old Lime-Kiln at Isles

Mr Ostler was a quarryman, and he used to take the donkey up there, you see, to pull the little trucks up to the top of the lime-kiln. Years and years after you could still see the bits and pieces of it, these iron rails like railway sleepers, relics of the axles and all of these trolleys. Us children used to go riding on the donkey! One used to watch in case Mr Ostler was coming!

Bluebells for Annie Boucher

Harbins Plantation was always called Bluebell Copse. When we kids used to go up there we'd pick armfuls of bluebells. You'd waste half of 'em coming back. I've seen mother have a bucketful of bluebells before now!

I knew every flower. In the country, you know every flower, don't you? You never hardly see any cowslips now do 'ee? Ploughing the fields killed the cowslips 'cos you'd see 'em all over the fields and meadows. Now they only grow around the hedgerows what haven't been ploughed. Several lots of orchids in the fields. One orchid we saw was called a *Granfy Griggle* – nice orchid he was , beautiful purple orchid. They used to grow in the fields just like cowslips and oxslips. There was moon daisies – we used to call them thunder daisies.

Listening to the Thrushes at Naish Barton

Down Yew Hill Rocks at the bottom of Primrose Hill there was hundreds of holes there, and that used to be sand-martins used to do those. There used to be hundreds of sand-martins. I haven't seen one for years now. There used to be thousands of thrushes round here, down the lanes and that – I used to watch them. If there was a stone or anything you'd find all snail shells around where the thrushes take the snails and crack them. I never seen any other bird having a go at snails, it only seemed to be the thrushes. In the evening, everything would be quiet and you could hear this tapping going on: 'What the hell was that?' like, and it was the thrushes banging their snail shells. We used to go out looking for glow worms. You go out at night and they shine out quite bright.

Dot's Magpie

It could talk and call all the children's names. Every morning it would come and tap on my bedroom window for me to open the window for it to come in. And if we were sat indoors in a crowd, you know, a lot of our relations used to come, I used to be the one that he'd pick out to come and rest on my shoulder. And then one night I went up to my friend's at Darvole – and of course I stayed up there too long – it had followed me up there, flying from tree to tree – and it got a bit dark and I didn't see it after. I was ever so vexed when my magpie went. I went all up round the next day calling it but I couldn't find it.

Scenes from the Upstairs Window

There was a garden behind our cottage, big garden. Th'other side there was a piece of garden where

Wesleyan Sunday School children in a field close to the old Methodist chapel, Moor Lane, 1919: here the children and Mrs Watkins of Hyde Farm (Superintendent of the Sunday School) are surrounded by thunder daisies. (l–r) from back: G. Bowsher; E. Stockley, C. Boucher, Mrs Watkins, G. Watkins; G. Bull, - Bowsher, E. Stevens, D. Bull; D. Watkins, A. Boucher, D. Boucher, S. Neville, C. Rawles, A. Bull; - Newman, J. Neville.

dad used to put mostly french beans, and a big apple tree. 'Twas an old-fashioned sweet apple, *Quarandine*. Peas were a treat mind. I used to go up with my brother and he'd scrounge some. Get a clip upside the ear, you know. Plenty of french beans, broad beans, cabbage, but peas were a treat. Gooseberry bushes were out there, 'cos that's where the babies came from, under there! In every garden you had your gooseberries, and currants, and raspberries. There was a plum tree up the side of the house, *Victoria* plum. I used to hang out the window at the side to reach the plums and Mrs Giles from across the road would tell mum when she came home – 'She's going to fall and break something one day'. Our next door neighbour, I can remember her husband died, and whether she lost her senses or not, or whether she was on the bottle I don't know, 'cos one day my dad came rushing in 'Come on quick, she's in the bloody rain barrel!' In the rain-water barrel trying to drown herself. They got her out, I can remember, and they took her off in a car. I went on the landing upstairs, I hung out of the bedroom window and I saw the black maria come for her.

Ralph Plays the Jack-the-Lantern

There was a story that men walking home along the footpath from the Foresters Arms *on a Saturday night might be tricked by the light of the Jack-the-Lantern, and be led down towards the stream to drown.*

WHEN my brother and I were children we had to go outside to the tap to get our fresh water, and if it was dark, I used to say 'I'm afraid to go up there' and my brother used to say 'You mind old Jack-the-Lantern's up there'. We were always afraid to go up the tap, and I didn't realise then what a Jack-the-Lantern was, that it was the glow-worm. Ralph was a scamp when he was younger. There was two or three children living next door. They were staying with their grandmother and of course at night they used to come out and play with us after dark. And my brother, he'd come out and where the saucepan had been on the fire he'd black his face. He'd come out and oh! we'd scream! We used to run up and down the field at the back of the garden and jump down under the wall, but if he knew we were going to do that, he'd be down under the wall waiting for us!

Gammitting About

THE lamp we had up there mother bought was a brass hanging lamp with a globe showing a lovely light. One hung down from the ceiling so that we boys gammitting about as we used to call it, just playing about as boys are before bedtime, wouldn't knock the table and knock it over. If it was knocked over the flame would all go up before you could do anything. She was afraid the lamp would fall and catch the place afire.

A Trick Too Far

WE used to tap people's windows with a button, put a button on a bit of cotton, hang it over somebody's window, and go back behind a bush and just pull the cotton, tap the window and people would come out their doors to see what's happening. The only thing I remember doing which we got into trouble over once, we'd been all through the village and unhitched everybody's gate, took everybody's gate off the hinges and just stood 'em up inside the posts, and then when people went to open them, they fell down. There was a row over that because one of the gates fell on some old woman's leg.

The Strap and the Birch

WASN'T no messing around in they days. If you'd done wrong you got caned for it. But it didn't hurt you did it? If you do wrong you expect to get punished. That's all it was, the end of it, wasn't it? I've seen a boy that had the birch, I went to school with him. All he did was wrote a love-letter to a girl. He was only a boy about nine, ten, and the mother found this letter and told the authority and he had the real birch from the magistrates. He showed me his back. My father would thrash me with a strap if I didn't do what he told me, or answered back or anything like that. That didn't hurt me though, did it? I didn't do it again, did I?

The Lads' Club

In the 1920s a Lads' Club was held in the Scouts Hall from October to April for teenaged boys who had left school for work. The club met on Tuesdays and Fridays, and for 2d a night they could play bagatelle, table skittles, cards and draughts, or learn how to box.

WE used to have a youth club in the old Scouts Hall. We had billiard tables, everything that you could wish to have in a sports club. You name it, it was there. Colonel Heneage he got it for us and he used to learn us boxing and all down there – his chauffeur was heavyweight champion of the Guards and he used to come down and learn us in the Scouts Hall. We didn't have any scouts, not in the period I'm talking about, if there was, I would have been in it.

Archie Learns to Drive at Longlands Farm

I could drive before I left school at 14 – on Revvy Crumpler's T-model Ford on the farm. Nobody taught very much them days, years ago – get in and drive! Round the lanes at Naish, into Yeovil. I got a motor-cycle licence when I was 14, and when I was 15 I thought 'Well to hell with this, I'll write for a car licence' and I got a full licence for everything. Said I was 17. You had to apply for it down at Taunton. No tests, no nothing.

There was no traffic really. I can almost tell you how many cars there were in the village: Jesse Crumpler had a car, he had an old Homberg; Mr Mayo had a car; Drake had a car; the Heneages; the people that went to live at Bubspool, they had a car; and the Maudslays at North Coker House naturally they had a car – they would! Mr Maudslay was the founder of the Maudslay

East Coker School children, c.1920:
(l–r) back row: Edwin Stevens, George Bull, Bill Ascott, B. Tucker, Jim Hutchings; third row: Miss Venn, Minnie Ascott, Louise Stevens, Alice Wills, Gwen Slade, Ada Bull, Lily Purchase; second row: Margery Lacey, Orpah Woolmington, Iris Gardiner, Gladys Pitcher, Hilda Whetham, Stan Haines, George Gillingham, Reg Tewkesbury, Charlie Boucher; front row: Bert Turner, - Higgins, Harold Symes, ?Ivor Gardiner, Ed Wellman, Frank Patten, Frank Hayward.

Motor Co. in Coventry. But apart from that, there was only just a few cars around.

Motor bikes became pretty popular right after the First World War because they used them in the war, they used motor cycles quite a bit. They were comparatively cheap in those days. The biggest firms were the BSA people – which is Birmingham Small Arms, they used to make the guns – and there was Triumph, and all kinds of other small firms making motor bikes. I could sit here and hear a motor bike coming up the road and I could tell you what make it was just by the sound of its engine. No helmets. They had like the old flyers used to wear, the leather helmet with the goggles – you needed one too on a motor bike – you'd freeze your ears off! We had leather jackets, they were handy if you fell. Quite a lot of people had side-cars. Swallow I think brought them out first. There were all kinds of fancy looking side-cars they had. The Harley Davidson had a wickerwork one. I used to do some grass track racing and one thing and another. There was always something going on, in a field, anywhere you could get. I used to go along and do a few repairs. The first motor cycle I ever owned, I was 14, it was a Belgian bike. I saved up, and my mother gave me some money. It cost four pounds. It was quite a lot of money really. Harold Symes, Sid Westcot and myself on a big old NUT motor cycle – one sitting on the petrol, one on the saddle, and one on the back! We used to go up Ham Hill. We fell off many times – I've got the scars to prove it! We used to pop down to West Bay sometimes and have a swim, something like that.

Schoolchildren c.1930 *(l–r) back row: Bill Turner, Jack Chick, Alan Whetham, Hubert Stevens, Arthur Hackwell, Bert Dyer, Kingsley Rendell; third row: Dora Hodges, Mina Munroe, Eileen Hunt, Edna Gould, C. Rendell, A. Lacey, Dorothy Baker, Lillian Stocker, Rose Thorne; second row: John Caplain, Margaret Hooper, Violet Cooper, Lenora Hooper, Betty Stroud, Irene Fisher, Ivor Turner; front row: Walter Baggs, Dorothy Cox, Joan James, Hilda Hallett, Violet Marsh, Henry Brown.*

Schoolchildren c.1927 *(l–r) back row: Bill Stroud, Cyril Perry, Eric Stevens, L. Runciman, Stan Russell, B. Best, R. Walbridge, E. Fisher; third row: Eddie Dunning, J. Webb, L. Pomeroy, Nora Rowe, V. Dunham, - Wey, M. Sainsbury, M. Dyer, J. Hilliard, Miss Broom; second row: E. Baker, M. Stocker, M. Sims, R. Hunt, I. Hughes, W. Hooper, K. Rendell; front row: Cyril Wey, J. Dodge, Joan Thorne, Eileen Pomeroy, G. Chick, Gladys Charles, S. Lacey.*

A Band of Children

THERE was four or five of us going to school from Bryant's Farm, Pendomer, at one time, and then there was another family down below, there was three or four of them. And then there used to be two cottages across the way and there was a girl used to come from there to school, and then we'd meet some more from the line cottages. When we did get up to the corner there was a couple of families at Isles, and there was the under-keeper's children used to go from there as well. Then we'd get up to where the keeper's family lived, top of Sleights, there was two or three more children there. All go on together. There was a good band of us. Well, if you got to the top of Lodge Hill and you heard what we call the first bell, we knew we only had so long to get to school before the second bell come and we'd be late for school then, you see. We were never late for school.

I was seven and a half when I first went to school 'cos we used to have such bad winters, of course the mud on the roads and all that, that mother didn't start me to school. She was going to start me on the Easter, course I jumped off the hay-rick and broke my leg so I had all that summer to get over it. Well, then she wouldn't send me to school, you see, in the bad winter in case I slipped down and broke it again, so I never went to school till the following Easter.

We had to start about eight o'clock from Pendomer for to get down to school. Of course there wasn't no tarred roads. 'Twas only the ordinary local stone and of course in the summer 'twas very dusty, and in the winter 'twas muddy. The first hymn I learned at school was 'Do no sinful action, speak no angry word'.

Walking to School from Up Coker

I can remember the big tithe barn at Bridge Farm, right there on the roadside. I can remember running up and down the steps as a kid, when we went to school. Old stone steps, big thatched roof. The steps were in the road.

I can just remember when we went to school, taking a basin on a Monday morning down to the cook in the kitchen at North Coker House, and when we left school we had to go back to get the basin of dripping. A penny or tuppence kept us in bread and dripping all the week.

We used to always carry our dinner to school – I've ate my dinner many a time before I got down cemetery! You'd be pinching apples dinner-time. Bread and dripping, bread and jam. Nothing else.

Dot Starts School

I was about five I should think when we came to Coker. My eldest brother had to take me to school. When we met Dot Andrews at the bottom of Back Lane she said 'What's her name?' and he said Dot. 'Oh,' she said 'two Dots together, bigger fools than ever!' I can always remember that.

We had little tables and we did sit round there. I used to sit to a table and course I did my work better, you know, than some of the others and they did put two or three kids round a table for me to teach. Show 'em how to do their sums and that.

I was always in trouble at school, that's all I know! I was always in trouble 'cos I did talk. And then I did help people with arithmetic answers and they did get the working wrong and the teacher would say 'Where'd you get this one? That's double canes again!' Out I go – had the ruler.

You soon get to know each other in the village, and going to school we kids met people and that. And of course on the farm – as soon as my brothers was about 12 they were on the farm too, before going to school, doing milking. They'd get a few coppers you know, not much, but every little helps.

Archie Rings the School Bell

I used to ring the school bell in the morning if I got there in time. The kids would probably be on the road out playing or doing something like that. When you ring the bell I think it was five minutes before nine and then they all came trooping in, and then the teacher would call the register, and we'd mark it on the board. The school as it was, there was about six or seven standards from the infants upwards, and there was only three rooms so you was kind of mixed. I was about eight years old when I started down that school there. I'd been to school in London but when I got down here I had to go in the infants because I couldn't understand what they were talking about! It's true. That didn't last very long. I suppose they didn't know what to do with me. I could read and write and everything when I started school there. We had a teacher, she was a girl who'd just left school. She was 14. She was our infant teacher.

In the mornings they used to have a Bible do. I was top of that believe it or not, the biggest heathen there ever was and I knew the Bible backwards practically. They'd question you about it, then once a year they used to have an inspector come and take us all day long for the Bible stuff. He'd be there sitting up on the old desk and asking us all these kinds of questions, and I'll never forget the first time he ever came, I can remember it as if it happened yesterday, he came in and we were all sitting there waiting for him and he said 'Stand up all children who are Christians'. Everybody stood up except for one. He said 'Well, what are you then son?' – 'I'm a Roman Catholic'!

You had the cane if you did something bad – bang, wallop, crash! That'll teach you! Then you'd come home and cry and tell your mother you'd had the cane 'What

East Coker School football team 1926–7 with headmaster Henry Headford (right) and teacher Arthur Childs (left). Back row: B. Woolmington, F. Hayward, S. Walbridge, T. Lambert; middle row: G. Hayward, H. Symes, L. Lacey, B. Andrews; front row: R. Rideout, C. Boucher, A. Moger, J. Hunt, M. Rideout, K. Gillingham.

East Coker School football team.
(l–r) back row: Mr Headford (headmaster), R. Male, H. Stevens, E. Bull, Mr A. Childs;
middle row: H. Brown, R. Haines, A. Hackwell; front row: C. Perry, E. Stevens, W. Stroud, B. Best, B. Turner.

for?', 'I didn't do anything', 'Yes you did!' – bang! She'd give you another whack. Children were kept in their place, they did what they were told. I think truancy in my day was very, very little really. You'd have just a few kids that would pop off occasionally. There was one girl called Alice, I used to very often have to go and find her. She'd be on her way to school and she never arrived, then the old boy would say to me 'Beales, go and find Alice'. I used to have to go out and search all around the Moors where she'd be playing, get her by the hair – 'Come on you, back to school'.

Keeping Your Hands Warm

You had plenty of potatoes and that. There was no shortage of any food. I can remember when 'twas bad weather, mum used to boil the potatoes in their skins – you'd go back to school with one of those in your hands and eat it on the way! If it was flooded at the sawmills you'd turn around and come back home and thought 'twas delightful.

I often used to wear Worthy Purchase's old boots to school. He might have been two years older than me. I had to make 'em fit – newspapers stuck up the toe-caps. Mrs Purchase only had the one boy, see; when he did grow out of 'em his mother passed them over and then Johnny or I used to have to wear them.

Mud on the Roads

It would get muddy, oh yes, when the cows was in the road. I've seen my old granny come down through, they used to all wear long skirts, I've seen her skirts dragging in the mud because the cows had travelled the road. Nobody ever wore shoes, they all wore boots. My granny always wore button-up boots. We used to wear hobnail boots to school. All rough roads, see. Up above the Marsh it used to flood in the road. We used to have to wait for a chap to come by with a horse and cart and take us through to go to school. Two or three feet deep – too deep for kids to walk through. There weren't no wellington boots in they days!

West Coker Cookery Classes

We girls used to go over to West Coker to cookery classes in the old schoolroom. The teacher, her name was Miss Walkinshaw, she was there for years and years. We used to go over there in a shooting-brake, sit facing one another, and the man used to stay there all day in the pub and he'd be real drunk when he drove us home. We used to be afraid of our soul, what was going to happen coming down around those roads through Green Lane and along.

Learning to Darn

You had to learn to cook, we used to have cookery lessons, and perhaps one morning a week we had to take something – a stocking or something – to mend, something to darn, learn the way to darn. And then we used to knit socks and they used to sell them out. And learn to patch things. You see you never forget it, what you learn there.

The School Allotments

We used to go gardening at the Mill Lane allotments. We'd get out there once a week, or summer-time twice. We had a little hut out there and all these tools, and they was all fit for youngsters, you know small rakes and spades. You had to clean them after you'd finished. You'd get an inspection now and again. Mr Webber used to come out occasionally when he wanted a smoke!

Rampant Peas

We used to march up there in military fashion once a week, something like that, up to the allotments – left-right-left-right, get your spades out and start digging! You'd go and start off the year double digging. That was bloody hard work. I had the best row of peas in the world. You were supposed to put the peas in just so, I put the whole packet in! I had a whacking for it, but I had the best peas! Peas everywhere!

In the Playground

The little ones could all play boys and girls together, they were in a playground at the back of the school, and the girls was in the front there, and the boys had another playground at the back of the school. Three different playgrounds. We had games out in the playground. The old shopkeeper, Mr Thorne, he used to shout across 'Play the ring games!' – you know, all join in – 'and the good ship sails down the alley-alley-oh!' Course we used to play hopscotch and spin-tops. And then we had the hoops you know, we'd get a crook made

Bert and Edward Best with other boys from the village school at work in the garden behind the headmaster's house. Boys were taught gardening, bee-keeping, and poultry-keeping, and had additional land to cultivate in the Mill Lane allotments.

East Coker School children c.1926:
(l–r) back row: Henry Neville, Maurice Barrett, Ron Welman, Doug Hooper, Jack Neville, Ralph Rideout, Eddie Hawkins, - ;
third row: Olive Walbridge, Lorna Withey, Dora Doddington, Arthur Childs, Vera Harris, Ella Dyer, Lily Turner;
second row: Raymond Lacey, George Cox, Nora Barrett, Sis Hawkins, Ron Stocker, Roy Haines;
front row: Ern Bull, Joyce Russell, Donald Webb.

by the blacksmith. Course we used to use them mostly going to school and coming back – you'd go a lot faster!

Rolling the Cricket Pitch

I used to play football when I was at the school, and cricket. I was never much good at that but we'd go up the cricket pitch to play. I don't know if they've still got that big roller – it used to weigh about 100 tons. Us boys used to push it on the cricket pitch, make it nice for the cricket players. You'd get a detail from school: 'You, you and you – I want some volunteers to go up the cricket pitch and roll the pitch'!

A Tragic Accident

Sydney Webber, headmaster of the village school for 27 years, was killed in a road accident in 1921 aged 49. His gravestone in the cemetery was paid for by parishoners and friends 'as a mark of affection and esteem'. Two years before, 330 subscribers had given Mr Webber a time-piece and cheque at a special evening entertainment to mark 25 years at the school.

Mr Caplen and our headmaster Mr Webber was killed at White Post in a motor bike and side-car. The gentry was out shooting up in one of the woods at Pendomer and the message came through that they were killed and they called 'em all off – 'cos he was so respected that man was.

Mr Caplen and Mr Webber are Buried

It was the biggest funeral ever been in East Coker when they were buried. I can remember we all lined the road from the school up to the cemetery. He'd been there a long time, he was a very popular man in the village.

LEFT: *William Ewart Murley, headmaster of East Coker School from 1932 until his death in 1952. The photographs on these and following pages all come from an album of photographs taken by Mr Murley through the 1930s and 1940s.*

BELOW: *East Coker schoolgirls* c.*1938. The older girls made all the uniforms using saxe-blue material provided by the school and sold to the girls' families.*

back row: - , Doris Withey, Alice Male, Nancy Vickery, - , Joan Male, Nora Barrett, Betty Cooper, Betty Morris, Hazel Shepherd, Rosemary Best, Dora Smith;
fourth row: Peggy Hodges, Sylvia Cooper, Beatie Vickery, - , Ethel Ackerman, Beryl Brown, ?Mary Hawkins, Betty Snaydon;
third row: - , Barbara Wiscombe, - , Grace Clayton, Betty Withey, Pamela Lambert, Edna Hodges, Joan Shepherd, Sheila James, Freda Dowell, - , Joan Stevens;
second row: - , Dorothy Sims, Joan Mead, - , ?Marion Lock, - , - , Trixie Walbridge, Lorna Norman, Ruth Dunning, Dorothy Rendall, Muriel Hill, Mary Brown, ?June Lacey, Molly Hillman;
front row: Stella Loader, Betty Snaydon, - , - , Ann Lewis, - (behind) Joan Purchase, Betty Giles, Doreen Baker, Pam James, Catherine Gill, Phyllis Dunning, Jean Male, - .

Piggyback rides in the playground.

The school's percussion band gives a performance on the lawn of the school house, 1934.

East Coker School takes two prize-winning floats to Yeovil's Jubilee Carnival in 1935: maypole girls in their white dresses and ribbons, and William Dampier's galleon.

Left: *Schoolboys inspecting the pigs and piglets on a visit to Bridge Farm.*

Below: *In the 1930s dairy work was taught in addition to ordinary classes. This photograph shows East Coker schoolchildren learning to make butter and Cheddar cheese under the supervision of an expert from the Farm Institute, Cannington. The children also kept bees, rabbits, poultry, and a variety of British and tropical birds in two large aviaries. During the Second World War a government agency bought all the eggs from the school, and rabbit skins from its blue rex rabbits were sold to make fur coats. The school even grew tobacco for Wills of Bristol, and in return Mr Murley was given a small amount for his personal use.*

FRIDAY BRISTOL EVENING WORLD SEPTEMBER 7, 1934

TOP: *The school sets up shop: (l–r) Audrey Gilley, Dorothy Rendall, Norman Gill, and Don Murley.*

ABOVE: *Making a beehive with the help of Mr Murley. The school produced its own honey, keeping the beehives in the school allotments. Richard Charles takes out a full frame of honey* (LEFT), *which Rosemary Neville decaps ready for it to be put into the spinner to extract the honey* (RIGHT).

Running Errands

SIDNEY THORNE,

General Grocery & Provision Stores,

THE POST OFFICE, EAST COKER.

I didn't have much time for play, I had to look after the young ones under me, or I used to go out to work before I went to school in the morning. Before I went to school in the morning, I had to go to Paddock Cottage to clean the knives, and the shoes, mind. Or I used to go and scrub the policeman's house and all that kind of thing. You had to hand the money over when you got home – that would be a loaf of bread or something or the other, see. 'Cos them days, what did your dad get? He'd get about 25 bob a week, if that.

I used to have to go up washing clothes or floors and all that on Saturdays. I used to like it though 'cos they'd give me some cake or something, see! She'd give me some money as well, but give me cake – 'You eat that here, my dear'. Course as soon as you went home 'How much did Mrs So-and-So give you today?' and you had to hand that over.

I went on errands for all sorts – butter or stamps or writing-paper, or bacon or cheese. Anything – 'baccy, tobacco for my father. I did have to run to the shop, they didn't shut till seven o'clock then. Sometimes I did have to go to Mr Thorne's. I'd take to my heels and run like the jiggers! I can remember once I was running back from Thorne's and there was two boys, they jumped out on me from that little copse at the bottom of Back Lane. I went home crying. Dad said 'I'll get hold of them!' He did give them a talking-to, mind. I wet myself in fright! I did, oh dear.

Do you know, I was about 16 before I went down to Holywell? We thought we were out of bounds if you went further than Thorne's or the school. All my young life I never went that other side of Coker for to go anywhere. I never went past The Tree!

Wood for the Kettle

Mother had five boys and two girls. It was a full house, but then we was all small, and of course when the evening come mother had a certain time early in the evenings after tea when she used to wash us – sit us up on the table and wash us – and put us all up to bed so that she could have some peace and quiet.

I can always remember we had a wooden box and when we came home from school that was our job, to go and get the morning wood, and we had to put enough wood in that box, chop it up, so that dad when he got up in the morning could light the range and 'twould be enough to boil the kettle. We used to yangle who should get the wood and who should do the other jobs. We all had our little jobs about the house – washing-up, cleaning the knives and forks and different things like that. When we were boys we had to once a week have the old knife-board and polish the knives up.

Going Sticking

WE had to go sticking and that for firewood. Anywhere – up Stony Lane, up Coker Marsh, and up the top where they had the ricks in the field and pick up all th'old spars.

Leading Charlie Thorne's Cow

THE earliest man I can remember living in Holywell was old Charlie Thorne. He was a mole catcher by trade. I've seen him up there in his shed with 60-odd moleskins. I don't suppose he got more than a penny a skin. Skin 'em, and peg 'em out, pin 'em down on a piece of board. He used to keep a cow, old Charlie did, up in the shed, but he never had no grounds at all. We schoolboys used to take 'un out when we came home from school. Take 'un out for hours alongside the hedges and eat all the grass. And if we had time we'd take his cow out in the morning before we went to school.

The Keeper's Sons

BEFORE we went to school, dad would have us out to help him – perhaps he may have had 25 or 30 chickens sitting on pheasants' eggs. He'd have to go round and collect the eggs, you see, and then he'd make up the nest, get a broody hen from a farm and used to sit them on pheasants' eggs. They used to make a big pen out in the Park somewhere and have the hens' coops about ten or 15 yards apart so the pheasants don't mistake their coop and get pecked. And then we moved 'em into the woods. I've been up four o'clock in the morning to help dad shift these pheasants into the wood. Then after they've been in the woods a little while, and they get wild and begin to roost – their wild nature about them, see – they begin to go up out of doors in the bushes. They're so wild I've known my dad have to take his boots off to creep up on the grass out in the Park to shut them in at night otherwise they hear you coming, they pop out.

Keeper's sons Alb, Fred and Eddie Hughes with vermin trapped for their father.

The Gallows Tree

A gamekeeper could live up there, and not do nothing, and lose his birds, and not worry about it. There'd be one tree just in the corner of the wood that they used to call it the gallows tree, have a bit of string and hang up any vermin killed so that their employer can see that his man is doing his job. We kids was brought up to do it. If we killed or trapped anything we had to hang it up to the nearest tree or fence that would show somewhere. Mrs Heneage didn't like to see it done, didn't like to see it hung up, so after that they were just buried or tucked away.

Earning a Few Coppers

PICKING up potatoes for Crumpler. A great big field of potatoes. You had to go and put them in the sacks. When the digger dug them up, you followed behind and picked up the potatoes. You'd get about tuppence, something like that, for breaking your back! I used to do it to get a few coppers to buy some sweets. All us lads round here used to do that, on a Saturday morning, you know, or after school, away you go picking up spuds!

Percy Crumpler used to own a farm at Burton, and I used to go clean the cows out for him on Saturday morning. I think he had about eight or ten cows – oh dear, what a job! I got sixpence for doing that. Some of the young lads – 12, 13 year olds – were doing the milking. There was never any milking machines in those days. Funny enough, those cows, you'd bring them in from the fields about six o'clock in the morning for milking time, and you know they all had names and those cows would go in the same stall every time. Each cow would go to its own place and they'd shove one another out of the way to get into their own stall. They had ones that used to kick like hell, and you'd put the bucket underneath and next thing you know you and the bucket were out in the middle of the yard! We used to have to hobble them, tie their back legs together, and tie their tails too! Tie their tails to their back legs or something because they'd swing their tails round when you was there milking away and WHACK! They was wicked! They'd start swishing that tail round, you had to get out of the way I'll tell you! Like a whip!

Bottling Milk at Longlands

IT was pretty bad in the late '20s, early '30s. 1926 was the general strike, that's when the rot set in really. Reverdy Crumpler drove up to London once or twice during the general strike in a good old model-T Ford since the trains weren't running. That was a hell of a journey in those days, I'll tell you. I think they used to distribute the milk at Hyde Park Corner at a big distribution centre there. I used to bottle milk for old Crumpler – during the general strike I was down there bottling milk. Hundreds and thousands of bloody bottles! During the strike it was night and day they were going because there was no trains going to London and the other farms in the village never had the facility like old Crumpler had for cooling the milk and bottling it, so he handled all their milk as well.

Pulling Weeds and Picking Stones at Pendomer

IF we were cutting thistles, the girls had to go out and help do it as well as the boys. 'Cos I always said it wasn't fair because when the boys come in at night they could play different games, whereas we had mending to do and this, that and the other.

You had to go and pull all the weeds in the corn, the charlock, that's wild mustard, or poppies. We had to pull them 'cos they'd spoil the sample of corn. You'd go through and pull the weeds – you learn the way to go through and not trample the corn. Farmers would get so much a hundredweight of corn, you see, so much a sack. What was called the West of England sacks – they were very thick sacks, he'd hold two and a half hundredweight of beans. The corn merchants, like Bradford's and that, they'd come and look at a sample when you were threshing. They'd knock back the price if it had got any rubbish in it.

You had to pick up all the stones in the field before you mow. After they'd chain-harrowed you could see if there was any odd stones about – if they get in the machine you break the knives in it. And the same with the corn you see, any big stones was picked up. I've been out days picking up stones where they was going mowing.

We used to have a bucket or something, or else put 'em in heaps and then they'd come out with a horse and cart and pick 'em up.

Duke Brings Dot James Home

THEY used to take the horses from Slade's Farm down to Pomeroy's to have them shod. When I got about ten or eleven my dad said to me 'When you come out of school today, you call in at the forge and Duke'll come home with 'ee 'cos he knows 'ee. Duke'll bring 'ee home'. So he told Pomeroy that I was going for this horse, so what they done was a man that was working in the smithy he got me up on top of this great horse. How I stayed on there I shall never know to this day, then when the horse walked into the yard and I was on there, oh my father rose the roof! The only time he ever slapped me, and he slapped my legs, to be a brazen thing like that and ride a horse home like that. I said 'Twan't me dad! They put me up there – I couldn't help it!' 'Cos I was scared all the way home, going from side to side, I had to catch hold of 'ee and put my arms round poor old Duke's neck. I think my father went down there and told him what he thought of him.

Everybody's Business.

It's everybody's business,
In this Old world of ours,
To root up all the weeds they find,
To make room for the flowers;
So that every little garden,
No matter where it lies,
May look like that which God once made,
And called it Paradise.

It's everybody's business
To be full of hope and joy,
And be as merry as they can,
Whatever may annoy.
For he who goes about the streets
Parading all his pain,
Will cast a cross on others hearts,
And have his own remain.

Alma. M. Pomeroy
20/10/24

Alma Pomeroy writes a poem in her friend Mabel Dodge's autograph book, 1924.

Hilda Brings the Trace Horse

MR Pomeroy was the blacksmith. Kids could always go in the blacksmith's shop. Wan't dangerous, you see, 'cos you didn't touch the fires or anything. He'd let you blow the bellows for to make the fire burn. My parents used to have their horses shod there – it was all according to how the shoes wear thin. If you were using 'em on a lot of road work they did wear out quicker. I remember taking a horse down there once when I was only seven or eight year old. And another time father had bought some beanholm for feed, and of course he had to come up over Lodge Hill and I used to take the horse down to meet 'un at the bottom of Lodge Hill. To put the extra horse on for to come up over the hill. I was only a kid!

Archie Neville at Longlands Farm

OLD Archie Neville was the cowman, when the cows were down that end of the village, he used to stand up about six o'clock in the morning, you could hear him bawling, yelling for the cows – they'd all come! He didn't have to go and round them up, like, and drive them; he'd shout at them, they were all ready to go milking, and then he'd drive them into the farm.

Fearless Archie

I went up Crumpler's farm apple picking for a few months with Archie Neville. Eating apples! That's really what I went up there for! Fearless Archie. Afraid of nothing, true. He was a masterpiece. Mr Jesse

Archie Neville at Longlands Farm, 1953: Archie worked for the Crumpler family at Longlands for 44 years.

Crumpler, he used to show bulls in those days, and they were big, mind. Some of they were about 25 or 26 hundredweight. Bloody great things they were, had horns on about that long, come straight out. And do you know when we used to get them ready for a show, I was only a boy with Archie, we used to have them out in the yard when it was fine, Archie used to hold the halter, we used to have a broken glass bottle and we used to shave the horns with it. Rub the horns and get them as smooth as you could get them, then rub linseed oil on them and do you know they were perfect after we'd done that. We was doing this one day up there and he started to get a bit stroppy, this bull. He were a big thing too, no doubt. And he started lifting his head – I thought to myself 'Jim, you'd better keep back out the way!' Well Archie was hanging on to him, see – 'Keep still!' Right, all of a sudden he took off with Archie hanging on to the rope! There was me back out of the way, mind, letting Archie go on with him! And he was trying to hold him back! He hung on to him and he went all down that lane, right to Chantry Barton and he's still hanging on to him! He stopped that bull down there and when he stopped the bull was like a dragon that blows out steam! He was snorting and going! Archie, he said 'I'll stop you, you *!#'*@*%!' – I wouldn't tell you what he said! And do you know he had that bull, he led that bull back up to Crumpler's, and he could do anything with him afterwards. When he found out he wasn't afraid of him, see; he knew that he wasn't the master of Archie. He could handle anything! Fantastic man, Archie was. Wonderful.

Cleaning the Looms

OLD Bill Poole used to keep the *Foresters Arms*. Great big fella he was, and he lived to a ripe old age. When I was a lad, about 11, although he was a landlord at the pub he also used to work down at the webbing factory. Every Saturday morning I used to go down there, other lads used to go in different parts of the factory and do 'em, but I used to go down there and clean his loom out. Mind you, in one week the fluff that used to congregate all up and round, and fly all about, was deep on the floor. I used to go down there and I'd get sixpence for that. They used to bag it up and burn it, see.

Going Shopping

There was three shops. Old Mrs Ray's here – Mrs Helyar that was then; Sidney Thorne, that was the post office, that was down next to the forge; where the post office is now, that was Rose Cox's little shop. Most of our shopping used to come from Rose Cox's. I used to go up there with a truck – couple of pram wheels and a truck – and bring back the groceries when we were kids. If my mother wanted a quarter of tea, then I used to go down Mrs Helyar's. Mother used to walk and push the pram to Yeovil on Saturday nights – father didn't get paid until five o'clock, then she'd set off for Yeovil to go shopping.

Rose Cox outside the little shop she ran with her mother and sister in North Coker (now the Post Office and Village Stores). Rose's father was P.C. Nathaniel Cox, the village policeman, who was killed by poachers in 1876. Money raised for his widow enabled her to set up the shop and make a living for her family.

Ralph the Errand Boy

It's a job to describe what it was like in them days. You had to go to work when you was big enough. 'Twasn't about your age. I was errand boy at Mrs Cox's shop – I took on from my brother when he went to the factory to work at 14. It's only a matter of one and six a week I had. Farthest place I used to go was right up the last house in Coker Marsh, and old Mrs Giles, and up towards Hardington on top of Primrose Hill. Old Mrs Giles used to always give me thruppence: 'That's for yourself, sonny'. I used to have a little Tate & Lyle sugar box them days – I had a pair of old perambulator wheels, and the axle, and put two handles on the sides. People would have a certain thing every week. And I had to run with it! I had to nip off quick in my dinner-hour from school, and then call in again in the evening, see if there was anything else to go. I had to call in half a dozen places going from here of a Saturday morning, get the orders – they used to have their little wicker baskets – and then they'd make these things up, Miss Cox and her mother, down in the shop, and I had to wait about there. Perhaps they'd put me on doing the wiping the floor down in the old kitchen, or brushing out the front, to keep me occupied. I didn't have to waste no time. If I was stumped for a job they used to have a chair inside the door and I could sit in the chair until such time as an elderly person or a lady come in. 'When any lady comes in, you go over there and stand up'. That was my orders, and that's how it always was.

Archie and the Blue Rabbits

Weekends mum would buy a joint or something like that. You could always fall back on a rabbit. You could roast them, boil them – it all depends on the age of them really. You get the young rabbits, you can make a nice rabbit pie or bake them. Rabbit stew is nice. Catching rabbits was a life-saver really. You always used to get men coming round collecting the skins. You'd get I think it was tuppence for every rabbit skin. I suppose they used to make coats out of them. What they used to call cony.

I remember I had a job once down where East Coker garage is now, and it was empty then. Mrs Mayo decided

LEFT: *Mrs Alice Helyar who in 1887 opened a little grocery shop in Up Coker. When she died her daughter, Mrs Ray, took the shop over.* RIGHT: *Mrs Ray's shop (now Silverweed Cottage).*

The interior of Mrs Ray's shop which remained unchanged from when it closed in 1967 until her death in 1979, aged 91.
(Photograph by David Pryor)

Haymaking at Darvole Farm in 1926. Farmer Bob Moger is on top of the hay wagon, his son Aubrey stands in front of the wagon on the left, with him is Sam Walbridge.

she wanted an angora fur coat. So she got 100 of these blue chinchilla rabbits, and they was all kept there in the dark. I used to go there and feed them, and where the roof was broken the rabbits if they sit in the sunshine for about half an hour they go brown, and she used to raise all kinds of hell about that. As soon as you let them out into the sunshine they go brown!

Catching a Rabbit

We could get in the harvest field as kids, but we were scared off, mind. Old Jesse Crumpler used to scare us off – 'You're going to get cut – you, go on! Go on!' We might catch half a dozen rabbits. If we knew somebody was having their field of corn cut, probably we'd be up there, see, perhaps evening time – they'd be just getting to the end of the field and that were the time when they did swarm in, you know, I mean you were glad to get a rabbit, they days.

Haymaking was hard work, especially they days when you had the pick, that's all you had, never had no machinery. Not only aching but black with the dirt out of it, from pitching it up. And we'd finish up – that's what we'd get paid with – with a sandwich of bread and cheese, and cider.

Bridge Farm, there used to be great ricks there, three or four in that yard right down the bottom where the barn is. Darn great ricks. I used to lead the horse – mind you, the horse didn't want no leading, 'twas only a matter of having somebody to take 'un anyway, take the horse and wagon, the load of hay, all down into the farm. Like I say, they horses know where to keep in the middle

Bill Best of Tellis Farm thatching a rick.

of the road, and then if you go through a gateway or whatever. I used to drive the wagon back when 'twere empty. Old Mr Lambert, he were the rick builder, he said to 'un, 'Here Boss, this lad here, he been very helpful. He haven't got no tea here, could he have a bit of food?' I went in, and I had more than I wanted! They looked after I then, after that.

Building the Rick

THEY used to take a pride in seeing a good rick built and a good roof on it. You used to have to take it off the wagon loose with a long-handled pick. You dab your pick into a load of loose hay, lug that great bundle up, and then the rick maker on there would keep on shifting it round into where he wanted it. Sweep it round, and put his foot on it and press it down. And then the one coming on behind him on the rick used to have to tread in his footmarks. That was the idea. They'd say 'Fill in the footmarks there boy, keep presssing it down'.

Child-Sized Rakes

WE never walked in the woods. No – we weren't supposed to, you see. Of course, my father he was a stickler for everything to be done right. Never had no play much, we had to work. You know, before I went to school my father had hand rakes made – small ones – for us little ones. They used to turn the hay by hand you see, and we were put in the middle of the field to turn the small lines there.

Praying for Good Weather

WE had a fortnight's holiday from school at Easter, but at Whitsun we never had hardly any. And then we used to have the month in August, you see. We used to pray for the haymaking to be finished before August because we had to work so hard! If you'd had bad weather for June and July, you'd be haymaking in August.

Alice Brings the Cider

MACHINERY for haymaking and that was pretty crude, wan't it? You had your mowing machine with the long blades out, and then you'd come on with the scythes. You used to cut all that by hand round the edges and corners, didn't you. I can see my dad now – his whetstone was sort of round and he'd catch hold of his

'Boy Harold' at Wicket's Beer Farm. With Harold are his niece and nephew, Frances Thomas and Wilf Turner, and someone who is just putting a kitten on Frances' shoulder!

scythe with the handle stuck in the ground, and they'd go on with this whetstone on the edge of the scythe to sharpen it up. They'd stop every so often to sharpen it. We used to go up and … I don't know about help, we could have hindered for all I know! What I did have to do was to take dad's meal up, you know, his dinner or his tea. 'Cos he was working till about nine o'clock then, you see. And of course for drink they did have the cider. And my sister Alice they sent her once and she came home drunk, they had to bring her home 'cos 'twas new cider and she'd sat and drunk the lot 'twas so sweet!

Boy Harold

HE'D do anything for Wilf you see, but he wouldn't work for nobody else. If he was in the mood he'd work. Course I mean years ago they didn't treat 'em as humans, if you can make out, they were like ashamed of 'em wan't they if you had a mongol child. And of course they didn't put 'em to learn anything, because he was like that. He used to think a lot of the animals, see. He used to feed the bull, and he were taken ill and while he was in the house – I don't know how long he was in – that bull never ate nothing nor wouldn't drink and he was going to a skeleton. When that Boy got better – 'cos they always called him The Boy – he'd go out and play his mouth-organ to 'un and thic there bull he did lick him and he went on eating then.

Working for the Post Office

I used to go over to the post office after school hours when I was ten. I used to get over there on a Monday afternoon and start quarter to four, finish seven o'clock on Monday, Tuesday and Wednesday. Thursday afternoons he used to shut the shop. Friday I used to go in there from quarter to four till half past eight, and the Saturday I used to be down there at quarter to eight and finished up about half past nine, quarter to ten. I used to run home to Holywell to dinner midday, then go back down the shop again. Two shillings a week I had for all that.

Very often at quarter to nine at night, especially on a winter's night, old Sidney Thorne he used to come out and say 'Jim, there's a telegram to go up to the Reverend Ransome up at Pendomer'. I used to have to run up there mind, run up there on a winter's night, dark as pitch, with a telegram. I used to be scared out of my wits. In they days I was only a youngster. I used to go up there, take the telegram out, knock on the door, – 'Telegram, sir' – and I used to run all the way back! I was afraid of my own shadow in they days!

Sidney Thorne's post office, with Mr Pomeroy's forge to the right. Sidney Thorne was sub-postmaster and grocer here for 39 years.

Postmen for East Coker and West Coker: (l–r) Harry Bull and Tom Smith (East Coker), G. Stacey and Mr Ring or Helyar (West Coker). The East Coker postmen would sort the letters at the village post office and postmark all of them 'North Coker' by hand.

EAST COKER
WITH
SUTTON BINGHAM

Coronation Festivities

WEDNESDAY, MAY 12th, 1937

Above: *Coronation festivities: flags and bunting on cottages in Up Coker to celebrate the coronation of George VI in 1937; standing in their doorways are Mrs Ray and Mrs Giles.*

Right: *Village children enjoy a tea to celebrate the coronation of Queen Elizabeth II in 1953.*

Darvole Races

I was born on the 2nd March 1914 at Darvole Farm. We used to have to walk from Darvole to Coker school, unless there was a horse and then we used to both ride down and leave it at Mr Pomeroy's, the blacksmith, till we went home at night after school.

Major Batten came to father in 1921 to know if it would be satisfactory to have the point-to-point races here from the Cattistock Hunt. Batten came to father with his leading hand from Ryme and one or two of his men and they started building the course round from Darvole. They went across to Moor Lane, and across to Pavyott's, and from there they came back round to Key and finished up at the last jump in front of Darvole. The Darvole races started in April 1923. People used to come to our place and say 'We'd like to bring the horse in the night before' and we used to accommodate them in the stalls or in the loose boxes that we had, 'cos we had plenty of room at Darvole then. And then they said 'Well, we ought to give your son something 'cos he showed us where the horses got to go' and most of the gentlemen that came there used to give me five shillings a piece, which was a very good day for me, that was. The first races was very satisfactory, and then they decided they'd stay there and of course the longer they stayed at Darvole, the more popular it got. In the course of the racing day, early mornings there was Barlow & Phillips coaches from Yeovil, and the National buses used to run to Darvole from the Borough in Yeovil for sixpence one way and a shilling return.

CATTISTOCK HUNT.

THE POINT-TO-POINT RACES

WILL BE HELD at DARVOLE FARM, EAST COKER

(Two Miles from Yeovil),

ON APRIL 10th, 1923,

FIRST RACE at 1 p.m. ENTRIES CLOSE 8 p.m., MONDAY, APRIL 2nd, to

MAJOR GUNDRY,
Red House, Dorchester.

For the following Races :—

1.—CATTISTOCK HUNT RACE.
2.—NAVAL RACE.
3.—CATTISTOCK HUNT FARMERS' RACE.
4.—ADJACENT HUNTS' RACE.
5.—ADJACENT HUNTS' FARMERS' RACE.

Tea will be provided by the Hunt for all Farmers over whose land the Cattistock Hounds Hunt.

An advertisement in the Western Gazette *for the first point-to-point races held at Darvole Farm by the Cattistock Hunt in April 1923. The races were watched by a large crowd standing on the 'natural grandstand' of a rising slope near the farm.*

29th of May, Shee-Shack Day

Oak-apple Day celebrated the restoration of Charles II on the 29th May 1660, and oak-apples or leaves were worn in remembrance of his escape after the battle of Worcester by hiding in an oak tree.

THEY had celebrations for Oak-apple Day, didn't they? Shee-shack day is what we called him – '29th May, Shee-Shack Day, if you don't give us a holiday, we'll all run away'. We used to sing that in school amongst ourselves. I used to wear an oak-apple and their

Coker Court estate workers enjoy an outing to Cheddar and Weston-Super-Mare. They stopped in a pub at Uphill, and when they came out the seats of the charabanc were too hot to sit on! Fred Acreman and Dick Andrews stand at the back of the charabanc; seated (l–r): - Thorne, Fred Foot, Mr Barlow, Ted Acreman, Keeper Hughes, Mr Foot, Frank Foot, Mr Cox, J. Hughes, A. Cox, Alb Hughes, Jack Humphries.

Villagers go on a bus outing: S. Vowles (driver) stands between the buses; back row: C. Rowe, F. Charles, T. Hackwell, H. Rendell, G. Rendell, Mr Daw, Dick Andrews, G. Neville, Nellie Andrews, Fred Foot, Mrs A. Neville, Mr Gilham; at front: I. Lacey, - Neville, Archie Neville, Alb Hughes, G. Cox, Stanley Stevens, Mrs Stevens, Mrs Rowe, Mrs Helyar, B. Helyar, Mrs Helyar, Mrs Gilham.

leaves. We kids used to always wear an oak-apple. I can remember going out to look for them. We used to wear them on our collars. In them days village life was everything, wasn't it? Nobody never went out of the village, did they. If they did they had to walk, didn't they? There wasn't so many people in the village when I grew up that had a bicycle, let alone a car.

Oak Leaves for the Milk Lorry

ON Oak-apple Day we used to trim up the milk lorry with oak-apples. Those lorries had hard tyres and they didn't have no windscreen in the front, they just had a piece of metal sloping up and a hood over the top, but no glass on the front. When he did stop, where he was stopped loading up the milk at Pendomer or Isles, we kids used to decorate the lorry.

A First Trip to the Seaside

WE didn't go to the seaside, not till we were quite big. When I joined the choir, that was the first time I went to Weymouth. Unbelieveable! Used to go up Sutton Bingham station and the train was going to take us on about half past eight; we'd be up there about half past six just to make sure we got our train! Old Jack Henning the porter used to say 'Now you boys behave yourselves, mind, while you're there!'

Bonfire Night – Gunpowder and Cannons

BONFIRE night was our biggest night, wasn't it. We used to go around the village letting off fireworks, putting them through people's letter-boxes. I can remember making cannons with a piece of pipe loaded up with gunpowder – put a fuse on him, hell of an explosion! That used to make a hell of a noise! A cousin of mine – he was a masterpiece for making weapons like that – had a piece of pipe on a block, rammed it with this here gunpowder and then put a fuse to it, to see who could make the loudest bang. Put one outside the *Helyar Arms* in the grating in the wall – he backfired in through the grating! Shook all the windows over at Mrs Sainsbury's cottage. Hell of a row about it – we ran away! Had to run when the copper comes on, mind. We've let they cannon off under The Tree many a time, and up in the Paddock. There was two big chestnut trees in the Paddock, big conkers on 'em. We'd go up there and put it under the tree. This cannon used to go off and shake all these conkers down!

Carol Singing

YOU'D start carol singing about a month before Christmas. I've got an old lantern we used to take, and father used to put a candle in him and we'd carry him around carol singing, see. You'd go to all the houses. If you were going to Up Coker you'd listen and hear somebody else up there singing and you might sing and they'd come to the door and say 'We've just had some-one'. Then you'd go to Colonel Heneage and you had a silver shilling, a new one. You'd go in the big hall and the butler would come out with the plate and you'd take a silver shilling each.

Christmas at Coker Marsh

I remember Christmas up Coker Marsh when all the whole family was in the cottage. All the Nevilles in Granf Boucher's house of a Christmas night – must have been 30 or 40 people in that little cottage having a party! House was full up. They'd get old granf drunk and dress him up in a skirt and bonnet!

The only time we had chicken was Christmas, mind. We had rabbits all the rest of the year! Father used to rear two cockerels for Christmas, keep 'em from April to Christmas and then kill 'em. Two or three big puddings mother used to make, boiling 'em in the copper.

Roast Turkeys from the Bread Oven

CHRISTMAS turkeys used to be put in the bake oven at Pulman's because the cottage ovens weren't big enough to put turkeys in. These old-fashioned ovens you might get a decent sized rabbit in there, but not a

Over 100 village schoolchildren took part in a special Elizabethan pageant and faery mask at the Tudor Fayre and Fête at Coker Court, June 1934. The fête was to raise money for the village-school funds, to help cover the cost of extra subjects such as music, gardening and handicrafts, and to provide sports.

PROGRAMME.

1. Entry of Villagers to Fayre.
2. Court Heralds.
3. Arrival of "Good Queen Bess" accompan by Courtiers, Essex, Raleigh and Drake.
4. William Shakespeare is presented to Her Majesty.
5. Faery Masque from "The Tempest" (where the Bee sucks).
6. Burlesque—Jesters Hobby Horse.
7. "Come Lasses and Lads."
8. Maypole Dances.
9.
10.
11.
12.

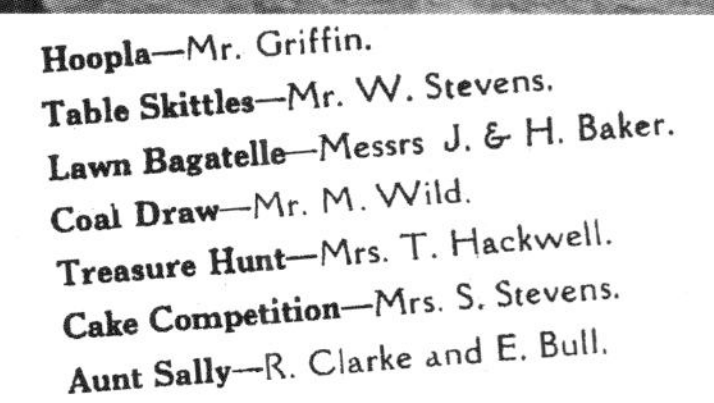

Hoopla—Mr. Griffin.
Table Skittles—Mr. W. Stevens.
Lawn Bagatelle—Messrs J. & H. Baker.
Coal Draw—Mr. M. Wild.
Treasure Hunt—Mrs. T. Hackwell.
Cake Competition—Mrs. S. Stevens.
Aunt Sally—R. Clarke and E. Bull.

Surprise Item.

Watch for the Lady with the Drum.

Mina Munroe, as Queen Elizabeth I, sits in the porch at Coker Court: (l–r) Stan Russell (as Sir Francis Drake), Roy Hartnell, Rose Hunt, Mina Munro, Joyce Dodge, John Mead, Bert Best (as Sir Walter Raleigh); pages Joyce Paddock and Peggy Sims; jesters John Caplin and Leslie Runciman.

turkey. We'd take them down to the bakery, and after they took the bread out the oven was plenty warm enough then to cook the turkey.

A Christmas Party at Coker Court

At Christmas time we had big Sunday School parties in the great hall at Coker Court. The people who were not so well off, the Heneages used to buy shoes or boots for the children, others had a toy, a doll or something like that. Otherwise at Christmas, because our parents were not very well off, we didn't have a lot of toys but we were grateful with a doll in a box, and a stocking with an orange, apple, and nuts in it.

The Farmers' Shoot

The only time we had a pheasant or a deer was Boxing Day. That was the farmers' shoot, they did let the farmers have the shoot up round Pen Wood. You could shoot what you liked, see. They'd divide 'em up. If they had a deer they'd give you a joint of it. The keeper had to skin it. You might get a brace of pheasants sometimes if they had plenty – they'd send a brace out to the farmers.

Ringing in the New Year

My father was always singing songs. When he did get drunk, you could hear it then, mind! When he came home at night, and if he was in the right mood and he wasn't overtired, we'd sit round the fire there and we'd say 'Dad, sing some songs' and he'd sit and sing all the old-fashioned songs:

> The lamp was burning brightly
> 'Twas a night that would banish all sin,
> The bells were ringing the old year out
> And the new year in.

And then he'd sing us lots of other songs. Dad's birthday was New Year's Day. They'd stay up to hear the bells rung – the bells used to ring and wake us kids up. And even till today if I hear those bells there's tears.

Tudor Fayre and Fete

AT

COKER COURT, EAST COKER

Thursday, June 28th, 1934

Opening Ceremony at 2.30 p.m.
by the
Hon. Deirdre-Lumley-Savile

Entertainments by Scholars
at 3 p.m. and 6.30 p.m

DANCING ON THE LAWN
TO MUSIC BY
Yeovil Town Silver Prize Band

Proceeds in aid of Village School Funds

A view of Up Coker, showing Slade's Farm on the right.

Girls learning how to tie bandages as part of a first-aid class. Pictured here in the conservatory at Coker Court: (l–r) Betty Morris, Joan Male, Dorothy Baker, Peggy Sims, Rose Hunt, ?Winnie Murphy, Nora Shorey, ?Susie Hodges, Molly Sainsbury, and Joan Hackwell (sitting on floor). Shortly after this photograph was taken, Molly Sainsbury left East Coker to go to a London teaching hospital to train to be a nurse.

Count Your Blessings

In her autobiography Molly Sutcliffe (née Sainsbury, 1922–1987) recalled moving to East Coker from Wiltshire when she was four years old. Her father came to work at Slade's Farm, and her mother was reunited with her family who lived in the village. Molly would spend every weekend with her grandmother and grandfather Baker who lived near the New Inn.

Whether Grannie Baker had to make up for four lost years or not I do not know but she certainly made a great fuss of me. I was to have Ovaltine before going to bed and no-one before or since ever made a nightcap for me to rival that of Grannie Baker's. It was associated with cosiness and security as I sipped it by her log fire, propping myself against her basket chair and all was always peace, for Grannie Baker believed fervently in the text 'Let not the sun go down upon your wrath'.

Molly Sainsbury who many years later was to write about her childhood in East Coker.

However naughty I might have been in the day all was peace at night. Then upstairs with the candle, prayers solemnly said and then Auntie Nan would sit on my huge feather bed and tell me a goodnight story, blow out the candle and tiptoe downstairs. This ceremony was to be repeated dozens and dozens of times in my life as years went on …

Home was a thatched cottage, rent and rates free, which belonged to Farmer Dunning… So we were settled in and mother no doubt felt very secure on 30 shillings per week, a free pint of milk every day and a dozen free eggs a week… Country life went on revolving around the seasons. Haymaking, harvesting, potato-picking, beet-harvesting, lambing time, primrose-picking, bluebell time, Easter bonnets, Whitsun fair, Sunday School outing, Harvest Festival, Michaelmas (Patronal Festival), Armistice Day, Advent,

Christmas, Lent, round and round and the endless Sundays after Trinity! …

The religious content made up about three-quarters of life and to have stripped that away would have left a huge vacuum. I personally never found it tedious or dull and was always full of enthusiasm for it. Each night that I went to bed all the day's affairs were put into perspective and all seemed right with the world. I always sang myself to sleep at Gran's … How my grandparents endured it downstairs I really do not know. Endlessly the choruses rolled on:

> Jesus loves me this I know
> For the Bible tells me so
> Little ones to Him belong
> They are weak but He is strong
> Yes, Jesus loves me
> Yes, Jesus loves me
> Yes, Jesus loves me
> The Bible tells me so

and

> Count your blessings
> Name them one by one
> Count your blessings
> See what God hath done
> Count your blessings
> Name them – ONE by ONE
> And it will surprise you
> What the Lord hath done.

So I could fall asleep, not counting sheep, but counting blessings – a much greater sustaining power than any of today's gimmicks to try and bring golden slumber to the disturbed and restless.

Visual aid is not so modern either. In my bedroom I had two pictures. One was of a pretty golden-haired girl chasing a butterfly and having just clambered to the top of a rickety fence on the side of a bridge over a fast-running river. As she leaned perilously out with her net to catch the butterfly a very much overworked guardian angel stood behind her with powerful protection. I used to reflect that I really gave my own guardian angel quite a busy time. The second picture in my room was an exquisitely-painted pansy, in pretty shades of mauve and purple. Underneath the text, in bold letters, declared:

KEPT BY THE POWER OF GOD

This again was a nightly meditation for me and at the age of seven I could dwell at length on the great majesty of God – creator of the universe – who nevertheless produced in such perfection this tiny, delicate little pansy.

A picnic at Tellis Farm: Molly's Grannie Baker with teapot in hand, and children (l–r) Violet Dunham, ?Nora Roe, Molly Sainsbury, Donald Sainsbury, Bert Best, Edward Best, Rosemary Best, Yvonne Sainsbury.

Sulphur in Treacle

PARENTS used to give kids sulphur in treacle, that was for worms. My brother, he used to like it, but oh I hated the stuff!

Epsom Salts

EVERY Friday night we were given Epsom Salts. You'd have your bath in front of the fire, have your bath there then you had your Epsom Salts. They were horrible! That was the remedy for all sorts them days, to keep your bowels going.

Well Water and Wash Days

UP Burton we had to pump our water. 'Twas all well water. In the winter our mum had great big baths of the water everywhere 'cos if it was frozen up you couldn't get it from the well. Wash days used to be fun. My mother would start at eight o'clock in the morning and sometimes she'd still be doing it at 12 o'clock at night. You'd have to light the fire to heat the water first, then it had to be blued and put through the wringer. I used to love to do the pillowslips in the wrong way round 'cos they'd come out like big balloons and our mother used to get so mad!

Wash-Houses at Chapel Row

FROM Holywell we moved to Chapel Row. There was seven houses there in those days. That's where they used to share the toilets, one between two lots, and the washing-houses there as well. One wash-house between two houses.

Bath Night at Naish Barton

ONCE a week we used to bath, and that end shed is still there. That's where the copper used to be and that's where the Lacey boys, there was three or four of them living over there, and I was with them and every Friday night, see who's going to get in the bath first! The older sister, she used to be the supervisor. She used to see that we made ourselves clean. There weren't any bathrooms down there. Boil up the water, ladle it into the bath, put the cold in, and get in and swim around in the tin bath.

Water for the Keeper's Cottage

THERE was a pump outside, out in the backyard, but it wasn't drinking water. I can remember once mother had a special kettle for tea and things like that, for our own water for to use, and I suppose the kettle got filled up with the wrong water once and we drank it and we was poisoned even though it was boiled. We had to fetch our drinking water right down from the reservoir in the Park here. We had to come all down along the side of the wood there to get our water and carry it all back up again.

The Holy Well

In 1923 Dom. Ethelbert Horne published an account of his visits to holy wells, or springs, in Somerset, including a visit to Holywell to see the spring that rises beside the Foresters Arms.

TO the south east of (*West Coker*) is a hamlet consisting of a few cottages, called Holywell. The well itself is a plentiful spring, the water coming through a pipe and falling between some great stones. These are squared and dressed stones, some of them being large steps, and they may have been part of a building in former times. No tradition, that I could find, existed in the neighbourhood as to why the place was called Holywell, nor were the waters considered 'good for the eyes'. Indeed, when I asked an old lady on the spot, who had come to dip up some of the water, if it was good for anything in particular, she replied, 'Yes, for making tea'! She added that 'across the Moor' was a spring the water from which was 'good for the eyes'. The directions for finding this well were so vague that I did not make the search.

The 'holy well' next to the Foresters Arms

Blackwell's Spring Water

Other springs in the parish, at Blackwell and West Wells, were both believed to have curative powers, as was the Beauty Spring, which Mrs B. Hackwell mentions in her little book The Story of our Village, *but the precise location of this spring is not known.*

I remember father going down to Coker Moor and getting water from Blackwell to bathe his eyes with. It was a cure for eye trouble. If somebody's baby had eye trouble my father used to go there and get the spring water.

Century and Agrimony Tea

AGRIMONY is a little yellow flower that grows out in the fields. There was century as well – it's a little pink flower. You never see it now much, but dad used to have bunches of that hung up. He'd pull it up at a certain time when it's all in flower nice and have bunches hung up in the old sheds round and indoors. He used to get that every now and again, break up a jugful, and put boiling water on it, cover it with a tea-cloth and leave it. And next morning the first thing you had was a cupful of this. It tasted terrible! I used to hate taking it!

Goat's Milk for the Baby

MY mother was old when my young brother was born, and she was ill all the time she was pregnant. When he was born he had gastro-enteritis and when he was a year old he was only about two pounds heavier than when he was born. Every day the doctor was coming and mother was worried. When he was a year old the doctor said to father 'Do you know anybody who has got a goat?' Everybody who worked on the railway kept goats then, they fed them on the side of the railway. Uncle Gilbert Neville was working on the railway, and he said to father he'd got a lot of goats up at Hardington Marsh. And he went up there one Sunday morning and bought this goat called Mary. We used to tie her down the bottom of the hedges and took her down the lane, down the Moor. Father used to go and milk her every day and that goat's milk cured my brother. He turned out to be a pretty fine sportsman. When he was growing up he won all the races, played football and he could jump over anything. Father used to say 'That's the bloody goat's milk!'

Brandy for the Baby

MY sister Mary and myself were born at Slade's Farm, and mother always told the tale of me crawling across the road and falling into the ditch. After that I was very ill with congestion of the lungs, my father finally helped me recover by giving me sips of brandy.

Cider and Ginger

CIDER and ginger – that's the thing for a cold. You want the powdered ginger, teaspoonful, warm up the cider, get it warm, put that in then I expect you add a bit of sugar, stir all that up and drink it. Half a pint of that would be enough for you, then hop into bed and forget all about it. I tell you what, you sweat it out! It's a really good cure .

Senna Pods

WE used to have senna pods every Saturday to keep your bowels open! Our mother used to boil them up in a special saucepan. Always had to have a dose every Saturday morning. Bloody horrible! Liquorice powder was another one – that wasn't very pleasant. I've seen my mother hold my sister's nose to give her castor oil before now, to make her swallow.

A Cure for Asthma

A very old method is when you get in amongst the sheep that's baaing and coughing and going. It's what comes off their throat that cures you. You've got to go in amongst them for a long time, every day if you can. Just for asthma.

A Gypsy Remedy

THEY always had their own remedies. My grandfather, I can't remember whether he was invalided out of the First World War or whether it was when he used to work sometimes in the mines in Wales and got rheumatic fever, but they brought him home on the train on a stretcher and they had to have somebody with a lorry fetch him home. They had the doctor and he said 'There's no way he'll ever walk again'. So when these gypsies came round, the gypsy man asked what was wrong and gran told him. He said 'I'll get him walking within a few months. What you do is you go and get some goose grease or some good-quality lard, and mix it up with the hottest mustard you can find, and rub that in his back two or three times a day'. And he walked, but the doctor said he never would. That was an old gypsy remedy.

ABOVE: *Loading milk-churns at Longlands Farm. The dairy was one of the first in Somerset to supply TT (tuberculin tested) milk, and sent 200 gallons per day to St Bartholomew's Hospital, London; another 100 gallons of milk, plus butter and cream, was retailed locally.*

BELOW: *Staff at Longlands Farm, March 1937: (l–r) back row: Bill Braine, Henry Lambert, Archie Neville, George Garrett, Reverdy Crumpler, Jack Neville, John Marsh; seated: Les Haines, Charles Lucas, Miss Burridge, Bob Besant, Peggy Partridge, Miss Woodruff, Charlie Boucher. The little boy is John Crumpler.*

ABOVE: *Staff at Walden's creamery, Bridge Farm. (l–r) Eddie Hughes, Elsie Hughes, Dot James, - , May Partridge and Lily Doloman. Butter imported from Australia, New Zealand and Russia was mixed on the premises and sold as Queen of the Vale brand butter; in addition milk from Bridge Farm was used to make clotted cream. Faggots, sausages, joints of meat and meat pies were produced from pigs slaughtered on the farm.*

BELOW: *Making butter using an end-over-end churn in the dairy at Longlands Farm – a small electric motor helps the dairymaid to turn the barrel churn.*

(Photographs of Longlands Farm from the Farmer and Stockbreeder*)*

Paddy Lacey delivering milk to East Coker and parts of Yeovil for Fred Dening of Redlands Farm. Paddy came to East Coker in 1939 as an evacuee, and went on to join the Land Army. She took over the Redlands milk-round after Eddie Neville was killed by a bomb that fell near Westlands while he was making deliveries.

In 1930 this advertisement for St Ivel cheese appeared in Punch *magazine. It shows East Coker Mill with the ivy on the building trained into the shape of a stag. Mr G. Lewis, who had run a family butchers and poulterers at The Poplars, came to the mill with his family in 1918. He set up business grinding barley meal for pigs, kibble maize for chickens, and crushed oats. The mill would start grinding when enough water had built up in the mill race at the back of the building, usually about two or three times a week. Scarce raw materials during the Second World War meant that the water-wheel finally stopped turning.*

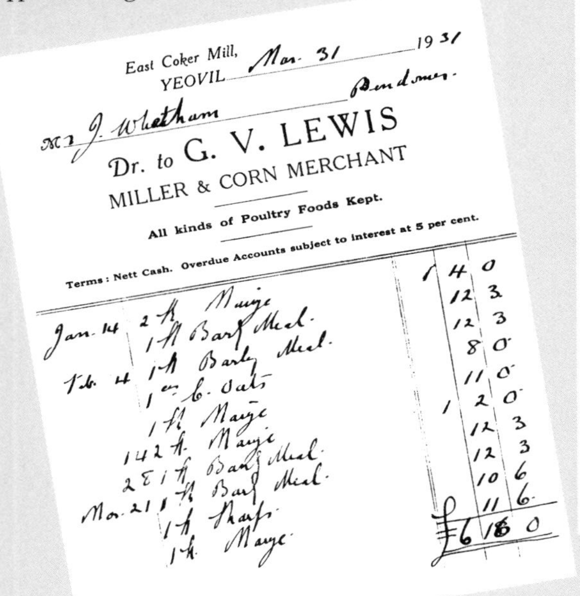

East Coker Mill, Mar. 31 1931
YEOVIL

Mr J. Whetham, Pendomer.

Dr. to G. V. LEWIS
MILLER & CORN MERCHANT
All kinds of Poultry Foods Kept.
Terms: Nett Cash. Overdue Accounts subject to interest at 5 per cent.

Date	Item	£	s	d
Jan. 14	2 ℔ Maize	1	4	0
	1 ℔ Barley Meal		12	3
Feb. 4	1 ℔ Barley Meal		12	3
	1 cw C. Oats		8	0
	1 ℔ Maize		11	0
14	2 ℔ Maize	1	2	0
28	1 ℔ Barley Meal		12	3
Mar. 21	1 ℔ Barley Meal		12	3
	1 ℔ Sharps		10	6
	1 ℔ Maize		11	6
		£6	18	0

The Vickery Man

OIL-LAMP and candles – that's all you had. You'd trot up to bed with your candle. The oilmen used to come round selling paraffin – old Vickery – they had lorries I believe, with all the brooms and buckets and brushes and everything hanging on the side. They used to sell practically everything – cups and saucers, soap, candles. They had their certain days, they'd be here say on a Tuesday, he'd always be here. You'd know when the oilman was coming, or when the fishman was coming with his fish. There were one or two of them. Old Bill Westcot he had a horse and cart; Bob Berry and his daughter, they used to push it round with a handcart, one of those big costerbarrow handcarts. Just fancy pushing that up Hendford Hill when you get half a ton of fish on there and shove them around.

The Butcher and Fishmonger Come Round

WE used to have a butcher come on here, George Rousell, Friday nights. He'd stop over here and serve the houses in a pony and trap. That was perhaps six o'clock at night, and then he'd be going all up round Up Coker. Nice old chap what used to come on with him, looking after the horse, you know, my mother used to go out with a cup of tea to him and a biscuit or cake, and he used to lap that up, mind. Poor old chap, he were crippled. Very badly crippled.

We used to eat salt fish – that was a cod split in half, dried and salted. It came in hessian bags and my mother used to carve it up in joints and take off whatever was

TAILORING

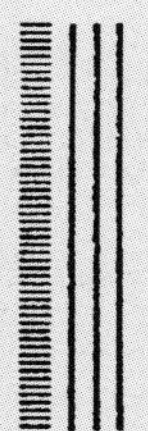

For both Ladies
and Gentlemen.

TAYLORS are real TAILORS
not merely RETAILERS.

FREDK. TAYLOR,
Phone 180. YEOVIL
The Super Store for Modern Attire.
LIFT TO TO ALL DEPARTMENTS.

A. WHALE,
Hardware and Oil Merchant,
Visits East Coker every Tuesday
WITH
China, Glass, Dinner Ware, Tea Ware,
Bedsteads, Bedding, Linoleum,
Brushes, Mats, Mangles.
76, Victoria Road, Yeovil.
Special Quotations for Paraffin Oil in Bulk.
Drums Rent Free.

A. Whale advertises weekly visits to East Coker in the Parish Magazine, *January 1938*

SIDNEY THORNE,

General Grocery & Provision Stores,

THE POST OFFICE, EAST COKER.

S. J. HAYNE,

MEAT PURVEYOR,

HIGH STREET, YEOVIL.

BEEF, MUTTON, VEAL and PORK of the very BEST QUALITY.

CORNED BEEF & PICKLED TONGUES. POULTRY ALWAYS READY.

Families Waited on Daily.

THE DEVON FIRE

Artistic
Economical
Labour Saving
For Wood or Coal

Large Selection always on View in our Show-rooms.

SOLE DISTRICT AGENTS:
HILL, SAWTELL & Co., Ltd.
YEOVIL.

Wireless Supplies ! !

We Stock a Large Range of WIRELES
COMPONENTS.

We Re-charge Accumulators

at Lowest Prices and Guarantee Satisfaction.

The British General Radio Comp
(Retail) Limite
36, Middle St., YEOVIL.

E. SOYER,

Fishmonger, Poulterer & Game Deal

22, Princes Street, YEOVIL.

Best Products of the Sea, Farm and Fore
FAMILIES WAITED ON DAILY.

J. TURNER,

Practical Carpenter and Joiner,

Painter and Decorator,

UNDERTAKER

ESTIMATES FREE. PRICES MODERATE.

NOTE ADDRESS:
Home Barton, EAST COKER.

John Gliddon & Co
YEOVIL

We Specialise in Millinery, Costu
Coats, Gowns, Ladies' & Children's Un
wear, Gloves, Hosiery & General Drap

Household Linens & Soft Furnishi

Funerals Furnished. Cremations Carried Ou
TELEPHONE 59.

TELEPHONE 280
ESTABLISHED 1847.

E. PRICE & SONS, LTD

Handel House, YEOVIL,

Specialists in Pianos and Player-Pianos.

Branches at Bournemouth, Boscombe, Andover, Amesbury, Devizes, Upper Parkstone.

Ask for Price List of Easy Payment System, or Cash.

More local shops advertise in the Parish Magazine, *May 1926.*

never used, tail or whatever, you know. It was soaked then for about two days to get the salt out. Change the water about every 10 or 12 hours. That was really good, mind, salt cod. Very cheap for that matter, them days.

Door-to-Door

The butcher came, the baker called every day at the house. Fishman come twice a week, push a hand-truck out through Yeovil. Old Bob Berry. Blind man. Had a truck, fish on a long truck, and his daughter used to come with him. He used to walk from Yeovil twice a week out here selling fish from door-to-door, sprats, mackerel, herring, kippers. Old Ernie Ball used to come on every Friday with greengroceries on a pony and cart.

Fish and Fruit

A couple of fishmen come on from Yeovil. I know. There was one called Westcot's from Yeovil. Bloaters and that. Used to wonder who was going to have the head or the tail of it. Fish and fruit they used to have. Fruit they did sell – oranges and grapes. In his horse and cart – some had 'em covered in, some had it open. One of 'em used to go in the pub for a drink, we used to sneak up round and pick some of the grapes off! They'd shout out 'Fish-O! Fish-O!' If they knew a customer they'd go to the door, but if not they'd shout. We used to creep up outside the *New Inn* as it was called then, and have a few grapes – that was from heaven, mind, because you wouldn't have a grape otherwise, it couldn't be afforded. Sometimes you'd pinch a banana and split it up between you, if it was a couple or three of us children.

Bread from Pulman's Bakery

I used to go round with the baker. A chap called Stuart Gould used to deliver the bread. He had a two-wheeled cart, and had the loaves up in the back. Used to be nice to pick those hot loaves and eat them! I went with him on a Saturday, just for the ride actually. I'd help him, I'd deliver the bread, take the bread to Mrs So-and-So up the garden path. People would have the same thing every week – two top and bottom loaves for her, and a tin loaf for her, and so on. If they wanted extra they'd leave a note 'One extra today please'. We delivered bread to Sutton Bingham, and Pendomer and all round. On Good Fridays we all had to troop down to the bakery to get the hot cross buns. I used to go and watch Jimmy Baker knead the bread. He used to make some lovely doughnuts – I can taste them now!

Reg Griffin delivering bread for Pulman's bakery c.1940. *Reg made deliveries to Coker, Closworth, Sutton Bingham, Ryme and Netherton. A different horse was used in the morning and afternoon, and when Reg went home to Garden Row at lunchtime the horse would be outside in the road with a nosebag. On Good Fridays hot cross buns were delivered throughout the village at four o'clock in the morning.*

Swans Visit the Bakery

I do remember when I was a very small child, two swans coming over from the lake at North Coker House, every Sunday morning they used to walk across the road and hit the glass of the door with their beaks for bread. They knew it was Sunday because they never came on a weekday when there was so much activity going on, ponies and traps coming up to fill with bread and going out, and then another one coming and loading up, another alongside. But on Sunday mornings, bang on the dot, they would turn up and with their beaks hit the glass.

The Coalman and the Tallyman

The coalman used to come round with a horse and cart. When the fire went out you got the ashes and you took them up the yard and you sieved it through and got what was left and re-burned it.

Then years ago, you used to have what they call the tallyman. People would come along more or less selling clothes and stuff like that. You'd buy something off him and you had your coat or shirt or pair of socks, and give him so much down and then so much a week after. I think my mother used to buy my clothes in Redwoods in Yeovil. But we used to get clothes handed on down from a bigger boy. You was always wearing somebody else's clothes.

The Rag-and-Bone Man

Half the time we used to have clothes given to us. Another time we'd have the old rag-and-bone man come round, old Johnny Hibbs. Johnny and Carrie. He'd collect anything he would. He used to go to all the big houses and they would turf out a lot of stuff they didn't want and give it to him, see. Then he'd come round and he'd sell it, just for a few bob. In those days, mind you, you could get a pair of trousers for about ninepence. He used to get it off the gentry, you know. I think that's why my mother used to get clothes from him really, because if you had a lot of cheaper stuff it would wear out quicker. He used to camp out round this way very often. I'll tell you where he used to camp a lot one time, Isles Lane. We was down the pub one night, down the *Foresters*, and he was in there having a drink with Carrie. So we went outside, we hitched the donkey out and put him back head first, with his head looking over the old governess cart! You ought to hear the language when he come out! I bet he cussed for five minutes and never said the same word twice!

On the If and Perhaps

PEOPLE didn't use to do too bad in them days, there was plenty to eat, money wasn't all that but when you come to weigh it up, say you had 28 shillings a week on the farm, you had no house rent to pay, you didn't pay for your milk, you didn't pay for your food from the allotment. You could go into any of the shops, like Redwoods in Yeovil, and if you wanted a new suit you'd go in and get it on Friday and he'd get your little book, put it in, and you'd pay half a crown a week or summat like that until it was paid for. You'd pay for it on the 'if and perhaps' – if I've got the money, perhaps I'll pay!

Teddy Ackerman of Placket Lane

TEDDY ACKERMAN used to live in a little tiny cottage at the end of the lane. Ever so little tiny cottage. The ceilings couldn't have been only about six foot high, if that. It was very, very old. Teddy Ackerman was the knackerman. He used to keep that little plot over the other side of the road. Teddy Ackerman used to bring say a skinter cow, maybe that had TB and had to be put down. Maybe there was a pig that might have had his leg broken and that kind of thing.

The Smell of Killing

OLD Teddy Ackerman he'd kill them anywhere but his place was at Placket, on the corner of Placket Lane. That was his house, and he used to do slaughtering and all up there. If you had a horse, you were driving a horse and it strayed, they wouldn't go by the place. You had to take the horse round the other way, he would never go by Teddy Ackerman's, he could smell when he'd been killing. I remember helping him skin a cow once, I was just a boy, 10 or 12 years old. They were probably cows that were on their last legs. He used to castrate dogs and cats and sheep and everything. If you

Teddy Ackerman of Placket Lane with his horse and cart.

had a horse or something that had to be slaughtered, he'd come and do it on the premises. I've seen him kill a pig, that's a hell of a thing too, screeching and screaming. They cut their throats. They used to do that every Christmas, they'd do a pig down the farm. They used to kill several in the course of a year, but they'd always kill a pig for Christmas.

Tom Keats From Winyards Gap

Some of these old men, mind, they had some fine old remedies, especially for their animals. I remember an old 'vet' called Tom Keats kept the *Winyard's Gap Inn*. He was never a qualified vet but he was the best vet around here for miles. He believed in all natural resources. He used to make his own medicine and that, see. Never had no letters after his name.

Ackerman's cottage on the corner of Placket Lane and the Yeovil Road (since demolished).

To Yeovil on Market Day

Everybody would go to Yeovil, Fridays. They'd buy their clothes, they'd buy their Sunday meat if they had any money. The first bus was a man called Bath, he used to drive it from Corscombe I believe it was. He had a bus, a real chariot. It used to come through the village and pick up. In those days they'd have their chicken, all kinds of things, on top of the bus, box of live chicken, take them to market to sell! A big rack on the top. A lot of people used to ride there when they couldn't get in the damn bus, hanging on all over the place like you see these coolies in India! I think it used to be either a penny or tuppence to go to Yeovil, or summat like that.

They didn't have any lorries, they used to herd the cows in to market. Drovers used to drive them all over. You'd get about 40 cows in front of you. One time in Choughs Garage, where I worked, there was a flat where the caretaker lived and stairs going up to it, and a cow got up there once. Poor Mrs Baker used to live up there, she nearly had twins! And of course you'd got a little passage – they had to take the cow into her room to turn it round to get it back out! They had a hell of a job to get the cow back downstairs. They'd be coming from all directions with their cows. It was organised chaos actually. They used to take the cattle in, and of course if they were sold in the market, the big butchers used to buy them and then they'd be shipped to the railhead and get taken away. Guys would take them to the slaughterhouse or somewhere and it was all over Friday night.

The Monday Market

We used to go in the cart with father and mother when they went to market, taking the eggs in Mondays, Monday market. Couple of great boxes, two or three boxes of eggs. What they used to do is throw a little bit of straw stuff in between them. They don't break then. You could take anything – apples, eggs, anything – in there to sell, you see. The auctioneer would sell them and if you had a certain person had been buying your eggs, they knew which were yours 'cos you had your name on them. Any produce you had, if you had it to spare, you could sell it there.

Home from the Market

Grandfather Newman came to Key Farm in 1894, and my mother was ten and her youngest brother was ten months old and he rode on her lap. They came from beyond Kingsbury. They'd go to market in horses and traps. They used to take these horses and traps down to the *Half Moon* and put their traps down. The *Half Moon* people used to have an ostler, and he'd to look

The first bus service to Yeovil from East Coker was run by Mr Bath who made a round trip from Corscombe and offered an hourly service up to 6pm. At weekends the bus ran until 10pm to bring people home from the cinema. Here Mr Bath is pictured with his bus in the road by the New Inn.

after the horses. When the farmers were ready to go home, when they'd had enough market and enough *Half Moon*, they'd get the horses and they used to say that the horses knew their way home! They didn't have to be guided! They'd say 'Oh well, the horses will get them home' and they did!

Down the Sandy Lanes at Naish Barton

A lot of the roads never had any paving at all. Naish Lane, it's all sand rock under here, it's natural sand. When the big ruts got deep they'd come along with a rake or shovel and fill them up, like, and start all over again! In the old days they dug those old sandstone rocks out and they used it for storing potatoes in. In fact, that wall opposite here, there was a potato cave over there.

Water for the Road

YEARS ago you see when they made the roads then there wan't no tarmac, no tarring nor nothing, they did have the stone. When they did do the roads they'd have a steamroller and they did put the stones out and the man did spread 'em all along like a blanket. Then the steamroller'd come on and roll 'em. Then they had to water that so they'd have a big water-barrel, about 200 or 300 gallons, and wheels you see and shafts for the horse to pull it. I've been down to Lyatts spring and filled up the water-barrel, and you'd pump and pump and wet the road for to help blend the stone.

Stonebreakers at Isles

UP on top of Lyatts Hill there, where you go in to Pen Hill, that was a deep quarry there. The men that was drawing the stone out of the quarries used to bring it out and pile it along beside the road. Up on top of Lyatts, and of course out there by Isles, the old men would sit and crack the stones. I remember seeing 'em up there – they used to generally wear goggles in case the stones fly, and they had a special stone-hammer. And then, you see, when they wanted 'em for to make up the roads, they could pick them up from where they'd been piling 'em.

RIGHT: *Bob and Margaret Mead at Gunville Lane* c.1913*: their home was said to have been built 'on sand and cider' because of the sandy soil underneath it, and the cider the men drank while they were building it. Legend has it that the house was built in 1899 but the foundation stone says 1900 because it was easier to carve!*

BELOW: *Shorthorn cows, Burton Lane. The roof of the Gospel Hall can be seen in the background to the left.*

St Michael's church choir, 1925, with Mrs Beatrice Hackwell the choir mistress and church organist. (l–r) back row: Tom Gilham, the Reverend Bailey, Cecil Pulman; third row: H. Headford, Sam Poynter, Jim Hunt, Tom Hackwell, Ken Gillingham, Ted Tucker, Arthur Childs, Sam Walbridge; second row: Ron Stocker, Douglas Hooper, Jack Neville, Len Parsons, Gerald Hayward, Ivan Lacey; seated: Ken Lewis, Henry Neville, Mrs Hackwell, Raymond Lacey, Roy Haines.

The choir in 1935: (l–r) back row: F. Bishop (who used to pump the organ), R. Stocker, R. Haines, I. Lacey, G. Hayward, T. Hackwell, Mr Headford, J. Neville, H. Stevens, A. Hackwell, H. Neville; middle row: A. Childs, E. Tucker, the Reverend Coates, Colonel Heneage, Mrs Hackwell, Mr Poynter, T. Gilham; boys at front: R. Griffin, W. Stroud, E. Baker and E. Stevens. Mr E. 'Teddy' Tucker (78 years old) retired from the church choir in 1949 after 65 years service from treble to tenor – he joined as a schoolboy after the then vicar Charles Powell visited the village school to look for promising singers.

The Passing Bell

Traditionally the passing bell was tolled when someone was dying; more commonly a bell was tolled after the funeral and interment, with the number of strokes rung depending on the age of the person who had died.

For a funeral they rung out the years: dong-dong-dong. Sometimes if it was a toff or that they'd have the coffin in the carriage, you know with special wagons, like. But anybody else you had to go on with the bier through the village.

St Michael's bell-ringers, August 1949. (l–r) Frank Foot, W. Loader, J. Rogers, G. Neville. The year this photograph was taken, two bell-ringers, E.G. Tucker, 78, and G. Neville, 73, had 112 years of bell-ringing experience between them.

Kept Away from Death

My parents' first child died before I was born, at Preston. She died when she was a baby.

When my mother died, father was desperate. There was eight of us children. We were put out to sleep that night – I had to go up with Mrs Cheney. I was in bed and I said 'Why've I got to sleep up here?', 'Oh,' she said 'your mum is dying'. I couldn't imagine my mum dying. The next morning I can remember I got up, had a wash and that and I was out in the backyard and the bell went and I said 'My mum's dead, what are we going to do?' I was th'oldest girl. After they came back from the funeral I thought to myself 'I'm going to see where they've put her' so I skipped away up the cemetery and Mr Baker was there filling her grave in. I remember him stood up and throwing the soil in, you see, so I looked down to see the coffin. I can always remember him taking hold of me and saying 'Now come on my dear,' and he gave me a sixpence and that was a lot of money back then 'now you run on home, there's a good girl, 'cos I want to cover her in'. I always remember, those words do live with me. Children was kept away from death and funerals.

Hackwell's: Funeral Directors

I was a pallbearer for a while. I remember pushing the bier down to Yew Hill, down to Holywell, and that was the farthest place we pushed it. We had to wear a dark suit if we had one, and a bowler hat. It was in keeping, really. Tommy Hackwell he was in charge. He was the boss so he used to be in front with his top hat. He told me that his hat was two inches higher than normal size because he was a little short man and he wanted to hold his own! I only used to do it because it was a bit of extra money – six shillings or 30 pence today. The funeral usually used to be at half past two, and we'd be released from the factory from two o'clock.

A Mark of Respect

You always pulled the front curtains if you knew a funeral was going to go by, people always stood still and the men tipped their hats when the funeral car passed them. It was just respect really. You either wore a black arm-band or some people wore a black diamond on their sleeve.

Laying Out

If anyone died and wanted laying out, my mother would go and lay them out. Mother used to wash them all over, and whatever they had to put on. They used to have white socks and a white gown to put them in the coffin. They always had that ready in the drawers.

East Coker Superstitions

These superstitions were collected by Mrs Joan Hughes (née Cole) when she was an evacuee in East Coker during the Second World War.

- If the church bells make an echoing sound when rung there will be a death in the parish before the week is out;
- One death will be followed by two others within a short time;
- When visiting a house you must not replace the chair you have been sitting on, or you will not visit there again;
- If the church clock chimes while a hymn is being sung, there will be a death during the week.

1. Every Ringer must be a *bona fide* Member of the Congregation at the Parish Church.

2. The affairs of the Tower shall be managed by a Committee, consisting of the Vicar and four Members elected annually.

3. New Ringers must be proposed and seconded by existing Members of the Tower.

4. There shall be an Annual Subscription of Two Shillings from each Ringer, to be paid in January of every year.

5. Each Ringer shall contribute Sixpence a month towards "The Tower Fund."

6. All Monies received from the Ringers shall be paid to the Hon. Treasurer, and shall only be spent according to a vote of the whole of the Ringers.

7. The Tower Bells shall be rung on the First and Third Sundays in each Month and on Great Festivals from 10.30 a.m. to 11 a.m., and from 6 p.m. to 6.30 p.m., and the Ringers shall meet in the Tower in good time so as to commence ringing punctually at these hours.

8. Practice Night shall be on Tuesday in every week from the First week in October until Easter from 7.30 p.m. to 9 p.m.

9. Meetings of the Ringers shall be held in the Tower quarterly, due notice of which shall be posted in the Tower one week previous to the Meeting.

10. All Ringers are earnestly requested to bear in mind that their aim is to work for the good of the Church and people, and to promote the glory of God.

11. Alterations in these Rules shall only be made after due notice, at a General Meeting of the Ringers.

January, 1927.

Whitby, Yeovil.

The Tower Rules for bell-ringers at St Michael's in 1927. Practice nights were only held between October and Easter so that the bell-ringers would be free to spend more time in their gardens and allotments during the rest of the year.

Hackwell's workshop: the business was started by Charles Hackwell whose house, Somerleigh, was next door to the workshop on Mill Lane (now Clewer). Mr Hackwell ran the business with his son Tom, and in 1913 Hackwell & Son advertised in the Parish News *as 'Builders, Contractors, Undertakers, Wheel-wrights, and House Decorators'. Traps and carts were built from scratch in the workshop, and were winched on a platform to the paint-shop above, away from all the sawdust. Tom Hackwell died in 1944, by which time the business depended on the undertaking and building-maintenance work. After the war the business was sold to Stanley Stevens and his son Eric, who worked together, along with Stanley's brother Ralph Stevens, for many years.*

A wedding group at Somerleigh: Charles Hackwell stands in the back row, far right, and his wife Kate is seated second from left. The door to Hackwell's workshop, where carts could be brought in and out, can be seen to the left of the photograph.

Above: *An early photograph of the sawmills on the corner of Halves Lane. Joseph Perry stands on the far right, with his sons Herbert and Sid in the middle. Joseph Perry was a blacksmith and engineer who made the twine-twisting machinery used at Drake's factory and elsewhere, and also iron castings for a horizontal log saw. Because one of these log saws was on the premises, by 1897 the business had moved into timber supply. A steam-engine powered the sawmill, fuelled by timber waste – sawdust and wood – and taking water from the stream.*

Left: *Men in front of the forge, 1965: on the far right is Jack Pomeroy who took over the forge when his father, Herbert Pomeroy, died in 1932. Jack was still working as village blacksmith over 40 years later, although by then most of his work was welding and repairing farm machinery. In 1932 there had been more than 100 horses in East Coker: one wall of the forge had nails all over it, each one with a horse's name above, and sets of horseshoes on each nail ready to be used for that horse.* (Photograph by Derrick Lumley)

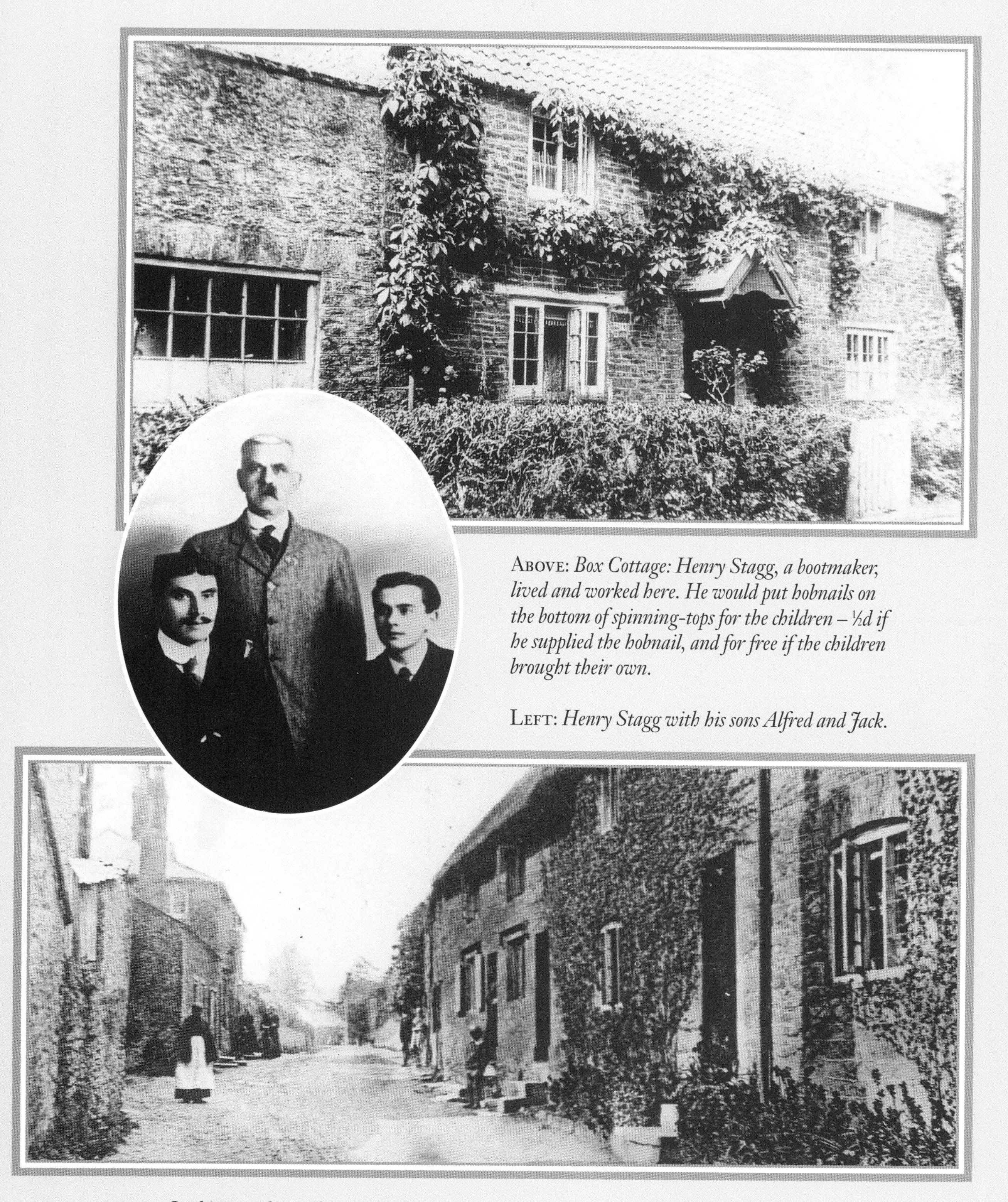

Above: *Box Cottage: Henry Stagg, a bootmaker, lived and worked here. He would put hobnails on the bottom of spinning-tops for the children – ½d if he supplied the hobnail, and for free if the children brought their own.*

Left: *Henry Stagg with his sons Alfred and Jack.*

Looking up the road towards Burton: Garden Row is on the right, and Mrs Cox's shop (now the Post Office and General Stores) is on the left. Garden Row backed onto the kitchen garden at North Coker House.

RIGHT: *Bunthams.*

BELOW: *The Granary House at Burton Cross.*

The Cricket Field

Cricket was the game East Coker was most passionate about. By the end of the 1920s Colonel Heneage was paying professionals to coach the village team.

NOBODY wasn't allowed to play football up at the recreation ground on Long Furlong Lane. That was sacred ground that cricket field! You wasn't allowed to go there unless you put on daps. After we left Inkson we went up there to play football, but we played outside the cricket pitch in the field next to it. East Coker had the best cricket team in Somerset barring the county side in them days. When Bill Andrews came here he was coaching a young team; older players was dropping out then – like Cecil Drake, Bernard Drake, Herb Dodge – and Colonel wanted to bring on some youngsters to take their place. I was never good enough to play for the first team – I played for the seconds! Course the war came and destroyed the very lot, didn't it. Colonel died before the war started.

The three Pulman boys – Edgar, Henry and Cecil – play cricket in the garden of their house at the Chantry, while their father, Tom, looks on.

Gentlemen versus Scruffs

IN the old days I can remember some county cricketers used to come down here and play at East Coker cricket pitch. Like all their friends, they'd have gentlemen versus scruffs or something like that. They used to be like Mr Mayo and all those people, what you might call the upper class, they used to have their friends come down, and old Ponsonby-Fane at Brympton he used to have a cricket team down there as well.

Village Professional

Bill Andrews (1908–89) was an outstanding all-rounder for Somerset County Cricket and played for the county in 226 matches between 1930 and 1947. Now and again Bill could be seen at cricket matches in East Coker where in his early 20s he had worked as a cricket coach for the village team. In his autobiography, The Hand That Bowled Bradman, *Bill Andrews describes his brief career as a Village Professional.*

IN desperation one March morning in 1930 I walked out of the office and bought the *Athletic News*, a well-known sports paper of the day. My intention was to see if there were any jobs going for a professional cricketer. Yes, there was one: 'CRICKET PROFESSIONAL/GROUNDSMAN wanted for EAST COKER CRICKET CLUB. Salary £3 a week for 22 weeks' engagement'. Frankly I didn't know

East Coker cricket team c.1920: *(l–r) back row: Arthur Mead, Stanley Stevens, Bob Mead, Bernard Hackwell, Ralph Stevens, Arthur Sims, T. Russell; seated: Bob Lacey, Doug Colley, Walter Stevens, Percy Crumpler, Bob Russell, Percy Ford, Percy Harwood.*

An East Coker ladies' cricket team in 1927.

where East Coker was although it happened to be in Somerset. I'd have gone anywhere. I applied and Larry Hawkins drove me down for the interview.

East Coker, I discovered, was a pretty village near Yeovil. The secretary of the cricket club told me he had received 140 applications for the job – a sure sign of the times. But he said he liked the tone of my letter and was impressed by my averages. I was appointed professional and groundsman for that summer. My salary was to be paid by the local squire, Colonel Walker-Heneage. The club had a lovely little ground, a good wicket and a strong fixture list.

I went back to Weston and gave in my notice at the solicitor's office. They offered me ten shillings a week to stay on. My former schoolmaster, Harry Saunders, said I must be off my head.

April came along and I set off for East Coker – with my dog. My first digs, with a sports-minded local schoolmaster, cost me £1 a week. I started cutting the grass and preparing the wicket, and getting in a bit of net practice. Almost immediately I got a letter from the secretary of Somerset, John Daniell. He wanted me to come to Taunton the following week to play in a pre-season trial match. East Coker gave me permission to go … you can imagine my surprise when the skipper came to me after the game and said he wanted me to play as an opening bowler in Somerset's first four county matches. I would be No.11 in the batting order. My terms were £10 a match and I had to pay all my hotels from this. But I felt like a millionaire.

Of course I accepted the invitation. But when I approached the East Coker committee about time off I met rather a cold reception. They told me bluntly that I should have to find a substitute professional as good as myself before they would let me go.

They were such a decent bunch and, after all, they had given me the chance to breathe the fresh air after being cooped up in a lawyer's office. I began quickly to look around for a substitute. There was only one answer – my brother Jack.

Bill Andrews with his brother Jack at the wicket in the garden of their home at Weston-Super-Mare

Roger and Joan Hackwell c.1936 with Bill Andrews' dog Ruff, given to them when Bill left East Coker to play cricket for Somerset.

He was nicely placed in an office with good prospects and a pension at the end of it. But he didn't give it a second thought when I asked him; he immediately said 'Yes'. My father was horrified that both his sons were now giving up steady jobs to have a go at cricket. He never really understood this great game.

Jack arrived at East Coker and we took digs together at the village pub. I felt I could make the grade at first-class cricket and land a contract. Then my brother could stay on at East Coker.

In fact, Jack did his stuff for the village club. Although really a wicket-keeper batsman, his bowling had benefited from hours of practice in the little lane near our Weston home. In his first match for East Coker he took six wickets. In his second he scored a century. My absence was never noticed….

Back in 1930 I had confidently left my brother in charge as the village professional and I headed for the county ground. My single-minded ambition was about to be fulfilled.

Bill and Jack Andrews Bring on the Team

WE had a darn good side here. When I was playing Bill Andrews come. The Colonel had a contract with him to teach the youngsters and play for the first team. I and my brother Walt, we were the only – we'll say we were outside the professions, you know. We were the outsiders, put it like that. Proper toff team here, I had a couple or three seasons with the first. I played for the seconds, but when Jack Andrews went away I played for the firsts. Jack used to train me. He used to bowl at me for over after over for me to keep winging, you know, and I kept winging for I think about three seasons. We used to play Yeovil, and Portland, and Dorchester, Weymouth, Petherton – they were all pretty keen on cricket during that period. I was playing for the reserve team previous to that. We used to have a rare bit of fun, the reserves: we used to play Cattistock, and Chetnole, and Yetminster and teams like that, you know, them days. After the game we used to go in the boozer up Halstock, *The Quiet Woman*, or somewhere or another.

Jack Drake, that was one of the big hitters, Charlie Mayo was another – he were a good cricketer mind. The firsts used to play the Somerset Stragglers, 'twas to do with the county side. I've never played in one of them games, 'twere always mid-week. Tommy Hackwell would be going on with his bat under his arm to one of these

East Coker cricket team c.1948:
(l–r) back row: Charlie Boucher, Basil Baker, Percy Maunder, Hubert Stevens, Len Purchase, Frank Waite, Bill Halfacre;
front row: Brian Boucher (scorer), David Foot, Doug Pilton, Eddie Rice, Jack Taylor, Jack Cornelius.

games. He'd be going off up there 'Cheerio!' Sam Young the wheel-wright there he said 'Hey, you want to look out at the job here, not go off up there playing cricket!' get rid of it. He wasn't going to put up with that. Bloody laugh it was!

Charlie Mayo

OLD Worsfold Mayo, he was a solicitor. The son Charlie, he used to go abroad to Canada, he'd ride in the saddle about ten hours a day. Fit as anything he was – he was as strong as a horse. We kids used to idolise him. He used to go up the cricket field, take up his golf clubs, one of us would go about a field and a half away over that way, somebody else this way, and he'd start hitting the balls. Good God Almighty! I wouldn't like to say how far he hit 'em!

I can remember the time when he played cricket for the first team of East Coker. He would go up on that cricket pitch and I have known him lose four cricket balls in one afternoon. I've known him hit 'em down the Mill Lane allotments, and over the pavilion, over the gardens, and pitch 'em on Buntham house. Terrific fella! There wasn't much he couldn't do, really. I remember he had a stock-whip, a little short handle with about a 24-foot lash on it. I've seen him at the back on the lawn with a cigarette packet cocked on a bough, and he brought that thing back once and then twice and then he'd crack it! Just like a gun going off! And he split that packet down through!

Another thing he had was a pet raven. When we used to go by there on our bikes, very often he used to fly out round and he'd go and peck you on the back of your neck! He was a sod he was. Then he got into trouble up the Court with the raven. A lot of the servants up there when they had their smalls out on the line, the raven used to go out and pick 'em off, take 'em back down to Charlie! That's the truth! And the Colonel made him

Charlie Mayo and his raven Grip – named after the raven in Dickens' Barnaby Rudge. *Like his namesake, Grip had a bad reputation and was exiled with family friends in another county. Charlie worked for a time as a cowboy for the Douglas Lake Cattle Co. in British Columbia. He died in 1943 in the Middle East where he was serving with the North Somerset Yeomanry.*

Football on Inkson

'TWAS a very heavy-going pitch. You know, very soggy. When we had rain we couldn't hardly move – your feet would sink. It was a grass field then, of course. I mind when Dick's father, Mr Andrews, and old Mr Helyar, used to come down from Back Lane and stay by the fence over the other side of the road, they'd be there watching us. We hadn't had a team for a number of years, not since the war I don't think. Jack Cox and Arthur Sims, they'd been in the services. When East Coker didn't have a team, me and my brother played for West Coker or Odcombe. These two teams played against each other one year in a final at the Yeovil Town ground – I knew all the players on both sides!

Scrumpy for Sunderland

In 1949 Yeovil Town FC made their historic FA Cup run, eventually travelling to play Manchester United before more than 80,000 spectators in the fifth round. But everyone remembers their remarkable 2-1 win over First-Division Sunderland in the previous round at Huish. Here is an account of a conversation in the New Inn *during the build-up to the big match against Sunderland.*

ONLY a mile and a half from Yeovil is the village of East Coker, with its thatched houses built of the ubiquitous Ham sandstone. Here is unspoiled rural Somerset.

By ancient custom the chair on the right of the bar in the *Helyar Arms* is reserved for a 73-year-old retired farm worker Gilbert Neville, who got married on 11*s.* a

East Coker football club, 1923–4, poses for a photograph in front of the vicarage: (l–r) back row: Mr Headford (headmaster), E. Watkins, J. Cronk, F. Crystal, B. Moger, F. Coombs; middle row: R. Stevens, A. Sims, Reverend Bailey, A. Millar, F. Beater; front row: A. Childs, R. Andrews, W. Stevens, C. Woolmington, E. May. Fred Beater worked for Slade's Farm and arranged for the team to play on a field called Inkson near the cemetery in return for them helping the farmer at haymaking time. At home games, the Legion Room at the New Inn *was used as a changing room for the away side.*

week because his best girl refused to wait until he got 12*s*. There he sits by the hour with a pot of 'scrumpy' (strong cider).

I asked him confidentially what he thought about Yeovil's chance against Sunderland. Gilbert pushed his battered felt hat on the back of his head, adjusted his choker, hitched up his trousers with their large Dutch pattern patches, wiped his grey moustache with the back of a gnarled hand and said: 'Us has our suspicions who stole un'. It seems that someone had pinched the ferret belonging to Mr Dunham, the Head Gardener at the manor; a ferret as cunning as Machiavelli, savage as a tiger, bred from a super line of ferrets.

After a few minutes I repeated my question about the match.

The mens' football team, 1948–9: (l–r) back row: S. Haines (treasurer), S. Gaylard (linesman), B. Hawkins, L. Purchase, J. Stroud, E. Rice (trainer), A. Hackwell (secretary); middle row: G. Colley, G. Hawkins, A. Moger, L. Johnson, A. Long; front row: R. Haines, B. Stroud, B. Gash. When the men's football club restarted in 1947, games were played on the cricket field which was now no longer exclusively for cricket.

'Yeovil'ul beat un if they get plenty of scrumpy before the match. There baint notting loike it. In my young day I used to drink five pints instead of breakfast. Three ha'pence a pint, it were' (now 8*d.*).

But pretty Mrs Betty Waite, the landlord's wife, advised me not to get 'scrumpy' on my shoes, because it rots the leather. She added that when she let some drip on her stone floor, it bleached it.

So it may be better tactics for Yeovil to let Sunderland drink the 'scrumpy'. With that and the Slope, Sunderland would not have a dog's chance.

East Coker Youths' Football Club at the old Yeovil Town Football Ground. In their 1948–9 season they were the Yeovil Youth Champions and winners of Yeovil Youths' Knock-out Shield. Peter Coombe, the team's captain, is held shoulder-high. Other team members were: A. Davis, D. Bellamy, D. Hussey, G. Hussey, W. Crossley, C. Hannam, N. Adams, J. Hancock, W. Hancock, G. Bown, J. Trott, J. Newman, D. Mortimore, A. Beales, C. Perrott, D. Rendell, P. Purchase, P. Lock, P. Denny, T. Edwards, A. Ellis and J. Frampton.

East Coker School's football team, Junior League Champions 1949/50: (l–r) back row: John Bishop, - , Robin Baker, Alan Haines, Henry Tizzard, Robin Annetts, Tony Rendell, Alan Stevens, Les Gould, Kenny Adams; middle row: Robert Harvey, Jim Jones, Dave Morris, Ron Smith, Roy Harriss, - , John Hodges; front row: ?Malcolm Lea, Bill Gould, Nigel Boucher, Gerry Smith.

Harvesting corn with a binder at Hyde Farm, c.1927. Alec Boucher sits on the front horse Flossie, the other two horses are Damson and Darling.

Hyde Farm in the 1920s

I'D been playing about Hyde Farm for about five or six years, always at the farm. Leading the horse and hay cart, played more than we worked. Boys in they days, they was always at the farm where there were animals about. Country boys were always on the farm. Dave Watkins and I, we were the same age, we were like brothers. Dave's father farmed at Hyde and I could go up there and ride the pony and all things like that.

I left school on the Thursday, I was 14 on the Friday, and started work on the Monday for 17 shillings a week. He always employed seven or eight men, Watkins did. He always had plenty of labour. As soon as we started work we were classed as one of the gang, we had to milk the cows, and I was ploughing when I was 17, mind, with two cart-horses. You learned with the older men. Mostly for the first two or three years – the old man was an invalid, he could only walk with two sticks – I was the old man's chaperon to take around the farm with a horse and cart. When he took over some land from Rock Farm, at Sutton Bingham, he had a lot of cattle all up round Coker Wood and every day about half past eight, nine o'clock, he used to go round and see the cattle and sheep. He'd sit in his old milk float and I used to get out to open the gates for him to drive it through. By the time we got there in the morning, the cattle were gone in the shade and we had to go in the bushes and count them all and see if they were all there, if there was anything the matter with 'em.

Alec Boucher on his 21st birthday: he worked for Mr Watkins of Hyde Farm, Sutton Bingham, from leaving school at 14 until he was 20 years old, starting on wages of 17 shillings a week, and finishing with a man's wage of 30 shillings. Alec remembered when he was 18 buying a pint of cider, five Woodbines, and a box of matches, and still getting change out of sixpence!

Everything was done by hand. The hoeing was all done by hand then, mind. I've seen old Bill Rawles and Jimmy spend weeks and weeks hoeing. Perhaps they had ten acres of mangel to hoe and they had to hoe that three times. They had to hoe 'em first, then single 'em, and then hoe 'em again. Hours and hours of work and 'twere only about ninepence an hour, weren't it! 30 bob a week. Old man Watkins was good – old Jesse Crumpler was another one – anybody out of work, old man would find a job for 'em. Crumpler employed a lot of men hoeing. He growed a lot of roots, sugar-beet, mangels. He used to hire casual labour, anybody that was out of work would go up there hoeing. He'd say 'I'll give you so much an acre to do it'. At Hyde you had your regular men, but still had strappers, see. Anybody were out of work, old man would give 'em a job.

I've done hours of hoeing, and mowing with a scythe, mind. They used to mow all the corn with scythes in them days. If the wind blew the corn down and the binder wouldn't pick it up, they had to mow it with a scythe. When they cut a corner field they'd go round the first two swaths, the first six-foot cut, by scythe not to waste a bit of corn. They'd mow all round these corner fields to give the binder a chance.

Scything, you had to learn yourself, didn't you. Go out with the men, they'd tell you what to do. Setting the scythe was the main thing, setting your handles. Being able to sharpen was the biggest thing, that was the biggest job of the lot, same with everything in a farm, if you couldn't sharpen you couldn't mow, and you couldn't use a hook if you couldn't sharpen. You had to spend half a day on the grinding stone when it was a wet day, grinding 'em down. 'Twas a skilled job, I never could sharpen. Herbie Lawrence was the best bloke to sharpen anything. When I come to Bramley Cottage first he cut my lawn with a scythe better than I could cut it with a machine. I used to take three hooks up for old Herbie of a night-time, he'd sit on his old couch there, got the stone, and sharpened them. You could shave with 'em they were so sharp!

We used to get up at four o'clock in the morning to go mowing. We were all together, 'twas a gang of us in the field with the horses and mowing machine. This was the amusing part about it, we'd start off mowing at four o'clock and work till it's very hot in the middle of the day then rest the horses. By the time it's 12 o'clock, the next bloody field of hay was fit, and we had to go on haymaking! Horses had no rest more than we! Every time you finished at 12 o'clock the next field was ready to be carried! I was only young and I was always late for work. I could never get up in the morning. I'd started doing the horses and had to go mowing. The carter said 'He won't get up! I bet he won't be up!' I said 'I bet thee I will', he said 'You'll have to stop up all night!' This particular night I went to bed around ten, woke up and looked at the clock – four o'clock! Christ! Get out of bed – had to walk all up across Merryfields and up to the stable. Nobody about. Had the horses in the Plot there, got the horses in to stable. Nobody were about. 'What the hell's on then?' I looked at my watch – instead of what I thought was four o'clock it was 20 past one! I had the horses all ready for our mowing at two o'clock! Cor – they pulled my bloody leg! I went to the stable and lay down on the hay and went to sleep! When I went on the farm first, all they did was cut the hay, made it into rows, and picked it up with pitchforks and put it on the wagon, took it over and pitched it up on the rick. By the time I finished, they had collectors, sweeps that used to sweep it in and elevators what would take it up on the rick.

There was always two carters at Hyde Farm. As the old man, Bill Rawles the carter, left off the horses, we youngsters took 'em on. I liked cartering. You had your own team of two horses which we used all the time. Horses were used for everything. Damson and Darling were my two horses. I've been up in Coker Wood, you know all the rides through the wood, I used to go up there and chain harrow 'em, and roll all them rides, mind, twice a year.

Everything was done in rotation wasn't it? 'Twas all done by hand in them days, see, sowing the corn, all things like that. The weather's the only thing that could beat you on the farm. They always had a job if it was wet weather. Dung-hauling with a horse and putt was the best job for wet weather – they used to say 'Can't go to plough, I've got to go dung-hauling!' Only time you had a dry job was when you were white-washing the cow stalls. You got used to bad weather. I've been soaking wet through. There weren't any wellington boots in they days, see. We used to wear hobnail boots and leggings then. Leather leggings come right up to your knees. Put 'em by the fire to dry by night, they were like boards in the morning! A job to get your feet in 'em! They'd soften up when they got wet again! Old man Watkins always wore button-up leggings, had a button crook to hook 'em up. We used to wear strap leggings with three buckles come down over your boot.

The men used to wear a sack bag most of the time. I always remember old Jimmy Stevens, when Jimmy used to wear sack round his shoulders, and he had an old fashioned button crook to keep him on 'ee. I can remember that button crook shone like a sixpence. You get one of them old sacks and he'll keep the wet out all day. And they'd wear another one around their waist mind,

Sheep-dipping at Hyde Farm – the workmen with Mr Watkins (far right) are Alec Boucher, - , Jimmy Stevens, - , and Charlie Boucher.

tied round their waist with a belt. They'd wear a pair of trousers till it fell off, then they'd get a new pair. They never had to wash 'em! I've seen some of the old cowmen putting their trousers by the fire to dry where they've spilled milk on 'em – their trousers could stand up on their own, and they still wore 'em! I always wore buttoned-up breeches. Most of the farmers wore buttoned-up corduroy breeches.

I used to like the harvesting best really. Harvesting was a good season. Catching rabbits out of the corn. It was a lot of fun. When they were cutting the corn, all the kids in the village used to go up catching rabbits as they ran out of the corn. There were hundreds of 'em. I've seen 'em knock down 60 with sticks up at the corner field. You could see the corn move with 'em. When I was riding the front horse taking the binder, you could see the corn move with the rabbits.

Every Christmas Mr Watkins used to sell a bullock in the Christmas Fatstock Show. A butcher used to buy the bullock, it was about a fortnight before Christmas, and then come Christmas the old man used to buy a quarter of that bullock and give all his workmen a big joint. They used to eat big, farmers used to, mind. Had breakfast at the farm – three eggs, five or six rashers of bacon, big plate of fried tatty. I'll tell 'ee what, when I was about 15 or 16, I had to go milking first see, milk several cows, then go in to breakfast, about eight of us all sitting down to breakfast, see.

I've seen ten or 12 horses and carts down at Sutton Bingham station with churns of milk to catch the eight o'clock train. Some had wagons, from out Halstock, Corscombe, all come there with 17-gallon churns. Big high churn. There were two men, one was Jackson, the other Johnson, they were milk retailers in London and they used to come down every year and have a contract with the old man for his milk. On the churn was 'Jackson & Johnson, Vauxhall' and on the other side was 'Edward Watkins, Hyde Farm'. They used to always bring us down a new football, they two old gentlemen. We had a good football team up at the farm. Good Fridays we used to go up in the woods and cut the goal-posts, and a long pole across the top. The horses would knock 'em down during the winter and break 'em. Every year we had to go and get another new set.

On market day I used to go on with the cattle with the old man. Drive 'em by road. Had three go in Percy's shop once, up Princes Street! We took a cow to market once, took us about three hours to get 'un in there. Sold 'un. And we were coming back up Hendford Hill in the pony and trap, Mrs Watkins and th'old man at the front, I at the back, and the bloody cow coming on behind! He got back up Sutton Bingham before we did! They used to sell the horses in Silver Street, by the *Pall Tavern*. I've seen 50 horses down there tied tail to tail. Drovers and that used to bring 'em in. Run 'em round there by the Pall, all gippos'd buy 'em, clap their hand. All in guineas.

There was always seven regular men on the farm besides the boys. By the time I left I was a man, wan't I? I was one of the men. I was only 20 when the old man died. Took him down to the cemetery on his milk float. I led the pony. Eight workmen from the farm carried his coffin. I was one of them.

Above: *Inside one of the loom shops at Drake's webbing factory,* c.1950.
Peggy Hampson watches over the looms in the foreground, in the background is Stan Guppy.
Below: *Drake's webbing factory looking across the orchard that is now the school's playing field. The old buildings, originally a powerloom sailcloth factory, are on the left; a new block was built to house modern high-speed Italian looms (right) and produced parachute webbing during the Second World War. In 1977 Sheila, Betty and Francis Drake gave land fronting Halves Lane to the village as the site for the new Village Hall which opened in 1981. The webbing business was sold by the Drake family, and subsequently closed in 1982; in 1987 the buildings were demolished.*

From Quilling Boy to Weaver

I was about 13½ when I went to work at Drake's. At the time quite a number of boys from Hardington was working there, and work was pretty scarce in those days. We all used to cycle together. We started work dead on the dot of eight o'clock, and they used to blow the hooter at ten to eight. There'd be hooters going from a lot of places in those days, some from Yeovil, but we all knew East Coker by its long, long blast because it was steam and it had a different pitch. We could hear it sometimes as far as Hardington church and we'd know then that we had to really pedal for to get over to East Coker by eight because the old foreman, Bill Pearce, used to be standing outside, looking at his watch.

There'd be six or eight quilling boys, and you'd have to keep all these looms going in quills for to put in the shuttle. Later on, when this new man, Mr Booth, come from the north, he revolutionised the whole factory. He brought an end to all the quilling boys and he brought three long quilling machines down. These machines was operated by two girls, and they used to do all the quilling on these machines which we used to do as boys with our hands. They still kept the boys on for learning to weave, putting 'em on with a weaver.

It was a question I would say not so much of your age, becoming a weaver, more of your manliness: when the quilling boy got big enough and strong enough he would go on a loom. As a quilling boy, his job was also to hand on the warp when the weaver was drawing a warp, so the quilling boy was learning all the time because he had to hand on so many warps to different weavers. The only thing was, it was a question not so much of learning it or doing it – it was a question of standing it because it was a boring job really, and the clatter of the shuttles going through – clack-clack-clack – the noise used to drive me up the wall! I suppose I was there about five or six years, but when I got a bit cheesed off, like kids do, I went down to the butter factory at Bridge Farm to work for a while. Jim Harding and Bill Poole used to work in the out-sheds – it was father-in-law and son-in-law – and they had old hand looms in there; they could make webbing much wider than any of the other looms – up to six feet wide. I used to watch their feet – they used to operate everything with their feet – with the treadles going up and down. Sometimes they used to have two men on one loom, one on each side, tossing the shuttle through. It was all woven in twine, and it was used for two purposes: one was as slings for loading cattle or horses onto boats; and the other was for straining soap when it was in a liquid form. It was a nice finish when it was all done because the string was waxed.

There was loads of fluff from the looms and it was difficult to burn. It came down so delicately as the weavers used to weave, and it would end up about a foot and a half deep. At times we had the floods up, because the river went right underneath the factory floor. We've had flooding when we've all had to stop work. The weaving shops were on two different levels – the top shop and the bottom shop. The bottom shop used to get flooded and we had to go on up and get all the fluff from the top shop – there used to be a lot of fluff underneath the looms – and chuck it all over the floors to try and soak up the water which would be perhaps a foot deep.

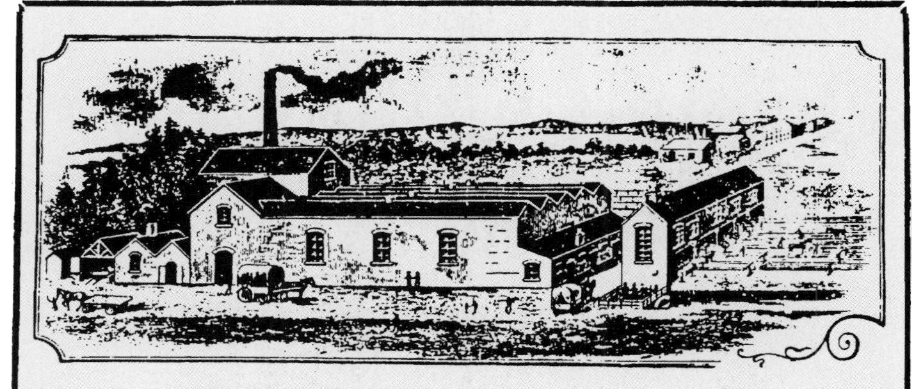

F. DRAKE & Co.,

North Coker Mills, YEOVIL, England.

Registered Trade Mark.

ESTABLISHED 1872.

CONTRACTORS
TO WAR OFFICE
AND ADMIRALTY.

Telegrams :
"DRAKE, East-Coker."

Telephone :
"WEST COKER 325."

MANUFACTURERS OF

COCOA BINDINGS, Fine, Stout and Fancy Chair and Tray Webs.

Linen and Woollen Saddlery Webs of every description.

Roller, Surcingle, Brace, Halter, Girth, Straining, Cavalry, Rein and Circular, and Army Webs.

Super Diaper, Twist and other Webs.

Union, Cotton & Worsted Webs.

Cotton Banding, etc.

Belt, Packing and Pack Webs,

Common Jute Rollers.

Best Twines.

Super Mattress, White, Packing.

Quilting and Sealing Twines.

Whipcords.

Motor Hood, Strap and Bonnet Webs.

Principal Makers of ELDON GIRTH WEBS for S. America.

AND AT

MANCHESTER : 45a Market Street.
NORWICH : 58 College Road.
BIRMINGHAM : 57 Albion Street.

Advertisement for Drake's webbing factory in the 1920s. Originally built c.1860 as a powerloom sailcloth factory, Felix Drake converted the premises for webbing and twine manufacture c.1879.

Men on the twine walks of the webbing factory: (l–r) Walter Stevens, F. Rendell, E. Purchase, T. Thomas, and T. Penny.

As well as the webbing factory there was a twine walk over the little brook at the back of the sawmills. The twine walk used to go roughly 100 yards, with six walks, and six men making the twine, each with their own walk. It was all men on the twine walk – like Arthur Sims, Edgar Purchase, Arthur Hackwell – and that would be their domain. First of all the twine was spun and twisted, then they would size it up and gradually it would get harder and harder till it came up a nice piece of string that was really shiny. The motor would be turning the drums when they were doing the sizing, and they used to let the twine run through their hands, and when they got enough on, then they'd hold their hands there and get off the surplus. When they'd finished making it nice and smooth, they'd take it all up ready for balling. They had a special way of carrying it so that it wouldn't be entangled – taking each length individually, tying it up in a skein, and carrying it round their shoulder.

Drake's had big competition from Harts, and Haslocks of Crewkerne, that was in the chair-webbing side of it. They were all competing against each other. There was a great big twine walk at Pymore near Bridport, and another twine walk was Dawes at West Coker.

Up the entrance drive by Cross Cottages there was a man named Joe Lawrence, who lived in the farthest one from the road. He had this black horse, a beautiful horse. Every day Joe used to take a wagon-load of webbing away to Yeovil stations, and I've known him take two in one day.

Arthur Board was the maintenance man, he was a mechanic, and he used to set the looms up and different things. He'd mend belts, and maintain the looms up to a point. There were two carpenters on site in the factory, and their name was Turner, young Jack and old Jack. They used to do all the woodwork, build ten-shuttle, twelve-shuttle looms from scratch. The iron parts of the frame were made by the Victoria Smelting Company in Yeovil. When this little fella named Booth brought his ideas down about the fly shuttles, they used to sit down together and this little fella used to give Jack a rough sketch and he would go from there, measure it all out, build the loom up. He was a real craftsman.

In the factory itself there were no women weaving. They had women working on the premises, but they were balling, spooling, and beaming, and things like that. The weavers were all men. And it wasn't until Mr Booth came and started the fly shuttles, that we had the first lot of young girls come in to look after them. And that introduced women to weaving at East Coker.

At lunchtime everybody stopped except the men who were on piece-work. If he was on an old-fashioned

Women in the overlooking room trimming and tidying loose threads on lengths of deckchair webbing.

loom he had to wind his own webbing by hand, and that had to be done more or less in the dinner-hour. Most of 'em was on piece-work, and that would save time because it was ever such a cutthroat job. Men used to take their lunch on in their big haversacks, with a bottle of cold tea or cocoa, and a piece of bread and cheese. We used to go out and sit on the grass, or in the winter-time we'd go over the twine-walk side where they had a stove and it used to be nice and warm in there. We used to all sit round and yarns would come out with different people. There were men of all ages. I can remember one old man, Jim Baker, he used to tell us all these stories about the deep snow in 1881, when you could walk from one field to the other over the roads which were filled right up with snow. He was a wonderful old man for telling tales. He used to smoke this tiny short clay pipe, broken off, it was only about two inches long.

On Armistice Day at 11 o'clock they used to stop all the works for two minutes' silence. Jack Baker would cut the steam off, then the whole lot would come to a standstill, and about five minutes afterwards it would all be starting up again. They had a steam-engine there with a massive boiler. If you can imagine the boiler of a steam train and magnify that about three times that would be the size of it. Jack Baker was shovelling coal all the time, just like a man on the railway, and of course the water used to be coming in from the stream. They had to keep the boiler filled up with water and keep it boiling to get the head of steam up to drive all the machinery and all the shafting. A great big flywheel would gradually start turning, and it would gradually speed up and speed up and then they get all the shafting working at the right speed for the looms to work. It was all overhead shafting, with the great big belts coming down driving the looms.

There was an old man called Neal, he was the dyer. He would dye the yarn any colour that they wanted in great big vats. And then they used to hang it out in the field on long poles, put skeins of it all over these, and then when it was all dry they'd bring it back in again. Out in the open field they could put out ten times more than they could up in the drying room with the steam pipes all along the floor; but if it started raining and they wanted it, then it had to go up in the drying room.

We always had a week's holiday in the summer. They used to close the factory down for a week, and they'd ask for six or eight volunteers for to go in and whitewash the factory, and have their week at some other time. The boiler had to be cleaned out, and also the flue going from the boiler to the bottom of the chimney. I had that job once when I was a boy because I was small. I had to get down in the flue, and crawl up through with an electric light, and we had to pull all the soot from the bottom of the factory chimney which was 20 or 30 yards away. In the process of doing this I broke the electric light bulb, and in the darkness I put my hand down and caught hold of the live element. Being underneath the factory – nobody couldn't hear me shouting down there in the dark. Fortunately it didn't kill me, and I had to crawl back to come out. I was given a new light bulb and had to go back in again!

Cooking for Queen Mary

When I came to Pen Mill station, William the chauffeur was waiting for me, and of course I was smart, little white bows on my sleeves and high-heeled black-and-white shoes. I didn't know where it was in the country, and I got in the lovely big car and he drove through the town, then down the lanes. I thought to myself 'Oh my God, where am I going? Give me a week!' because I'd never been in the country before. When we come to the gates, we didn't go up the drive, we went all the way around to the back door. When I got to the door, he opened it and I went in the passage there and I could hear all banging of saucepans and things like that. I went upstairs into my bedroom, put my luggage up there, and put my print dress on – because we used to wear print dress and aprons then – and so I come back down to the kitchen.

I never went out for the first year or two! I used to go out when I had a day off, walk around the fields, and I never come down the village. I went out for a walk one Sunday morning in the fields to Spin Wood and back, so Alfred the footman said Mrs Heneage wanted to see me and I thought 'Oh my God, I hope I haven't walked anywhere where I shouldn't walk' because she was terrible particular. And so I went upstairs and changed, and I went through with Alfred. Mrs Heneage said 'Oh, Joan, Colonel Heneage and I have been wondering whether you would like to take the cooking on?' and I said, 'Oh yes please, madam', straight away and she liked me because I didn't hesitate.

Joan Boucher (née Barry) who was 19 when she first came to East Coker in 1930 to work as a kitchen-maid at Coker Court. Within a few years she was made the cook, and her younger sister Doreen came to the village to work with her as the new kitchen-maid.

I did a big party up there for about 300 or 400 people. I stayed up all night making 700 bread rolls. I rang Pulman and said 'Send me up as much yeast as you can'. We had four waiters from Fortnum & Mason's and they wouldn't believe I'd made everything. Our Doreen said 'Come in the larder' and it was packed out with the hams I'd cooked, and the tongues garnished with apple jelly, and pieces of chicken all different ways. Everything turned out lovely. When the party was over I had dinner to do as well!

I had Mrs Heneage's scones to make for breakfast at half past seven every morning, the big range going hot for that. Doreen had to light the fire and everything, push the dampers in to get the ovens hot for me before I got up. I used to have six big buckets of coal in the morning, and six at night-time. I had four big lovely ovens, all my stock-pots and the kettles on top of the range boiling away. Colonel used to come to the kitchen at nine o'clock every morning. I used to get the book on the table for him, and a chair for him to sit down, and a pencil and all that ready for him and he'd say 'Now what shall we have today Joan?' and I told him what I had in the larder, and he would decide what to eat and put it down in the book.

We had two big larders with marble shelves, and a lovely icebox. I used to have freezing-salt and two big blocks of ice from Soyer's, the fishmongers in Prince's Street, every morning. They'd drag it to the larder by the back door. It was always cool in the larder. I used to go in there and make all my puff pastry on the marble slab, and all the sweets I made went in there. Mr Wilfred the butler would cool bottles of wine from the cellars in the icebox.

When I worked at the Court as a cook I had sacks and sacks of everything. I was never short of nothing. Sacks of caster sugar, and ground almonds, and all that come by train from Fortnum & Mason's every three months. A big lorry used to bring it from there to the Court. When I was cooking I just had to turn around and all my sacks were there. In my top cupboard I had a bottle of brandy, a bottle of rum, a bottle of sherry – and I never touched a drop! I used to put it in the trifles, or make a brandy omelette for the Colonel.

In the scullery we had two big sinks with big brass taps. We had two big dressers there – one was full of copper and brass, and the other one was china. We never had no china from the front of the house at all – that was kept in the butler's quarters. In the butler's pantry he had

The South Wing, Coker Court, to the left of the picture was built in 1900 to house a modern kitchen, boiler room and additional servants' quarters.

two really big cupboards, all of the silver was in one and all the glass in the other. All the china with the cockerel on he had underneath. They used to wash all that in there.

Every New Year's Eve the bell-ringers used to come into my kitchen, the Colonel used to have the bell-ringers in, plenty of food and drink for them. On my big, scrubbed kitchen table I used to put all the cold cooked ham and tongue for them. When they'd finished they went into the servants' hall, because Colonel's bedroom was up over the servants' hall, and they'd sing 'For he's a jolly good fellow' at the top of their voice so he could hear them!

I was working at the Court when Queen Mary came up. I didn't know she was there. I don't know if it was seven or ten for lunch that day, and the butler brought all the silver dishes and things out just the same, no different at all – it all went on silver every day whether Mrs Heneage had somebody there or not, so I didn't know nothing about it at all. Mr Wilfred came out for the coffee and he said 'Joan, what do you think? You've just cooked Queen Mary's lunch, and she's staying for tea!' After lunch we ran up the stairs to the window overlooking the front door and we seen Queen Mary and Mrs Heneage going to church.

The shops in Yeovil used to be open until ten o'clock at night. I finished working at eight o'clock at night and used to get my bedroom slippers down. The chauffeur come in one evening and said 'Joan, coming into Yeovil?' I said 'I can't come into Yeovil like this!' and he said, 'Come on, you'll be alright, I've got a nice fur coat in the back you can put on'. So I went but I couldn't get out the car because I had my bedroom slippers on!

Christmas Eve all us girls used to go to church. Lottie, Mabel, Eileen, Doreen and me. We used to wish one another a happy Christmas and when we were back in the Court we used to have the Christmas presents all on the stairs going up to the attic.

Queen Mary visits Coker Court and St Michael's on the 25th June 1941: 'although her visit, until the very day, had been a well-guarded secret, the village gave her a Royal reception, in most Royal English weather,' wrote the vicar I.G. Saunders.

The Girls from the Court

I was 15 when I came to the Court first, that was in 1934. I had my 16th birthday up there. I had an autograph book and everybody signed it. Everybody up the Court wrote in it.

They wanted a kitchen-maid up the Court and I came up and the chauffeur met me at the station. I thought I'd come to Land's End because it was all country, after being used to the town. I went in there then, and went upstairs and when I went along the corridor they let me in my bedroom. When I come down there was all these bats in the corridor, and of course I hadn't seen a bat before, and I started screaming – nearly everybody come up, wondered what had happened!

When I first went there all I had to do really was keep the kitchen clean and doing all the washing-up by hand. And no detergent then, it was soda and water, and soft soap to soften the water. Drying the plates, we had all these wooden racks going right across the walls. If you went into the butler's pantry and seen Mr Wilfred and Alfred washing-up, when they washed the silver they never put it on a draining board, they had to put it on a green baize cloth so they wouldn't scratch it. When you think of all the silver we used to clean – knives and forks and spoons. And in the kitchen they had a dresser and it was full of copper and it was always gleaming. We used to go in the pantry once a week, take all that copper down, and clean it with sand and vinegar. Silver was done with Goddard's powder and methylated spirits.

We were up about half past five, six o'clock the latest, because we had to get the fire going. The first cup of tea in the mornings we used to have an oil-stove so we could put the kettle on. The range was going all day then. All the time we cooked on a coal fire. It was only the one fire in the centre, two ovens either side and then you could put the top down and cook on the top. We never had a thermostat, we just put our hands in the oven and thought to ourself 'Oh, that's hot enough' and put things in. Mind you, it was hot work cooking on the range! You had to have all the windows open, especially in the summer, all the windows was flung open because we used to get so hot. When you got in the kitchen and the scullery, the windows was high up – you couldn't look out of the window there except to see people walking in the garden at the top of the slope.

The Heneages used to love soufflés – you know when you make soufflés they can go down flat? Mr Wilfred used to just stand at the kitchen door waiting for the soufflé to come out of the oven, to put it on a silver platter and run with it! Everything had to be arranged properly on a silver tray, broad beans and anything, you never chucked them in a tray and put a bit of butter on. You had to arrange them all in rows. Another thing we used to do was we had to pluck everything, you see. If you had a goose, you never had the goose come all ready for the oven. Grouse, chicken, goose, turkey – everything had to be plucked. And I know the grouse used to be hung in the cellar and they never had it till the maggots was on it, when it was ripe, and you used to pull those feathers out and the maggots used to be crawling underneath!

I expect by the time we'd cooked the lunch and cleared up all the dishes we used to finish about half past two, and then we used to have that time free. We used to get back down in the kitchen for the dinner about six o'clock. Of course we couldn't go out, we had to stay in. You weren't allowed to go out anywhere except on your day off. That's why in the summer Colonel Heneage very often used to say to William the chauffeur 'Go and see if the girls would like to go out for a ride this afternoon'. We used to put our coats on and get in the car and go off. Downstairs the butler, chauffeur, footman and kitchen staff was Colonel Heneage's servants; and upstairs the lady's maid, and the housemaids they were Mrs Heneage's. He paid our wages, and she paid their wages, and there was a bit of controversy because we were given higher wages than the housemaids. The Colonel used to have all these tickets to the police balls, and the opera, and he'd say 'Give them to the girls, I expect they'd like to go'. Not that I liked operas, but we used to go just because it was a night out. Of course we used to dress up in all our finery going to the police ball in the Assembly Rooms.

They all knew us in the village, we were called 'The girls from the Court'. Whenever there was anything on at North Coker Hall they used to say 'I expect the girls from the Court will come down'. That's what we were known as. We had to be in by ten o'clock, but if you was going to a dance or anything you'd let them know and then somebody would come down and let you in, or they left the pantry key out. I remember when we went in the pantry window once because they'd forgot to leave the key out! The pantry window was open and they were shoving us through the window! Oh dear! When Mrs Heneage said we couldn't go to a dance, what we used to do, we used to go down the fire-escape so she wouldn't see us go out. There was four of us come down that fire-escape, we were all in our evening dresses, all these flounces. Anyway, we got down the Hall and when we got down there the dance wasn't until the next week!

Charlie Dances the Twilight Waltz

I was born in South Wales and I came to Somerset to live in 1920. In my early years, my teens, I used to be very fond of dancing and concert-going. There were several of us chaps of all of the same age, and one of the places we enjoyed going to most of all was the North Coker Hall. At one end there was a gallery which was known as the musicians' gallery, and in this gallery there was a full grand piano, a German Bechstein. On one side of the wall there was a huge stone fireplace, large enough to accommodate a young tree, and very often during the winter when we went dancing they did put a tree on this fire and that was our only heat. The dance routines were foxtrot, waltz, quickstep, lancers and so on. But the thing that used to please us young chaps was that every so often they used to have what they called a twilight waltz, and they used to put the lights out, which incidentally were oil lamps, and the dance was carried on by the light of the fire, no other light. The fireplace was big enough to provide enough illumination, and being young and romantic us young chaps and girls, we thoroughly enjoyed that and in the romantic light of the fire all you heard was the band playing and the swish of the ladies' long dresses.

The Sixpenny Hop

I got to know a lot of the people in East Coker working at the factory, and we used to come down from Hardington on a bike and go to the Village Hall for the sixpenny hops. East Coker was always a very popular place for dances, all the way round all the villages, you know, you'd get girls and boys would come from Barwick and Stoford, Hardington, and Pendomer. Marvellous spirit really. You'd probably get one once a month, something like that. Lots of 'em used to come from Yeovil to East Coker dances, they were so popular. The Village Hall had a very good floor. I remember up Hardington it was full of knots so that you couldn't glide along, you had to just hop over the knots more or less. Quite a lot of 'em had proper dance shoes, shiny ones. I did in the end! I remember one band was called 'The Melody Four'. They'd always have refreshments in the hall, always a good crowd of people laying it on and looking after it. It was more strictly supervised in those days, but I never saw any real trouble at East Coker. There'd be posters all round, up on the parish notice-boards. We'd put on our best clothes. In those days we used to have Sunday suits. Despite how poor everybody was, you was more or less expected to have a suit for Sundays.

Stan Russell and his Collegians

I was 14 when I played at Crystal Palace with the Yeovil Boys' Band. Played cornet with the Yeovil Boys' Band. It was the last time the band contest was held at the Crystal Palace because it burned down. The first band I got together was when I was 17, and we used to play in the Village Hall, or perhaps in Yeovil at the Liberal Club or something like that. Of course if you wanted six to play you had to go around and get a couple more. In those days there was an MC, and you had three tunes for

Stan Russell and his Collegians: a popular band that played at many of the dances in North Coker Hall. This photograph was taken at the Liberal Club, Yeovil. Stan is seated at the piano and Ernest Bull is playing the drums. In 1941 Stan Russell and his band played at fund-raising dances to send gifts to men and women of East Coker who were in the services, adding the band's fee to the contributions.

the waltz, three for the foxtrot, and three for the quick-step. At the end of the three you'd sit down. We used to get ten shillings each for the whole dance. But when you played down Coker you ended up in the balcony so all the floor was for dancing. But you want to play up in top with all the smoke coming up! Your throat was like a rasp! Terrible! There were dances most weeks – it was always a full hall. When the war started the RAF was down here, they wanted to join their band with ours, so we done that.

Blue Skies and Spitfires

I remember being at school and seeing Spitfires taking on German planes above us. I can picture it so clearly – the blue sky above the school, and Mr Murley, the headmaster, getting us back inside in case of shrapnel or anything. The planes were miles up in the air, but you could see it, and hear the rattle of the machine-guns.

Pre-War Preparation

I think somewhere around 1936 it began to strike people there might be a war. They extended the aerodrome at Westlands in 1938 to take larger fixed-wing aircraft, so the airfield was much bigger than it is now. They built Houndstone Camp in 1938 in preparation. The Royal Naval Airstation at Yeovilton became a fighter-station from a training-station, it was put on a war footing as far back as 1938. They started building quite a few small aerodromes around here, at Ilton near Ilminster, one at Warmwell near Dorchester which was quite a big fighter aerodrome during the war, mostly Polish squadrons. It was on a Sunday morning, the 3rd September 1939, that was the day that war was declared.

Redlands preparing for war: building an air raid shelter, 1939. (l–r) Mr Brooks, Stan Symes, Mrs Symes, A. Haines, Mrs S. Haines, Mrs E. Dening, Mrs Purchase, Anthony Dening.

The Lights Go Out

When the war began early in September 1939, I was on holiday in Weymouth, and I remember that it was quite a traumatic experience because suddenly in a town that had been absolutely bathed in light – the whole of the promenade, the pier, and all the rest – there was no street lighting of any kind. It was simply blacked out. I remember crawling back to the guest-house, bumping into lamp-posts and falling over kerbs!

My uncle Charlie was a Territorial in the North Somerset Yeomanry and my mother drove him to join them on that Sunday morning, the 3rd September 1939. My grandmother and I were left alone and we got the announcement at 11 o'clock that war was declared, and I remember my grandmother crying. There had been a big crisis the year before, in 1938, and I remember going to Yeovil and assembling gas masks.

The 'Coker Court-ites'

The majority of evacuees arriving in East Coker came from south London, and from the Charles Edward Brook School for Girls in particular. By 1943 the school of 156 girls, billeted in villages around Yeovil, had 34 Somerset girls among its pupils. In addition to the Charles Edward Brook School, there were primary-age children who came with their teacher, Miss Whale. The Mission Room on Long Furlong Lane became their school until they merged with the village school in April 1942.

We moved to London in 1938 and we were living in Camberwell. My father was a headmaster and he liked us always to live near his school. Now at the beginning of the war the evacuation took place on the 1st September 1939. War wasn't declared until the 3rd. Our school was Charles Edward Brook School, it was a girls' grammar school. Our school came down to Yeovil and then we were all separated out into the villages around. My father stayed in London to look after the children who hadn't been evacuated and that's how he happened to be there when our house was bombed. Fortunately it was a time bomb. Our school was found Yeovil High School to share with three days a week. All the East Coker contingent had a bus which used to pick up at the *New Inn* to bus us into Yeovil.

We were at Coker Court the first Christmas. There was great rejoicing because there were ten of us girls there when we joined them, and that made us equal to the 'North Coker House-ites' and we could have two

The 'Coker Court-ites': evacuees from the Charles Edward Brook school for girls who were billeted at the Court. This photograph was taken at the back of the stables there. (l–r) at the back: Edna Dowers, Barbara Hill, Olive Hull, Joan Cole, - , Pamela Webb, Nancy Madge, Peggy Gerhold; at the front: Hilda Huff, Pamela Huff, Vera Hutt, Peggy Cole.

equal teams for games of netball. We used to come in by the back door to the South Wing. There was a long stone corridor and off it on the right were the various places like the servants' hall and the kitchen. We were not allowed to run or talk in the corridor in case the noise went through to the front of the house.

The Siren Sounds

I suppose really the first thing we knew about it was around the third week of September when a plane flew over here and the siren blew. Obviously a reconnaissance plane of some sort. There was some anti-aircraft guns at Barwick Park, and they fired off half a dozen shells. The siren was on the top of the *Quicksilver Mail* at the top of Hendford Hill; another one was on top of the old police station in Yeovil.

Route Marches

I can certainly remember before long route marches were coming through the village. Hundreds of soldiers, initially British soldiers, in little platoons, groups of eight or so, and then a little break and another eight whistling and singing. They were going on 20-mile route marches.

MINISTRY  OF FOOD.

REASONS FOR RATIONING

War has meant the re-planning of our food supplies. Half our meat and most of our bacon, butter and sugar come from overseas. Here are four reasons for rationing :—

1. **RATIONING PREVENTS WASTE OF FOOD** We must not ask our sailors to bring us unnecessary food cargoes at the risk of their lives.
2. **RATIONING INCREASES OUR WAR EFFORT** Our shipping carries food, and armaments in their raw and finished state, and other essential raw materials for home consumption and the export trade. To reduce our purchases of food abroad is to release ships for bringing us other imports. So we shall strengthen our war effort.
3. **RATIONING DIVIDES SUPPLIES EQUALLY** There will be ample supplies for our 44½ million people, but we must divide them fairly, everyone being treated alike. No one must be left out.
4. **RATIONING PREVENTS UNCERTAINTY** Your Ration Book assures you of your fair share. Rationing means that there will be no uncertainty—*and no queues.*

YOUR RATION BOOK IS YOUR PASSPORT TO EASY PURCHASING OF BACON & HAM, BUTTER AND SUGAR

The Western Gazette *for the 12th January 1940 prints an announcement by the Ministry of Food giving the reasons for rationing.*

The First Regiment Arrives

THE first regiment to be stationed here was the Queen's Own Regiment, and it was stationed in the old Village Hall, and also in the yard of Bridge Farm and in the Scouts Hall. They went off to France with the British Expeditionary Force in 1940; and after that came the Guards Armoured Brigade of which David Heneage was a Major; and when they went, in came the King's Own Scottish Borderers. Then the Royal Air Force came, they took over the headquarters at Bridge Farm.

Restrictions Come into Place

I was 17 when the war broke out. It seemed like a phoney war to start with. Very little seemed to be going on. All the restrictions were being put in place, like the black-out, the hoods on the headlights of the vehicles, and not showing a naked light. The food restrictions came in pretty quickly. And of course there was the restrictions of movement with the lack of petrol, and all the signposts came down. In one bedroom we had a stock of mainly tinned food in case of emergency – it was government property. It was never used, they came and collected it at some other point.

The Seafront is Barricaded

YOU weren't allowed within 20 miles of the coast without a special pass. That had been in existence since 1940. The whole of the seaside, all the beaches were mined, and all the fronts were barricaded with barbed wire, and most of the houses or the hotels along the seafronts were taken over by troops, and most of the roofs had anti-aircraft guns on top of them.

From Saucepans to Spitfires

During the war, local scrap-iron collection was organised by Charlie Hackwell, and bags for waste paper were kept in the yard of the New Inn *and at Hackwell's workshop on Mill Lane.*

PEOPLE were digging up their lawns to plant vegetables and things like that. Waste paper, aluminium, rubber – anything that was useful was collected. And then they took most of the iron railings to use to make tanks. They even came around collecting aluminium saucepans from the women to make Spitfires. They sent a lorry round and asked people to donate all their aluminium saucepans!

The Men From the Beaches

The Queen's Own Regiment was among those despatched to the continent with the British Expeditionary Force which was cut off in Belgium and withdrew to the sea. The evacuation of 338,226 men of the British Expeditionary Force from Dunkirk began on the 26th April 1940.

THE Queen's Own were stationed in the old Village Hall, a lot of them, and they used to blow a bugle at six o'clock in the morning to wake everybody up. They went away to Europe in the Expeditionary Force, and when they got through at Dunkirk some of them came back here again without any officers, no arrangements, no food, no nothing. Just the clothes they stood up in. Mrs Meech and Mrs Andrews, up in Back Lane, cooked those soldiers a dinner every day.

Cooking for the Soldiers

AT the time of Dunkirk there were about 50 or 60 men brought from the beaches at Dunkirk straight to East Coker to occupy accommodation there, and my mother and her next-door neighbour in Back Lane, a Mrs Andrews, they agreed to cater for the Dunkirk men. For me it was an amazing period of excitement. We had army lorries backing up Back Lane and sides of beef being unloaded, and massive supplies of food, at a time

East Coker's Special Constables, also known as the Police War Reserves: (l–r) Frank Foot, Mr Taylor, Jack Mead, Percy Lock, Joseph Whetham, and Bill Richards (seated).

when rationing was just beginning to take a hold, and I think the men who'd come from Dunkirk were really so relieved to be alive they spoiled me terribly. For two or three weeks this went on, with Mrs Andrews and my mother providing breakfast, lunch and an evening meal for about two dozen of these soldiers.

On Sutton Bingham Platform

I remember the soldiers coming back from Dunkirk, seeing them on the station, and I remember going out with socks for them because their socks were worn through. They were in a dreadful state. We knew that they'd been evacuated from Dunkirk, and we thought that we'd lost the war then.

The Bells are Silenced

The first attacks by German aircraft over the West Country came two months after Dunkirk. Church bells could no longer be rung, or even chime the hours, and were to be used only to signal an invasion (St Michael's was able to resume chiming the bells at hours in August 1942). In July 1940 East Coker's new vicar, the Reverend Ivor Sanders, wrote about the silencing of the bells of St Michael's.

WITH what pathetic innocence I said in my letter last month – 'The Christian bell will still be rung in England' – and now for the time being the Christian bell even is silenced, to be used only as a warning of the approach of the enemy; and if that enemy had his way a great deal more that is Christian would be silenced beside the bell!

Leaving the Billets

ALL the soldiers would march from Yeovil, like it could be the Scots Guards, and they'd all march to West Coker and pick up, follow the band on to East Coker and pick up from there, and then they'd march on to Yeovil Junction or Sutton Bingham and get on the trains. That's how they would leave. And then a couple of days later another lot would move in to the billets. Then as they built at Barwick Park, they stopped billeting soldiers in the village and they all went in the Nissen huts up there. Lufton and Houndstone camp was built and they moved troops out there as well.

Men and Women in the Services

The East Coker Services Fund Committee was set up in February 1941 to raise money to send parcels to men and women of the village who were in the services. The Minute Book is a good indication of the number who were full time members of the armed forces, and lists 175 men and women. Of the 175 nearly a tenth were women. Its Joint Honorary Secretaries/Treasurers were W.C.V. Cornelius and R.B. Oaksford.

Rota of First Aiders on the "Alert" from dusk to dawn.

Monday.	Mrs Lacey. Mrs Lambert.
Tuesday.	Miss Peggy Morris. Miss Mary Jones.
Wednesday.	Miss Welch. Miss Willcox.
Thursday.	Mrs Wiscombe. Miss B.Wiscombe.
Friday.	Mrs Oaksford. Miss Blaxham.
Saturday.	Mrs Hampson. Miss Mary Baker.
Sunday.	Miss Edna Hodges. Miss Betty Morris.

In the event of danger the party on "the alert" will report to the Senior Warden or Warden in charge at "The Tree" The First Aiders will then proceed to The First Aid Post and will remain there ready for instructions for duty or until told to dismiss by the Senior Warden or Warden in charge.

14.December.1942.

As part of the Air Raid Precautions for the village, there was a permanent First Aid rota.

ARP, WVS and WI

In March 1938 East Coker Parish Council selected Captain W. Broadhurst to become the first Head Warden for Air Raid Precautions, and he was succeeded by Mr Boxall who became the Head Warden in 1940. Other ARP Wardens included Arthur Sims, postman Rendell, Ewart Murley (the headmaster of the village school), Arthur Board, and John Pitcher.

Their first task was to distribute gas masks to the entire village. Principal duties were to make sure the black-out was observed, and to report any air-raid damage.

The ARP had associated groups, for example Mr Boxall had a Volunteer Fire Party: S. Stevens, F. Griffin, A. Tuck, J. Pomeroy, E. Newitt, and J. Baker. The Volunteers were issued with a manual pump, stirrup pump and other equipment.

Another group was the Women's Voluntary Service for Civil Defence which set up rotas for First Aid cover, and for washing-stations in the event of a gas attack. The East Coker branch was formed by Mrs Drake and one of its first efforts was to assist in the placing of evacuees.

In 1939 the East Coker Women's Institute began weekly work parties which were held at North Coker House. They sent parcels of knitted socks and scarves to the Red Cross for those serving in the Army and Royal Air Force, and to Liverpool for the men in the Atlantic convoys. In August 1940 the Ministry of Food set up a scheme for making surplus autumn fruits into jam to sell at local shops at government regulated prices. Twice-weekly jam-making sessions at the Estate House led to a total of 1,289lb of jam being made by the East Coker WI! Perhaps the most valuable task of the WI was to organise the National Savings campaigns in the village, as well as arranging whist drives and flag days to raise money for causes such as Aid-to-Russia and Aid-to-China. In 1945 its members responded to an appeal to send anything that could be spared to help bombed-out householders in London.

Black-Out and Search Lights

THE black-out made the village a sombre place after dark. With the fall of France in 1940 the ominous throb of German aircraft on their way to bomb South Wales or Bristol became a frequent nightly occurrence. Consequently there soon followed the emplacement of searchlights in the area and not long after barrage balloons were sited in the north of the parish.

The barrage-balloon site between Longlands Lane and Gunville Lane was part of a ring of 24 balloons protecting the Westland Aircraft factory from air attack. The hydrogen/air-filled balloons had three stabilising fins and were attached to a mobile winch lorry and large concrete blocks. The balloons were grounded or close-hauled until there was an alert so that they did not pose a threat to aircraft from local airfields. On the 21st June 1944 the Yeovil barrage was sent to the south coast to combat the V1 'doodle-bug' menace. Two fields in the parish are still known by farmers as 'Balloon Site' and 'The Balloon Field'.

Barrage Balloons

The Westland Aircraft factory in Yeovil was protected by a ring of 24 barrage balloons. The sites were manned by the RAF, later supplemented and largely replaced by the Women's Auxiliary Air Force.

THE RAF took over the barrage balloons. There was four sites this side of Hendford Hill: one up by White Post, one up past Tellis Cross, one up by Placket, one on top of Hendford Hill. All they chaps were stationed in the village. They let the balloons up when there was an alert.

DEFENCE COMMITTEE

The following is a list of the members of the Defence Committee for the Parish of East Coker, with their allotted duties:—Mr. W. B. Drake, chairman; Rev. I. G. Sanders, deputy chairman, organiser of shelter and feeding scheme; Mrs. Maudslay, billeting officer; Mr. C. W. Hackwell, voluntary food officer; Mr. A. J. Boxall, head warden, Medical Services; Mr. W. E. Murley, school representative; Mr. F. Gilley, Platoon Commander, Home Guard; Mr. J. Whetham, Police and Special Constables; Mr. T. Griffin, Auxiliary Fire Service.

The Western Gazette *for the 21st November 1941 lists the village's Defence Committee.*

Watching the Barrage Balloons Go Up

THEY usually started going up before you got the air-raid warning. They had a first alert before we did, and sometimes they would put them half-way up and then you'd know when they started pulling them back down that it was nothing. The balloons went up as high as the cloud cover – on a clear day you could only just see them, they were that high. The wires were on a winch on the back of a lorry, and then they were anchored down on big concrete blocks all the way round the lorry. There'd be one at each site, and there were barrage balloons right round the whole of the Westland works in a complete circle. When we've had lightning storms here, you'd see as many as 10 or 15 of them catch fire, they'd come down all aflame when they've been struck by lightning because whatever gas they used to inflate them with was highly inflammable.

Balloon Site 8

ONE was just up the road from us at Burton. I got very friendly with the crew, in fact two of our dog's puppies went there, they christened them Riff and Raff and they were two hound-like dogs that trotted round the village following the RAF rations bicycle. The barrage balloons stayed here till 1944, then one day they were all gone. Because of the flying bombs they put a string of these balloon barrage across the south-east coast. The sad part of the story is that a flying bomb hit the cable of Site 8's balloon, came straight down the cable in a vertical dive, and exploded on the unit, killing its entire crew, including Riff and Raff.

An Air Raid Shelter at Coker Court

AS the air raids began to progress against Bristol and Bath, in 1941, as soon as the siren blew all the children had to run up Back Lane to Coker Court to the cellars as the air-raid shelter, tiny ones and all. We were up there sometimes for two or three hours at a stretch, then come back to classes.

Chocolate in the Cellars

I was at East Coker School when the war began, and I can remember one of the first signs of the effect of the war on us was that we had an air-raid exercise, and the only air-raid shelter we had were the cellars at Coker Court. We were all marched in a crocodile from the school up to Coker Court. On the happy side, I remember that when we arrived at Coker Court, in one of the cellars Colonel Heneage had put a table absolutely laden with half-pound blocks of Cadbury's Dairy Milk chocolate. One for each child.

Digging for Victory

The village school closed for a week in June and October 1941 so that older children could help local farmers with haymaking and potato-lifting. Village boys had always had gardening classes, with allotments at Mill Lane, and when the school opened its canteen in 1942, they grew vegetables for the cook Mrs L. Colley to use. The same year the girls were given their own gardening class on land given to them by Mr C. Maudslay of North Coker House. In 1943 East Coker school had four teachers, and 123 children (19 were evacuees).

'Big Berthas' at Barwick Park

We would always know if the German planes were going to Bristol, or locally, or going on up to the Midlands to Coventry, by the height that they were. If they were down low we used to say 'Bristol tonight', and the guns used to fire at them. They had the big guns at Barwick Park which they called 'Big Berthas', and the shrapnel used to rattle down on the roof at Tellis Farm.

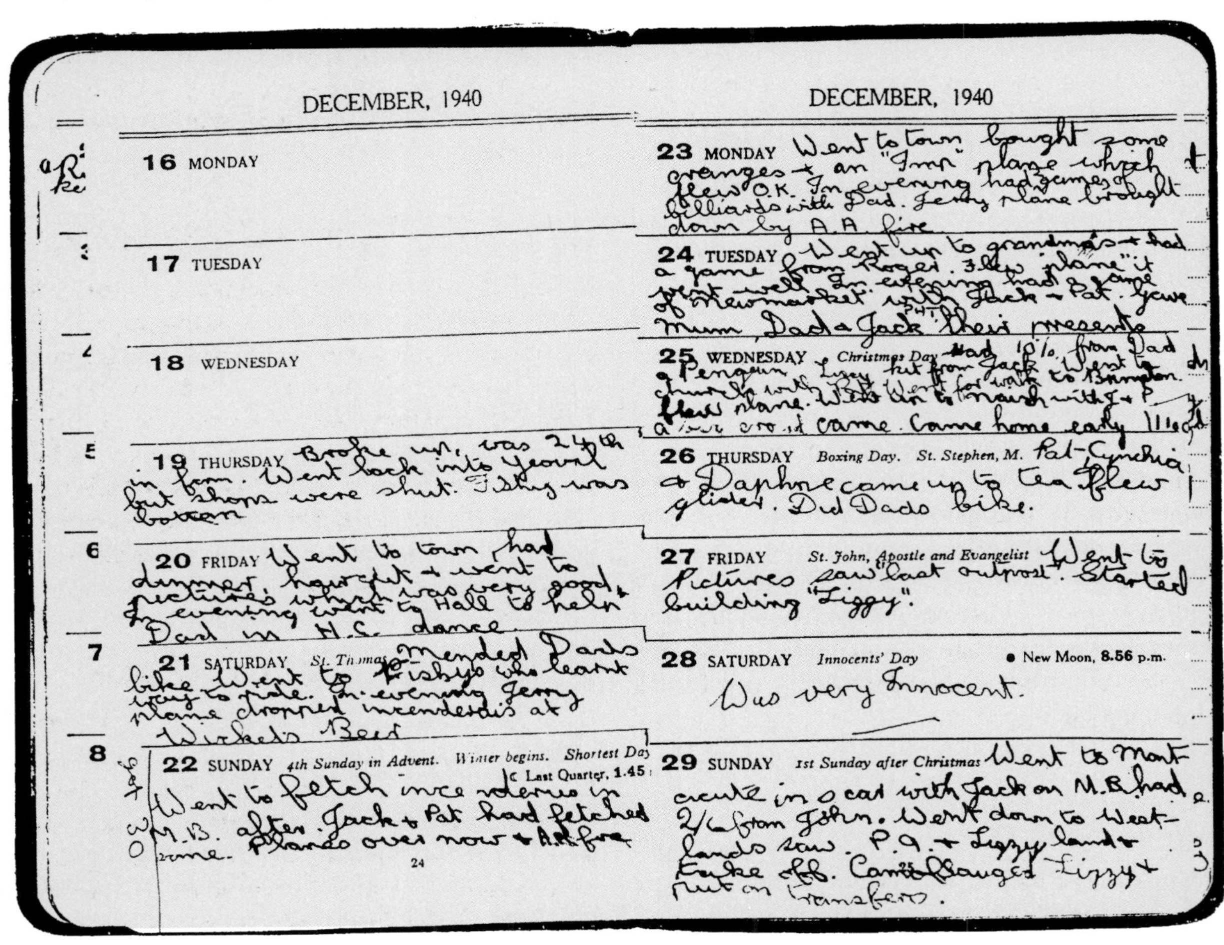

DECEMBER, 1940

16 MONDAY

17 TUESDAY

18 WEDNESDAY

19 THURSDAY Broke up, was 24th in form. Went back into Yeovil but shops were shut. Ishy was [illegible]

20 FRIDAY Went to town had dinner, haircut & went to pictures which was very good. In evening went to Hall to help Dad in H.G. dance.

21 SATURDAY St. Thomas Mended Dads bike. Went to Frisby's who learnt [illegible] to [illegible]. In evening Jerry plane dropped incendiaries at Wicket's Beer

22 SUNDAY 4th Sunday in Advent. Winter begins. Shortest Day. Last Quarter, 1.45
Went to fetch [illegible] in M.B. after Jack & Pat had fetched some. Planes over now & A.A. fire

24

DECEMBER, 1940

23 MONDAY Went to town bought some oranges & an "Imp" plane which flew O.K. In evening had games of billiards with Dad. Jerry plane brought down by A.A. fire.

24 TUESDAY Went up to grandma's & had a game from Roger. Flew "plane" it went well. In evening had a game of Newmarket with Jack & Pat. Gave Mum, Dad & Jack their presents

25 WEDNESDAY Christmas Day Had 10/- from Dad a Penguin Lizzy kit from Jack. Went to church with Pat. Went for walk to Brympton. Flew plane. Went [illegible] with J. & P. [illegible] came. Came home early

26 THURSDAY Boxing Day. St. Stephen, M. Pat, Cynthia & Daphne came up to tea. Flew glider. Did Dads bike.

27 FRIDAY St. John, Apostle and Evangelist Went to Pictures saw "last outpost". Started building "Lizzy".

28 SATURDAY Innocents' Day New Moon, 8.56 p.m.
Was very Innocent.

29 SUNDAY 1st Sunday after Christmas Went to Montacute in a car with Jack on M.B. had 2/- from John. Went down to Westlands saw P.9. & Lizzy land & take off. Camouflauged Lizzy & put on transfers.

25

A wartime schoolboy's diary: Alan Cornelius, then 13, records the Home Guard's fundraising dance (19th); incendiary bombs at Wicket's Beer (21st); going by motorbike and side-car to collect the fins of fire-bombs that had burned themselves out (22nd); air raids and anti-aircraft fire (22nd/23rd); building a model of the 'Lizzy' (an affectionate name for the Westland Lysander aeroplane) and seeing the real thing taking off and landing along with the P9 – a twin-engined fighter later to be called the 'Whirlwind' (27th/29th).

A Near Miss

THE nearest I ever got was stood at the back door of our house and my father said something and I stepped back inside – a piece of an anti-aircraft shell from Barwick Park hit the ground right beside where I was stood. As a lad I'd go across to Wicket's Beer and Pendomer where a lot of incendiary bombs fell – you used to find them in the fields, nice German eagle engraved on them.

Raids on Westlands and Bristol

I shall never forget I was out walking and I heard this plane come over and there was a German swastika across it. He was going to Westlands and I thought 'Christ, Westlands is going to have it now'. When they bombed Bristol they come over here in crowds the German planes did – hundreds of them. It was a hell of a drone. The noise was terrific.

Ray Listens to the Pheasants

IN the Park there was a big chestnut tree, and one October time I was up the tree and the early warning you'd get was from the pheasants – you'd hear them making a row and you knew something was about. And then, from over Pendomer, up the railway cutting a German aircraft came out of there, firing guns. I was out of the tree and into the hedge! And then the balloons slowly started going up, and the aircraft went round the back of town and bombed Houndstone Camp. I had a grandstand view from up there.

The Fires at Bristol

THERE were raids on Bristol every night. And Bath. When they had the Baedeker raids in 1942, the retaliatory raids on all the cathedral towns and cities, when they bombed Exeter, Coventry and Bath, it was terrible. Some of the big raids at Bristol you could see from here – the sky lit up. You could hear them come through here about half past seven or eight o'clock of an evening, and they'd be going back over about five o'clock next morning.

Aircraft Overhead

THERE were attempted attacks on Westlands more than anything: because it's low-lying, the Germans flew over it before they realised it was there, you see. Do you know, once when I was on my way home from Yeovil there was a German aircraft coming over firing at the balloons. I remember climbing into a ditch with my little boy Christopher, about three or four, and hearing the bullets zing-zing-zinging around me. And another time I remember going out of our cottage at Sutton Bingham, we heard a terrific noise of aircraft going over and they were on their way to Bristol. Too many to count. And I remember saying to my sister 'Is nothing going to stop them?' They seemed to just go over, wave after wave.

Machine Guns and Lysanders

WHAT we could hear was almost constant machine gun fire from Houndstone Camp, especially on a cold morning, you could hear them practising. And then they used to build Westland Lysanders in Yeovil, the Army Co-operation planes. They used to land the spies and all that sort of thing because Lysanders had short take off and landing, you see. They used to build them at Westlands, and practically every Saturday morning you'd see an Avro Anson bomber come in, bringing the pilots to take the Lysanders away.

Following the Railway Lines

WE had the barrage balloons to protect Westlands; Barwick Park was all ack-ack guns that used to fire at the Germans, but they were artful, see. They'd fly up the railway line. They knew there was no balloons along the railway lines, so they could fly along the line which passed Westlands, bomb Westlands, turn and fly back. The aircraft guns couldn't fire at them 'cos they was too low.

Planes Over Darvole

THE most German planes we ever saw, was a formation of 90. That was a September morning, probably

George Vickery (Royal Air Force) and Eric Stevens (Royal Naval Air Service): before joining the services Eric was one of many teenaged boys in the village to join the Local Defence Volunteers (later Home Guard).

in '42. We were up at Darvole, I was with the tractor, and father said there was a lot of noise, there must be a lot of planes. We stopped the tractor and then they came over, that was the day I think they were going Bristol way. Another time we were up there at Darvole, working in the field, and my father said 'Look at that plane coming up the railway line – look there's the pilot!' and I said 'And look what's on the back!' It was a blooming German aeroplane, and we could see the pilot's head.

Rosemary on Look-Out

One thing I did when they thought we were going to be invaded by the Germans, when it was a crisis time, I went towards Pendomer and sat for days and days looking for paratroops, to see if they came. I can remember watching the trains coming along and the Germans flying over the top and shooting at the trains as they were going along the railway line. And they dropped incendiary bombs all along there as well, all through Pendomer and that area.

Incendiaries at Wicket's Beer

There were bombs all around Pendomer, the incendiary ones. The wood was alight up there. And then they had the big bombs 'cos they had an unexploded bomb that went down in the clay. They had to come and take it out. And there was a couple of them dropped at Wicket's Beer out near the pond. Well, they exploded and afterwards they could never shut one of the doors at the farmhouse properly – how it shook it.

Bomb Damage

The incendiaries and high-explosive bombs that fell around East Coker during the war were random bombs that were either intended for the Westland Aircraft factory, but failed to find their target, or were jettisoned by enemy aircraft that had come under fire and needed to make a fast retreat. More common was shrapnel falling onto the parish from the anti-aircraft guns at Barwick Park.

In 1940 three bombs falling close to Pavyott's Farm killed a bull in its stall, and a fox that was nearby; shrapnel injured a foal. On the 10th October 1940 one oil bomb and three big high-explosive bombs landed in a field near White Post, and several cows were injured and had to be put down by the vet. While this was going on, and village lads were collecting pieces of bomb casing in the field, another bomb that had fallen in the road between Culliver's Grave and White Post exploded, hurling pieces of roadstone high into the air. A slight dip in the road's surface still shows where it fell. In May 1951 East Coker Parish Council noted that an unexploded bomb had been seen in the stream in Coker Moor.

Look, Duck and Vanish!

On the 14th May 1940 Anthony Eden, the Secretary of State for War, broadcast an appeal for Local Defence Volunteers. The Army was busy reorganising and re-equipping itself after the evacuation from Dunkirk. Arms and ammunition were scarce and the initial allocation of rifles for the whole of Somerset was 200, plus 2,000 rounds of ammunition. Here Eric Stevens writes about joining the Local Defence Volunteers in East Coker, soon to be rechristened the Home Guard.

Jack Cornelius, a despatch rider for the Home Guard: Jack was a member of the East Coker platoon from its formation in May 1940 until he joined the Royal Signals in 1942.

How proud we felt when they signed us on. As soon as we heard they were starting a Local Defence unit, chaps my age, 17 or 18, and men too old for the services, or in reserved occupations, signed on. We had an armlet at the beginning with LDV on it – Local Defence Volunteer – but translated by everyone else as 'Look, Duck and Vanish'! Then bits of uniform started to arrive, tunics without trousers, forage-cap but no boots. There was a lot of jealousy then if you didn't get something. Then a few American rifles arrived. At the beginning there wasn't a gun between us, we used to drill with anything, broom handles, etc; some, especially farmers and the like, had shotguns. The headquarters was the British Legion Room at the *New Inn* – more plans were made in the bar than up there – and our look-out post then was the railway bridge at Sutton Bingham. We used to sleep in the station in between the time we were on duty – sleep! Just as you were about to drop off the Plymouth to Waterloo would go through at about 60 miles an hour!

The Watcher-Post

By the spring of 1941 the Home Guard had a watcher-post up in Isles Lane: it was built into the side of the bank. That was one of the highest points, and we could see the other watcher-posts – the church towers at Corscombe and Odcombe. Usually the watcher-post was manned by about five men, and there was always two on duty, all night. We used to be patrolling the village in pairs, or else we had a check-point under the bridge at Sutton Bingham which had a panic button connected to the watcher-post, so if any vehicle didn't stop you'd press that and there was always somebody at the top of the hill that could fire at it.

The Home Guard on Parade

Fred Gilley was the Platoon Commander of the East Coker Home Guard. The senior ranks were mostly made up of men who had been in the services during the First World War. Home Guard duties were at night-time and weekends as many of the men were working in reserved occupations, at Westlands or on village farms, during the daytime.

We had parade every Sunday morning in the *Helyar Arms* yard, which was then the *New Inn*. We did our training in the village, sometimes you'd get an instructor from the regular Army. There was a miniature rifle range in the old laundry at Coker Court *(now Lyneham Bungalow)*, but when we had our .303 rifles we went up to Odcombe to a valley to shoot there, and to practise throwing hand-grenades. We kept our guns and ammunition at home.

The other place we did a lot of training was the Park. We used to do patrolling, seven people I think it was, with leader, number-one rifleman, number-one bomber, number-two rifleman, number-two bomber, and three 'on the bar' practising outflanking movements. And then we did bayonet drill with some bags of straw. I was a local guide in the Home Guard, and we wore yellow and green armbands. There was two of us, and in the event of an invasion we had to make our way to the post office and the regular Army would know that they would find one or two chaps with local knowledge of the terrain there.

They thought one night that a German plane had come down between Crewkerne and Hardington, and we went up in the dark, and marched line abreast across the fields there in the dark, right the way toward Haselbury. We came back in the morning quite early and we slept in West Coker School. We didn't find anybody, it was a false alarm.

Ammunition at Tellis Farm

After a slow start, the East Coker Home Guard became very well-equipped. As well as rifles and hand-grenades, the ammunition store included anti-tank weapons. Phosphorous-filled bottles were stored in the stream near the sawmills; a 40-gallon barrel of diesel and petrol was buried in a bank so that it could be run across the road and set alight if any German tanks came. Italian POWs dug a secret ammunition dump in a field near Halves Lane.

On a number of occasions the Home Guard had meetings at Tellis Farm, and we had all the ammunition at our place – bullets, rifles, small bombs, hand-grenades. It was anywhere and everywhere, all over the house, under the stairs, outside in outhouses. Anywhere that we could put it! If a bomb or an incendiary had landed at Tellis Farm, we would have gone up just like that.

The East Coker Boys' Club c.1942. During the war the Boys' Club used the great hall at Coker Court as its club-room after the RAF took over the Scouts Hall to use as B-Flight headquarters. Photographed in front of the porch at Coker Court: (l–r) back row: Raymond Groves, Harry Whitby, Gerald Colley, Graham Whensley, Ronald Loader, Raymond Murley, Ivor Rogers, Derek Loader, Leonard Stocker, Dennis Boucher, Gordon Hawkins, - , Hector Bell, Dennis Frampton, David Foot; front row: Nicky Skelton, Ken Schooling, Dennis Stocker, Kingsley Rendell, Mrs Walker-Heneage, the Reverend Sanders, Bill Hawkins, Alan Cornelius, Jack Boucher, Clement Richards.

The Village Lads -v- the Guards Armoured Division

DAVID HENEAGE was a Major in the Guards Armoured Division and they had a short spell billeted around here, because the Home Guard did an exercise with them. It was intended to be for real, the Home Guard manned their fixed defensive positions. It was known that the object of the armoured group was to penetrate into the fringes of Yeovil, and the job of East Coker Home Guard was to delay them as much as they could. I was at that time a messenger with the Home Guard, and we had flour bombs and were throwing them down onto the scout cars going along the road into Yeovil.

On the night before the exercise, the Guards Armoured Division was camped on the Sleights, all the vehicles had gone in and were forming an encampment, and there were tents and so on in the field next to Spin Wood. We all went up and crawled along the hedges after dark and did a spying mission! If anyone had actually said 'Halt, who's there?' and fired a shot over our heads we'd have run a mile!

Peggy the Bicycle Messenger

EAST COKER had an invasion plan because I was a messenger. I was supposed to have my bike always at the ready and batteries in my lamp, and you had to practice so that you could dress in two minutes. And when it was action stations, then I was to take messages to the outlying farms that weren't on the phone that the invasion had happened, so I remember having to learn where all the outlying farms were so that I could pound over there. There was supposed to be a rehearsal but it was called off at the last minute.

ARP Messengers

East Coker's invasion plan was put to the test on the 7th September 1940 when, at the height of the Battle of Britain, an invasion scare set the church bells ringing.

IN the event of an invasion, we would be messengers for the ARP wardens, the Home Guard or the WVS.

A fighting angel in wartime: in January 1941 the parish magazine introduced a new design for its cover, showing St Michael with his sword drawn, for when 'there was a war in heaven Michael and his Angels fought against the dragon and the great dragon was cast out into the earth'.

One night here the church bells rang which was the sign of an invasion, and it had been pre-arranged that all the boys had to report to the Village Hall. If they had bicycles they had to bring them and be messengers. It would be about 30 of us.

The Church Bells Ring a Warning

WE had a scare once when there was a false alarm. All the Home Guard were out on duty, and the vicar, who was Mr Sanders in those days, skinned his hands pulling on the rope to ring the church bells.

Waiting for the Invasion to Arrive

In the middle of the night the church bells started to ring and that was the signal that there was an invasion. The church bells were silenced during the war and it was Mr Sanders, the vicar, who was ordered to ring the church bells. I can remember I'd been made to come downstairs and sleep in my mother's room and my mother got very nervous. Somebody arrived on a bicycle next door, to Cecil Drake, and got off his bicycle and said 'The Germans are here, sir'. And we got dressed. I was told to go and gently wake my grandmother, which I did, so she got completely dressed except for her curlers underneath a mob cap, and she had a bag with her jewels in it and she put them down the front of her dress. We all went and stood at our front gates to wait for news of the Germans. Everybody got up and the village was very awake. And the vicar rang and rang and then stopped and came to somebody and said 'What do I do now?' and they said 'Go back and keep on ringing'.

Making Khaki and Air Force Blue Webbing

At 14 I left school. In those days the thing was to go out to service. I went to work on the West Coker Road for five shillings a week, starting from half past eight until five. When the war started and they were dropping bombs at Westlands, and one fell at White Post, my father said that was enough, and so he got me a job in the webbing factory. I started as a quiller, winding the cotton onto quills and bobbins to put into the machinery and the shuttles, and then I became a weaver.

There were men working there who were too old for the Army, they'd been working there for years. Some of the women were weavers. Most of it during the wartime was for Army and Navy – the bigger looms made the wide web for haversacks, in khaki or air-force blue; there was a webbing that was for spats, and this narrow web for the little straps that did them up. I can remember there was a time when we did 12 hour shifts. We had an air-raid shelter, and then when the siren went everybody switched off and went into the shelter.

Revolvers at the Ready

My formidable grandmother – my uncle had all his cowboy equipment including revolvers – she tried to get ammunition for these revolvers because, you see, we were expecting the invasion. And also there were my uncle's lassos in a long passage at the back of the house, and she was hanging up one of my uncle's lassos and she said to me 'Now darling, if I ever hold up a German parachutist with your uncle's revolvers, and I say to you 'Get the rope', this is where it is'. During the Battle of Britain there were dogfights, and on one occasion a parachutist came down at the other end of the village and my grandmother was out on the lawn at the back of the house with the revolvers.

Black Monday

On the 30th September 1940 Westlands was obscured by cloud cover and at 4.40 p.m. German planes bombed Sherborne mistaking it for Yeovil. On that day 18 people were killed, and 50 injured. In East Coker villagers saw a Hurricane shot down – it crashed at the top of Newton Road, Barwick, where it could be seen burning, with its ammunition exploding. The pilot parachuted to safety.

The Pilot in the Apple Tree

Of course they had an horrendous raid on Sherborne. I wasn't in the forces then, I was working for Mr Drake in the gardens at Devonshire Cottage. We stood on the flat roof of the house, we could hear them coming, and there was about 100 and some odd planes all in one formation. There was a lone Hurricane that came from Warmwell took them all on, and they shot him down. The actual aircraft came down the other side of Stoford. He ejected from the plane before it crashed and took a long time to parachute down, as he was quite some way off. There's an orchard up the road from here at Tellis Cross and he landed in that orchard in a tree. All the women left here with pickaxes and forks because they thought it was a German pilot. When they got to the orchard he was tangled up in the apple tree, and he couldn't speak English, because he was Polish, and he had to undo his RAF uniform to show his wings!

An advert in the Western Gazette *for the 15th March 1940 urges farmers to plough by day and night for the war effort. Throughout the war years Britain experienced double summer-time, with clocks put forward two hours instead of one, which meant that farmers could still be working in 'daylight' at midnight. British summer-time was returned to normal in 1945.*

Tractors from the War Agricultural Committee

DURING the wartime, that was the first tractor we had. The county bought up these tractors you see, and then sold them out to the farmers. War Agricultural Committee. If you bought a new one 'twould have been expensive. These tractors had been used before, but they were in good order. They gave you orders how much you had to plough and what you had to put in and that. Sometimes they made them plough the places that wasn't fit to be ploughed.

Crops and Machinery

THE War Agricultural Executive Committee was formed. Usually a farmer was chosen to come around and he would look at your acreage and say 'You've got to grow 30 acres of wheat, and five acres of flax' – you had no choice, and that's how it was organised. They got us growing wheat and flax and potatoes. They made certain implements available. In the case of binders, they imported a lot from Australia – Sunshine, Massey-Harris binders – and they were bought over in a kit form, you put them together.

Double Summer-time at Wicket's Beer

HAYMAKING was the busiest time 'cos everything was done by hand. Whetham's used to get blokes come up from East Coker, blokes that worked in the twine factory. They only come at night. By day, we spent all day getting it ready – you had to turn it and get it all ready to bring in at night, see. After work they'd go home and have tea, and then they come up to the farm in the evening. They'd start perhaps seven o'clock, you'd still be there at 11 o'clock. You stayed until dark; until you couldn't see no more. During the war you had the double summer-time – clocks were put on two hours. You were still haymaking at midnight. The sun was still shining at 12 o'clock at night.

Evacuee Sheep at Slade's Farm

LATER in the war, we had about 50 evacuee sheep from Romney Marsh in Kent, from when they had the doodle-bugs going over.

Chocolate for the Cows at Longlands

DURING the war, for the cattle-feed dad used to have lorry-loads of bombed buildings from Cadbury's. They used to bring down all the rubble and they used to pick out the chocolate for the cows to eat. And if we could get there first we would take the best picking! They used to come by the lorry-load and they'd tip it and then they'd put it out for the cows to sort through. I can always remember if we could find something wrapped up we thought that was a real good treat.

A Land Girl for Key Farm

Mildred 'Midge' Hoare was a farmer's daughter from West Buckland near Wellington in Somerset, and was a member of the Women's Land Army from 1942 to 1946. For two of those years she worked for her cousin Harold Newman at Key Farm. This extract is taken from Midge's written record of her years in the Land Army.

I contacted the Women's Land Army headquarters at Taunton and requested a move to cousins of mine, Mr and Mrs H. Newman, at Key Farm, near Yeovil. This was in October 1943. It was a beautiful old farmhouse built in Hamstone, with leaded windows. It was situated on the main Yeovil to Dorchester Road two miles from Yeovil. The farm was about 200 acres supporting a dairy herd with also sheep and poultry. There were three cottages where the employees lived. I lived in as one of the family with my cousin Harold and his son Fred. We all did various jobs on the farm. The buildings were all in one complex, which was very convenient. It was a busy main road so we had to be careful driving tractors and trailers.

My main job was tractor work. I drove the green standard Fordson, with a combined clutch and brake, and a very uncomfortable iron seat, popping up and down like a yo-yo – although padded with sacks, I was glad when the job ended. I often had to cut a field of grass for a neighbour, as it was wartime, farmers helped each other. My cousin grew sugar-beet and flax. Tons of sugar-beet were grown by farmers which took the place of cane-sugar. Fred and I often transported many loads to Yeovil Junction, from where they were taken to sugar factories. I found sugar-beet-pulling very hard work. Many mangolds were also grown for cattle-feed, which were cut up in a hand-turned machine with cake of another type of feed. Flax-pulling was done by hand and was very back-breaking. It was used as an oil-seed for cattle. We had to hoe mangold and sugar-beet by hand, which meant thinning-out and weeding during breaks in haymaking.

There was an American camp only a quarter of a mile away from Key Farm at Barwick Park. Many times whilst driving a tractor with trailer, if American trucks passed by full of American soldiers they would throw out oranges and cigarettes – pennies from heaven – they felt sorry for us!

The Great NAAFI Raid

Wartime could be full of adventures for children: some village boys staged their own mock battles with complex rules on a 'battle field' that included the Park and Spin Wood. They were armed with wooden rifles and sub-machine guns, meticulously modelled from plans in booklets. The boys, who had seen soldiers on manœuvres in Spin Wood (the Americans even let them fire their bazookas!) used the trenches there for their own battles.In 1944 the East Coker 'army' invaded the territory of the awaiting Preston 'army' – the boys speeding down Bunford Hollow in pram-wheeled carts towards the fields at Preston! On another occasion there was a daring raid on NAAFI chocolate supplies, here recounted by Don Murley.

THERE was a NAAFI hut on the Hymerford House premises, but later the stock was moved into what had been the caretaker's quarters of the Village Hall. There was *real* chocolate (not the gritty, bitter muck – 4 oz. per week – wrapped in grease-proof paper stencilled 'RATION' that children received) and cigarettes: and a very small window overlooking the corner of the road by The Tree. Somehow, by some mysterious means, the children from that part of Coker knew and, as soon as it was dark, congregated at The Tree. A very small boy was lifted up to the window, which was obligingly easy to open, and vanished inside. He kept reappearing throwing the goodies from the window until the NAAFI was depleted of chocolate and cigarettes. The older boys shared out the cigs and most of the choc was distributed to the younger. The following day two detectives toured Coker grilling whichever children they could find. The next day they came again, and the next, and then went away none the wiser, never to be seen again.

Prisoners of War at Slade's Farm

SOME of them must have come from the North African campaign and they were stationed at Houndstone, to one side of the barracks. I used to go at one time and pick four or five up every morning, and bring them back to work on the farm – hoeing, potato-picking, harvesting, threshing. They came with their own rations, but I think my mother used to supplement them, she was a bit soft-hearted. And then in the end we had one – Carl – who lived with us for the last two years of the war. We'd usually get the same men – they seemed to be familiar with farm work, and were good workers. One of them had been to the Russian front, and he said how cold it was – they'd put paper underneath their uniforms to try to keep warm. They could speak quite a bit of English, and we learned a bit of rough German as well, mostly of the baser sort!

In March 1942 East Coker was given a fund-raising target of £3,000 for the Yeovil and District Warship Week – and raised £15,000, which was £15 per head of population!

Wings for Victory

National fund-raising drives included: Warship Week 1942; Wings for Victory Week 1943; Salute the Soldier Week 1944. The East Coker Women's Institute formed a National Savings Group and organised these and other collections.

DURING Wings for Victory Week, a national savings campaign when in the week we were all supposed to be raising as much money as possible for the war effort, the RAF put on a boxing tournament on the lawns of North Coker House. I wasn't allowed to go by my parents who thought boxing was a very bad thing, but I secreted myself into one of the WAAF bedrooms in North Coker House and looked down from a bedroom on the ring and that's the first boxing match I ever saw. It was in the same week that my mother went to an effort for Wings for Victory Week at Sutton Bingham Manor, and Methodists in those days didn't take part in raffles, but unknown to my father she brought some tickets for the raffle and won a pig – which was something of an embarrassment but also a blessing at the time of rationing.

National Savings

WE used to have special savings weeks, you know national savings. My mother could probably give my brother and I sixpence a week each for a stamp, but these special weeks you'd perhaps put 2/6 on. And then we used to have little draws, just to buy more savings stamps to do something for the war effort.

Red Cross Bazaar at Coker Court

One of many fund-raising events in the village during the war, in May 1943 a sale at Coker Court raised £310 for the Red Cross, St John Parcels for Prisoners of War, and Aid-to-Russia funds.

WONDERFUL bazaars were held in the great hall at Coker Court during the Second World War, for the Russian Red Cross and various things. The Heneage family used to give the most exotic things, and old Mrs Keppel was staying there and she was on one of the long trestle-tables in front of the fire selling the most gorgeous *objets d'art*. As everybody knows, she was Edward VII's mistress and she was with him when he died. This wonderful old lady was all rouged-up, with a great feather boa and looked absolutely wonderful. All painted-up – and people didn't paint-up much in those days, especially in the country. London people did. She said to me 'Now come on, you must buy this' and it was three guineas for a little snuff-box. My mother made me buy it and I have never regretted it, a Battersea enamel snuff-box that came from the Honourable Mrs Keppel.

Then when Queen Mary came through, she was staying at Longleat, she was a great friend of Mrs Keppel and Mrs Heneage. We used to sit on the garden wall and wait for her and wave. There was great excitement during the war when the Honourable Mrs Keppel's daughter, Violet Trefusis, came to stay for a period. She was friendly with Hore-Belisha, the Minister of War. That was very exciting because she sort of woke up the village. When she left, she said they were so wonderful to have her when the blitz was on and everything else, but she had to go back to her house in France and then eventually back to Italy because she thought living in East Coker was a rehearsal for retirement!

'White Christmas' and Gang Shows

THE RAF were billeted in the village, mainly they were servicing the barrage balloons, but they brought a little bit of glamour to the place in a way because they had certain facilities. The Village Hall was turned into a cinema – great problems with black-out, they had to stick all sorts of things on the windows – and I saw 'White Christmas' and things like that because the village kids, with a bit of persuasion, could get in and watch the films provided for the RAF.

And the Ralph Reader Show came here, which was the leading service show in those times, and I'm almost certain Tony Hancock was in the Gang Show that came to East Coker in the Village Hall. And several others – I think Peter Sellers was in the RAF Gang Show so it could have been any of those. And also they did their own variety shows, and I think they had one or two girls who'd been in rather tatty revue beforehand, because I remember a girl doing a Sophie Tucker semi-strip-tease – terribly exciting for a ten-year-old boy to watch this!

East Coker
28th. Aug. '44

To All Wardens
East Coker.

The next meeting will be on Tuesday the 5th. Sept. at 20.00 hrs at the School.

There is a demand in our area for both Helmet & Mickey Mouse Respirators. There are none in the store.
Would Wardens please see that as far as possible all necessary changes up to the end of September are completed before the meeting so that we may then prepare an accurate list of our requirements.

A.J.Boxall
S.W.East Coker.

A copy of a letter to all ARP Wardens from Head Warden A.J. Boxall regarding the shortage of gas masks – Helmet Respirators were for babies, and Mickey Mouse Respirators were designed to look less frightening to the small children who might have to wear them.

West Bay Opens

We went exploring on our bikes – our parents sent them down for us because otherwise there was no transport. We went to West Bay when it was opened. It was closed for a long time, but when the invasion scare was over they opened a gap in the barbed wire, which we heard on the grape-vine so we cycled there for the day!

A Christmas Treat

The United States Armed Forces first arrived in Somerset at the end of 1942. The GIs quickly became favourites with the children and treated them to candy and chewing-gum.

Americans were at Barwick Park in these huts and tents, and they used to march through the village. They used to go on manœuvres up to Coker Wood. I can remember once going to a Christmas party up at Houndstone Camp, from the school. We went in big lorries and had a fabulous time. We had sweets and all that kind of thing which weren't very plentiful at the time.

Throwing Oranges from the Train

I used to play with Yvonne, her dad was the stationmaster at Sutton Bingham. I was up there playing when an American troop-train had pulled into Sutton Bingham Station, but gone beyond the platform, and

East Coker Junior Red Cross Link, 1944. (l–r) back row: Pam Appleyard, Catherine Gill, Doreen Baker, Daphne Quick, Pam Robins, Joan Crawshaw, Jean Colley; middle row: Janet Boucher, Pam Vowles, Sheila Robins, Marion Loader, Miriam Jones, Joan Harris; front row: Brian Boucher, Richard Boucher, Clifford Snaydon. The Junior Red Cross was run by Alison Oaksford and Dora Willcox (a teacher at the school), and had its base in the stables at North Coker House. The Red Cross was very popular in the village and in 1943 had a Medical Officer, Lady Superintendent, nine full members and ten probationers, a cadet unit, and Junior Link.

was actually on the bridge. We were just playing there in the road under the bridge, and I came home with boxes of candies, oranges, and all sorts of things. They just threw it out of the carriages. I suppose we were eight or nine at the time. 'Got any gum, chum?' we used to say, then you'd get a packet of chewing-gum.

Americans at Barwick Park

I always remember when they came first, about the first couple of days they came in file, some on each side of the road, from Barwick Park, walking along by the sawmills. Jim was there and he said to me 'Who do you reckon they be then?' I said 'They're American soldiers' and he looked a bit closer and said 'They be a bit like we to look at , don't 'em'.

The First Black Soldiers

LATER, when the Americans came into the war, we had our first sight of black troops. And that was an eye-opener, of course. They were a curiosity, which is an awful reflection, and the kids were running down the road with eyes open, you know, eyes popping out.

Dances for the Soldiers

I remember all the American soldiers that were billeted up at Barwick Park and they used to come right through the streets of Coker and up Coker Woods doing manœuvres. I was six or seven then and they used to give us chewing-gum. And that was when dad used to organise dances in the Village Hall for all these soldiers: I used to go into the hall and look over the balcony and watch.

D-Day Convoys

Somerset was a concentration area for D-Day, with ammunition, transport and armour collected and ready to be moved off. The assault on Normandy was launched on the 6th June 1944.

BEFORE the D-Day landings, a convoy would start say at three o'clock and they'd be going on all through the night, right through to the same time tomorrow. And I've known the main road to be about a quarter of an inch deep in a white powder where the tanks had chewed up all the tarmac all the way through. Night and day, non-stop, for about a fortnight before the D-Day landings. And all down the Dorchester Road by every hedge was all boxes and boxes of ammunition. All lined up beside the road. And when they'd done all these boxes of ammunition, there were big ack-ack guns all along the hedges, covered in nets. Jeeps, tanks, lorries – just stored there – and as it came, so it went. The next morning it was all gone. Put on the boats to take over. These convoys were going through all the time.

Tanks and Equipment Disappear Overnight

I was in the Land Army, I'd learned to drive by then and I was delivering and going around. And one day there was all the tanks in every space possible, armoured cars, by the road, lined up with camouflage nets over them, and next day there was nothing, they'd gone. Everything had gone. It was all moved overnight.

Ammunition on the Dorchester Road

I can remember coming home on leave just before D-Day, in the March of 1944, and there was Americans everywhere, the whole of Yeovil. Houndstone Camp was all American, including one of the biggest celebrities of all time, Joe Louis – the World Heavyweight Boxing Champion, he was a physical training instructor at the camp at the time. There was a massive American build up in this area. I got a lift home from Yeovil with an American soldier in a Jeep, but he had to go to Maiden Newton first, and the whole of the roads, either side, from the top of Hendford Hill right till we went to Maiden Newton, either side of the road was stacked solid with ammunition. They said it was like that all the way to Weymouth. You couldn't get another box of ammunition anywhere. All lined up ready for D-Day.

The East Coker platoon marches through the Borough, Yeovil, as part of the stand down parade of the 3rd Somerset (Yeovil) Battalion Home Guard, on the 3rd December 1944. At the time of the stand down the Yeovil Battalion had 2,112 officers and men and 34 women auxiliaries.

Planes and Gliders

One of the most vivid things I remember was when we invaded France, D-Day, and one day all the troops were here, and then the next day they were all gone. And the planes were going over, that was something I shall never forget, there was all these gliders going over, being towed by the other aircraft, with all the troops in them.

Victory in Europe

In the Parish News *of June 1945 the Reverend Ivor Sanders writes in a spirit of thanksgiving for the victory in Europe.*

We should also here record what happened in this parish; especially perhaps for those who in some far distant future may rewrite the parochial history of our times; and of what will be to them 'the noble works that Thou didst in their days and in the old times before them'.

Awaiting the long-expected (but at the last moment somewhat retarded) news, on the 8th May – Victory in Europe day – at the pre-arranged hour of 7pm (when country dwellers can foregather) we met, with one accord, at the parish church, to give thanks to Almighty God for our great deliverance.

And it was in the same spirit of devout – and very heart-full – thanksgiving that numbers of faithful communicants came, spontaneously both on the morning of that day and the following day to make their Communion.

The more formal occasion of thanksgiving was, for us, at 11am on the following Sunday. It was, I think we all felt, not only a most notable, but a deeply gratifying occasion. The church was full (not however actually overflowing out on to the gravel paths at the west door, as on one of the occasions of national prayer in 'the terrible days' of 1940 – future generations will not easily realise how terrible they were). The various services paraded; colours were carried, and a band played them to church; while the bells pealed again, as they had done for several hours on Victory day itself.

Service of Thanksgiving

I do remember the service at church when it was over. That was quite emotional, although we were very young. I know we sang 'Now thank we all our God' and when we sing that in church now I still get quite a lump in my throat because I can imagine myself back all those years singing it now that the war was over.

EAST COKER

WELCOME TO PRISONER OF WAR

A hearty welcome, with church bells ringing, was accorded Pte. Henry Neville, R.A.O.C. who arrived home from the Abbotsville Convalescent Home, Wiveliscombe on Friday after being a prisoner of war in Germany for nearly five years. He was met at Yeovil Town Station by Mr. Lucas of the New Inn, and, as the car entered the village, it was stopped by the crowd, who carried a banner "Welcome Home to a Hero" and sang "For he's a jolly good fellow." By the green the factory workers gave him another great welcome. Private Neville was introduced to the schoolchildren by Mr. Murley and they presented him with a parcel of cigarettes and a cheque from the Red Cross Junior Link. On nearing his home Private Neville was met by the Rev. I. G. Sanders and in the afternoon he was entertained by Mrs. Walker Heneage. at Coker Court. Later in the evening Private Neville returned to the Convalescent Home, where he will remain for another three weeks

In May 1945 East Coker celebrated the return of Henry Neville who had been a prisoner of war in Germany for five years. Sadly, four years earlier, his brother Eddie Neville, a Private in the Home Guard, was killed by a bomb that fell on Yeovil on the 26th March 1941. At Eddie's funeral the coffin was carried by his comrades in the East Coker platoon, and his name appears on the war memorial in St Michael's church.

A Farewell Letter

The incumbency of Ivor Sanders, the vicar of East Coker, coincided with the war years. In September 1947 he wrote this farewell letter to the parish he had served.

WHAT days – and nights – were those in the early days of war! I came to East Coker actually in the early spring of 1940. So that you might almost say that my incumbency has been the wartime incumbency of the war of 1939–45. And we have seen great changes together in that time: strenuous days – and strenuous nights – both in the dark and dreadful days, and again when the tide of war began to turn; and near to the coast as we are, when night marauders went overhead almost every night; enemy bombers to begin with, going to Bristol, Bath, Weston-Super-Mare, Cardiff and South Wales; later streams of planes going south instead, to Brest for the Scharnhorst and the Gneisnau; and then at last those unforgettable streams of lights in the twilight skies and all through the night on their way to Normandy.

What comings and goings of troops too, within the village itself, and at the Court. How well I remember Mrs Heneage saying 'Well, you see I seem to collect brigadiers, you must come and meet them'. Later it was American officers – 'hands across the waters' – beneath her ever-hospitable roof: and we met them too, and have many interesting memories of what we now so blatantly, or so cynically, call World War II. Then, of course, all our evacuees and what numbers of them I prepared for confirmation together with the children of our own parish, so many of whom I had so constantly about me in those war years. One could then: there were not so many counter-attractions!

Nor may we ever forget those harrowing but halcyon days when Dunkirk came even to East Coker, and 'men from the beaches' slept away their weariness, and were fed, beneath the shady trees and lilacs of the Paddock. You remember the almost heart-breaking loveliness of that first spring of war?

But perhaps we sometimes forget that we had great times in those days at the church. But some day, when I too am only a name, one of the vicars of 'the good old days' as they will be by then, our children grown staid and white will say so too. For in the desperate days, 1940,

On the 8th September 1945 East Coker had its Victory party. Villagers in fancy dress gathered at the New Inn *and then made their way to North Coker House where a party was held for 700 people. There were teas and games in the afternoon; as darkness fell the lawn was flood-lit for dancing, and a bonfire, with an effigy of Hitler on top, was set alight.*

1941, 1942, the Days of National Prayer saw the churches full. Man's extremity was God's opportunity it seemed with a vengeance! Full, and more than full I must remind you. How well I remember one, the first I think, when the church already full and the west door open (in just such glorious weather as this) the rest of the congregation stood out on the gravel paths of the Court drive.

All through the war (or until we grew cocksure in our own material power), despite the black-out, despite the Sunday afternoon evensongs we never really liked, we kept up a good standard of church attendance. This is largely forgotten now; but it will be remembered in days to come.

Armistice Day, 1946

In his book, A Country Reporter, *David Foot writes about changing attitudes in post-war East Coker.*

That evening, on the day I left school, I pondered for the first time on the way the village was changing. East Coker tugged at me emotionally. Without being able to articulate the sensation, I knew that post-war attitudes were different, more defiant. The hierarchical levels were disappearing. Village boys were back from the fighting in France and Italy, looking older and more cynical: saying radical things their fathers would never have dreamed of saying...

There were 43 members of the local branch of the British Legion who grouped up outside the headquarters, a quarter of a mile from the church. Some of them had pinned their medals to their faded lapels; some were in their demob suits. Almost all looked hollow-cheeked and serious. They lined up in three ranks with a minimum of formality. No question of shortest-on-the-left, tallest-on-the-right. Officers lined up with Privates, of which there were many more. 'By the left, quick march!' ordered someone with a quiet, self-conscious voice. It was almost as if he had forgotten what he used to say. And they moved off, all of them instinctively in step, standard-bearer at the head. They didn't swing their arms high but the old drill-square discipline had not deserted them. They were all of a sudden consumed with patriotism and sad memories. The rest of us walked behind them, equally serious and contemplative.

To celebrate the end of the war, Mr and Mrs C. Maudslay of North Coker House presented every household with an aluminium horseshoe hanging from a red, white and blue cord. Cyril Maudslay was Chairman and managing director of the Birmingham Aluminium Casting Company. He was also Chairman of Sterling Metals Ltd of Coventry which cast the majority of landing wheels for British aircraft during the war. Victory horseshoes can still be seen nailed to walls or doorways around the village.

In the church the flag was lowered with reverence and the names of 31 men from the parish, who had lost their lives in two world wars, were slowly read out... 'AB Albert Ackerman, RN Division; Gunner John Baker, RM Artillery; Private John Boucher, Grenadier Guards; Private Henry Farnham, Dorset Regiment; Captain Howard Helyar, Rifle Battalion; Lance-Sergeant Walter English, Somerset Light Infantry...'.

The Estate is Sold

Colonel Godfrey Walker-Heneage had died on the 6th May 1939, before the outbreak of war; his widow Dorothy Walker-Heneage (née Helyar) died on the 15th June 1947. At the funeral her coffin was borne from the church by six old employees and tenants (W. Dunham, J. Dunford, Frank Foot, Bert Turner, J. Hughes, and J. Pitcher). For someone who had always loved the trees on the estate, it was fitting

Major John David William Graham Walker-Heneage, MBE, of Coker Court. Originally intended for a career in the Navy, he attended the Royal Naval Colleges at Osborne and Dartmouth, before going through Sandhurst and receiving a commission in the 3rd Battalion, Grenadier Guards – his father's regiment. He left the Army in 1928 because of illness and joined Fortnum & Mason, becoming managing director, but rejoined his regiment on the outbreak of war. He served with the Guards throughout the 1939–45 war, including the liberation of France and Germany. Major Heneage died on the 9th August 1950.

that Dorothy's grave was lined with moss gathered from the woods. Two years after her death the Western Gazette *for the 6th May 1949 announces that the bulk of the Coker Court estate has been sold to Green's of Chichester.*

Coker Court Estate Sold

Death Duties and Taxation

Most of the tenants of Coker Court Estate have received letters notifying them of the sale of the property. Major David Walker-Heneage, who inherited the estate on the death of Mrs. Dorothy Walker Heneage in 1947, has told the tenants that the burden of death duties and taxation has caused him regretfully to take this step after many generations of ownership.

The *Western Gazette* is informed that The Court itself the policies and park, with certain agricultural land adjoining, has been retained by Major Heneage and will remain in his occupation. The property sold, which includes 10 farms and covers over 2,000 acres, represents one of the most important sales of agricultural land in Somerset for some years. Negotiations were carried out by Messrs. Jackson-Stops & Staff, Yeovil.

A Time to Rebuild

WHAT happened then, the estate started to break up. Green's of Chichester, who were timber merchants, bought most of the Coker Court estate, with the whole of Coker Wood, Pen Wood and a part of Spin Wood. Green's had their own personnel, mostly Latvians and Lithuanians, timber people from the Baltic states most of them, they were here in the Army during the war. There were a lot of them worked around this area timber-felling. That was the sort of job they did where they came from. Axes and saws, that's all they used. After a few years, when Green's had taken all the timber they wanted, which was only the best of it – oak, beech and ash – they decided to sell the estate.

The railways had gone into decline because all through the war years they'd taken thousands and thousands of troop-trains and no money had ever been spent on them. Everything was in an absolute state of ruination. Nothing had been done – railways, roads (imagine the roads with tanks and transporters on them), houses. With the massive bomb damage in London and places like that, the timber was used for rebuilding houses.

RIGHT: *Clearing Pincushion Corner, 1949: this plantation was a popular place for villagers to go and listen to the nightingales sing in the evening. It is said to have got its name because the ground was cushioned with a soft bed of moss.Men from the village sawmills pictured here (l–r) Paddy Percal, Tony Younger, Arthur Long and Pete Granger.*

BELOW: *Alb, Eddie and Fred Hughes preparing their nets and snares ready to go to the tiny Channel Island of Herm to catch the thousands of rabbits which were infesting it in 1947. Herm had been under German occupation during the war. The three brothers took half a ton of equipment – traps, snares and nets – and expected to catch 600 rabbits a day, which would be sent by boat to other Channel Islands for food.*

The 'Coker Co-Eds', 1950: perhaps inspired by the Gang Shows that visited East Coker during the war, a group of teenagers staged their own variety shows doing all the writing, producing, and performing themselves. Two shows, 'Showtime Follies' and 'All at Sea', even toured surrounding towns and villages. (l–r): Joan Purchase, Dennis Frampton, Rosemary Neville, Ivan Lock, Betty Snaydon, Len Stocker, Lil Charles, David Foot, Dorothy Rendell, Peter Denney, Catherine Gill, Dave Mortimer, and Daphne Quick.

East Coker School's pantomime production in 1947 was Aladdin: (l–r) back row: Vera Quick, Sheila Robins, Jean Gray, Don Murley, Eric Walker, Peter Burgess, Gwen Edwards, - Thorne, Pamela Robins, Janet Spencer; middle row: Heather Lacey, - , Marion Loader, Miriam Jones, Graham Colley, Sylvia Harris, Jean Lock, Daphne Quick, Iris Axe, Rosemary Neville, Cecil Turner, Michael Walker, Jill Mintern, Helen Neville; kneeling at front: Alan Stevens, - , Tony Quick, R. Harris, David Lee, John Cambridge, - .

Gregg's Riding School, Furzy Knap, c.1947: the school was established in 1946 by Leslie Dicks – here his daughter, Amelia, is pictured in a basket saddle riding Molly the pony. In the background is one of the Nissen huts used by the RAF who manned a barrage-balloon site nearby. In 1996 Amelia Bennett and her family, together with many friends and former pupils, celebrated 'Golden Greggs', the 50th anniversary of the riding school.

Robert Oaksford showing children from the village school around the sawmills. He bought the business from the Perry family in 1937 with the object of producing specialist joinery in addition to the sawmill trade. With the outbreak of war, joinery production was suspended for war requirements, and the sawmills produced railway sleepers, oak and softwoods for railway-truck construction and repair, and timber props for coal-mines. A new company, The West of England Saw Service Ltd was set up on the premises to service the saws and keep up the speed of production, and handled saws from sawmills throughout the West Country. When the war ended the sawmills received timber from the Riechwald Forest in Westphalia as part of war reparations: the timber was full of shrapnel and an 18-foot long band-saw would snap if it hit a piece. The sawmills were sold by the Oaksford family in 1975, and four years later stopped trading.

Above: *The 16th May 1952: looking across the future site of the Sutton Bingham reservoir. A dam would be built to impound 540 million gallons of water, creating a reservoir that could supply two million gallons of water a day. The scale of the project was impressive with over half a million tons of earth moved, and 40,000 tons of concrete laid. The scheme involved a total of 264 acres of land, and eight families living in Sutton Bingham had to be re-housed. The construction of the reservoir was completed at the end of 1954.*

Left: *November 1952: the first task was to dig a cut-off trench, six feet wide and 75 feet deep, to reach a natural, impervious layer of clay. The trench was dug using shovels and, working deep in the bottom of the trench, if the workmen looked up they could see the stars in the sky, even at mid-day. The cut-off trench was filled with puddled clay in a concrete casing. If an air bubble was found in a sample, they had to puddle the clay all over again.*

(Photographs on this page by Maurice Bramwell)

St Michael's church choir as it appeared in the Bristol Evening Post *of the 28th June 1949. The choir had recently increased in size from 20 to nearly 50. Mrs Beatrice Hackwell, who was the church organist and choir mistress from 1925 to 1952, stands to the right. Her assistant, Mary Baker, took over from her in 1952 and has been the organist at St Michael's since then. The choir: (l–r) girls, back row, Mary Baker, Ann Lewis, Joan Purchase, Dorothy Rendell, Muriel Hill; front row: Jean Lock, Stella Loder, Betty Snaydon, Rosemary Neville, Marion Andrews, Betty Giles, Lily Charles; men and boys, back row: David Lacey, Clifford Snaydon, Arthur Hackwell, Roy Snaydon, David Foot, Walter Stevens, Paul Harvey; front row: Robin Baker, Tony Quick, Michael Walker, Nigel Boucher, David Morris, Malcolm Lee, Johnny Hodges, Royston Harriss, Jimmy Harriss, Ronald Smith, Jimmy Jones, Robin Harvey, Michael Jessop.*

The Reverend George Mullard, vicar of East Coker from 1948 until 1979, pictured here with Joseph Whetham. One of the new vicar's first undertakings was the renovation of the old Mission Room on Long Furlong Lane (now The Old Chapel) which had been closed for ten years. On the 18th October 1948 it was re-opened as St Luke's mission church, Burton, and provided an alternative place of worship especially for older people living in North Coker and Burton.

EAST COKER

This poem was written by C.G. Rendell of Hunt's House, in September 1943.
In the middle of wartime, he speaks of the timeless beauty of the parish.

'The lines are fallen unto me in pleasant places' PSALM 16, v.6.

I gaze at thee from 'Redlands'
Across the farmland and moor,
When refreshing dew lies on the grass
And the night is scarcely o'er;
The herdsman's call and the quiet flock,
While the lark sings to God its theme,
The sun's first rays in the Eastern sky
Unfold to me the scene.

Nearer I draw to the valley
Where the stream its course doth trace;
Then cross to the wooded hillside -
Thou art nestled at its base -
That hill adorned with stately trees
Elm, Oak, and Cedar's bole,
Shading Church and Court, and humble Cot
From 'Primrose Hill' to 'Darvole'.

I see thee in the Springtime
Like a bride in lilac dress,
On carpet bright of Daffodils
With Violets at thy breast;
Where Peacocks in their splendour walk
And grace the Court so fair,
Laburnam, May, Wisteria,
With fragrance fill the air.

I see thee in the Summer
When soft winds blow from the sea,
Through 'Isles' and 'Pen' and 'Springclose'
O'er 'Sleight', 'Tellis Hill', and free
Over the corn where the passing fan
Causes a wave and the moving crest
Bends, as if God's providing Hand
Softly the crop has blessed.

I see thee in the Autumn
When woodland tints flame near
The reapers working in the field,
And the Squirrel stores her fare.
The Swift and the Swallow gather
Ere Southward they depart,
When rise the song of Harvest Home
To Heaven from thankful hearts.

I see thee in the Winter
When trees are bared for strife,
And snow winds blow o'er 'Burton Cross'
Or from 'Aldon' in their might;
But the pure white Snowdrop, too, I see
With its promise of the Spring;
While hopes are high, and hearts are brave
When the bells ring the New Year in.

T.S. Eliot

T.S. ELIOT wrote the poem 'East Coker', one of the *Four Quartets*, in 1940 having visited the village on only a few occasions. East Coker had been the home of Eliot's ancestors until their emigration to New England in the late 17th century, and this was the connection that drew him back.

On his first visit to East Coker in 1936, T.S. Eliot came to see the memorial stained-glass window to the Eliot family, which had recently been placed in St Michael's church by an American cousin. He had stayed in Yeovil on the previous night, and walked from there to East Coker to visit the church, also stopping at the *New Inn* (now the *Helyar Arms*) where he was amused to find 'I made so good an impression upon the landlady of the *New Inn*, that she asked me, was I not a cousin of Colonel Heneage?'

EAST COKER

"LITERATURE OF THE WEST"

In this series on the B.B.C. West of England Home Service on Sunday next, at 10.38 p.m., and repeated on Monday afternoon, T. S. Eliot will read his poem, "East Coker." The village was the home of Mr. Eliot's ancestors.

From the Western Gazette 15th March 1946.

The following year, T.S. Eliot called on Sir Matthew Nathan at West Coker Manor. If walking from West Coker to the church at East Coker, he would have taken the lane that narrows and climbs between faces of sandstone rock from the crossroads at Yew Hill Rocks – perhaps this was the inspiration for the 'deep insistent lane' of the poem. T.S. Eliot's last visit to East Coker is said to have been in the late summer of 1939, when he took some photographs of the village and church, and gathered the impressions that he later set down in the poem 'East Coker'.

T.S. Eliot died on the 4th January 1965, and his ashes were buried in St Michael's church on Easter Sunday, the 17th April 1965, near the Eliot window that he had first come to see nearly 30 years earlier. At a memorial service in the church five months later, on the 26th September 1965, the 77th anniversary of the birth of T.S. Eliot, a memorial plaque to the poet was unveiled bearing the first and last lines of his poem 'East Coker':

> In my beginning is my end
> In my end is my beginning

The publisher, Sir Rupert Hart-Davis, gave an address in tribute to T.S. Eliot, closing with these words:

> 'Now the end and the beginning are one, and as you pass this tablet on the wall, say a prayer, by all means, for the great poet it commemorates, but above all, say a prayer for the great and good man whom we remember today, on his birthday, with gratitude, and with love'.

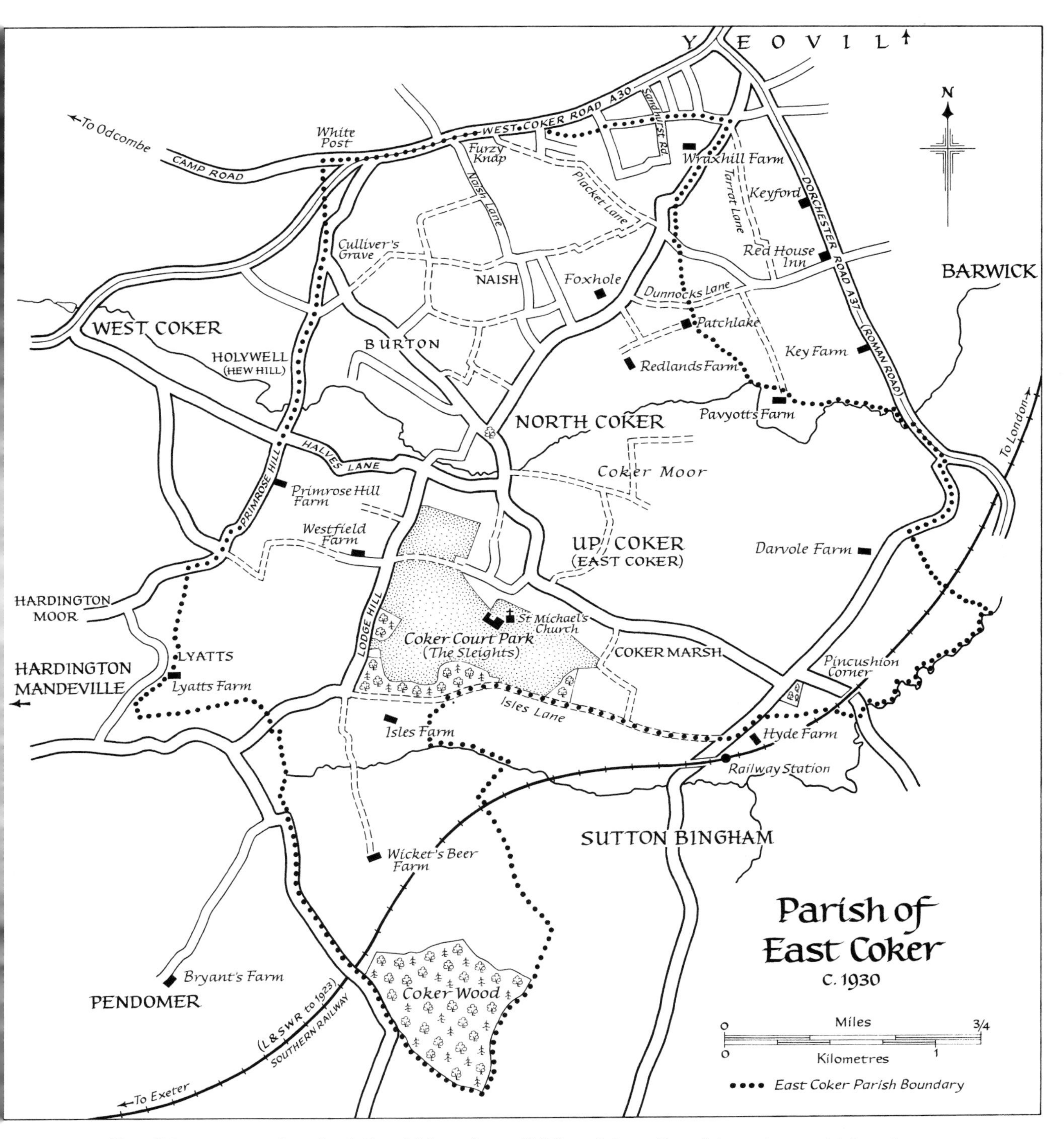

East Coker c.1930, when the civil parish boundary still followed the outline of the ancient parish boundary, and what is now the Lower East Coker Road was the main route from the village into Yeovil.

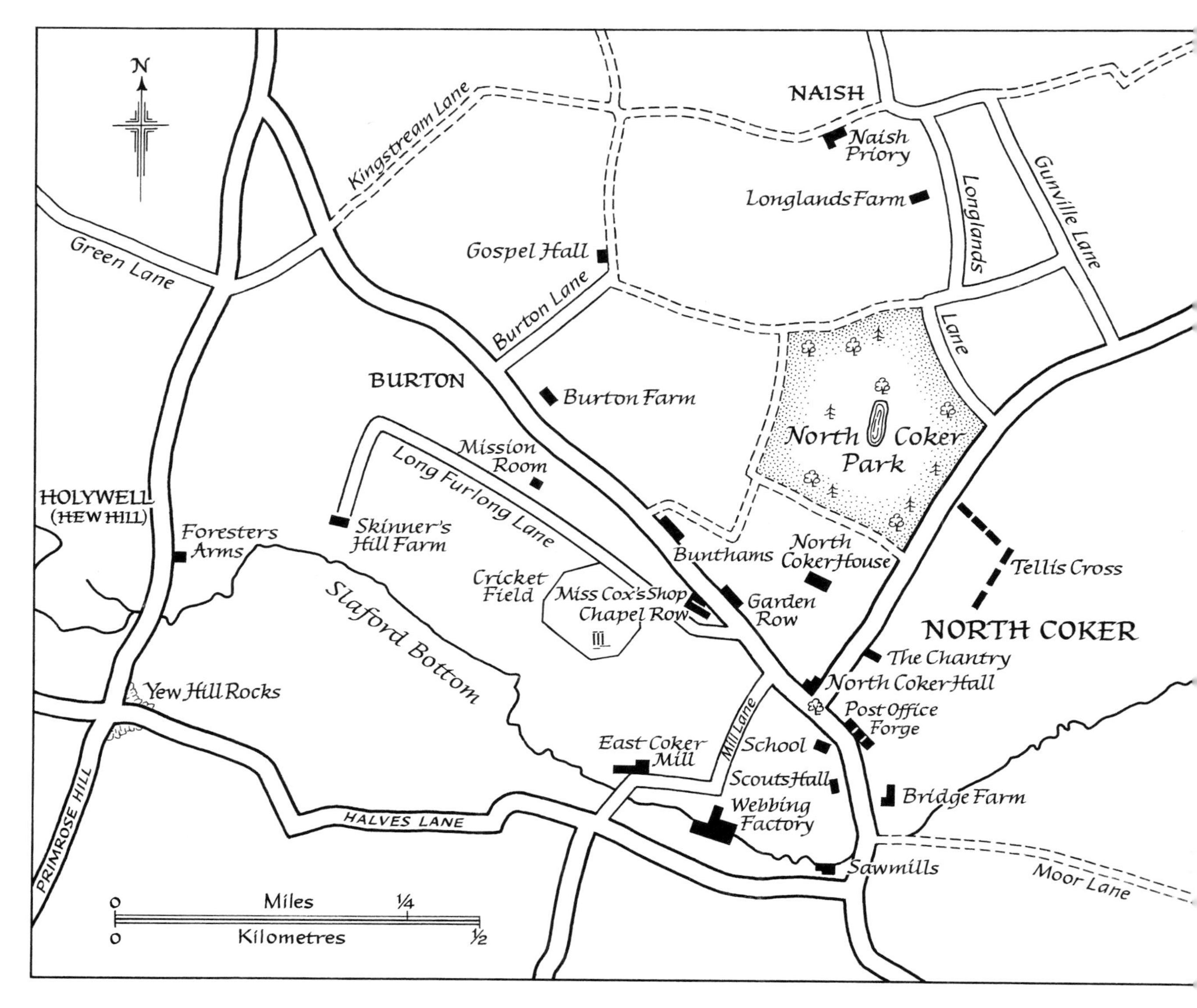

Maps of North Coker and Up Coker c.1930 showing some of the places that appear in this book.

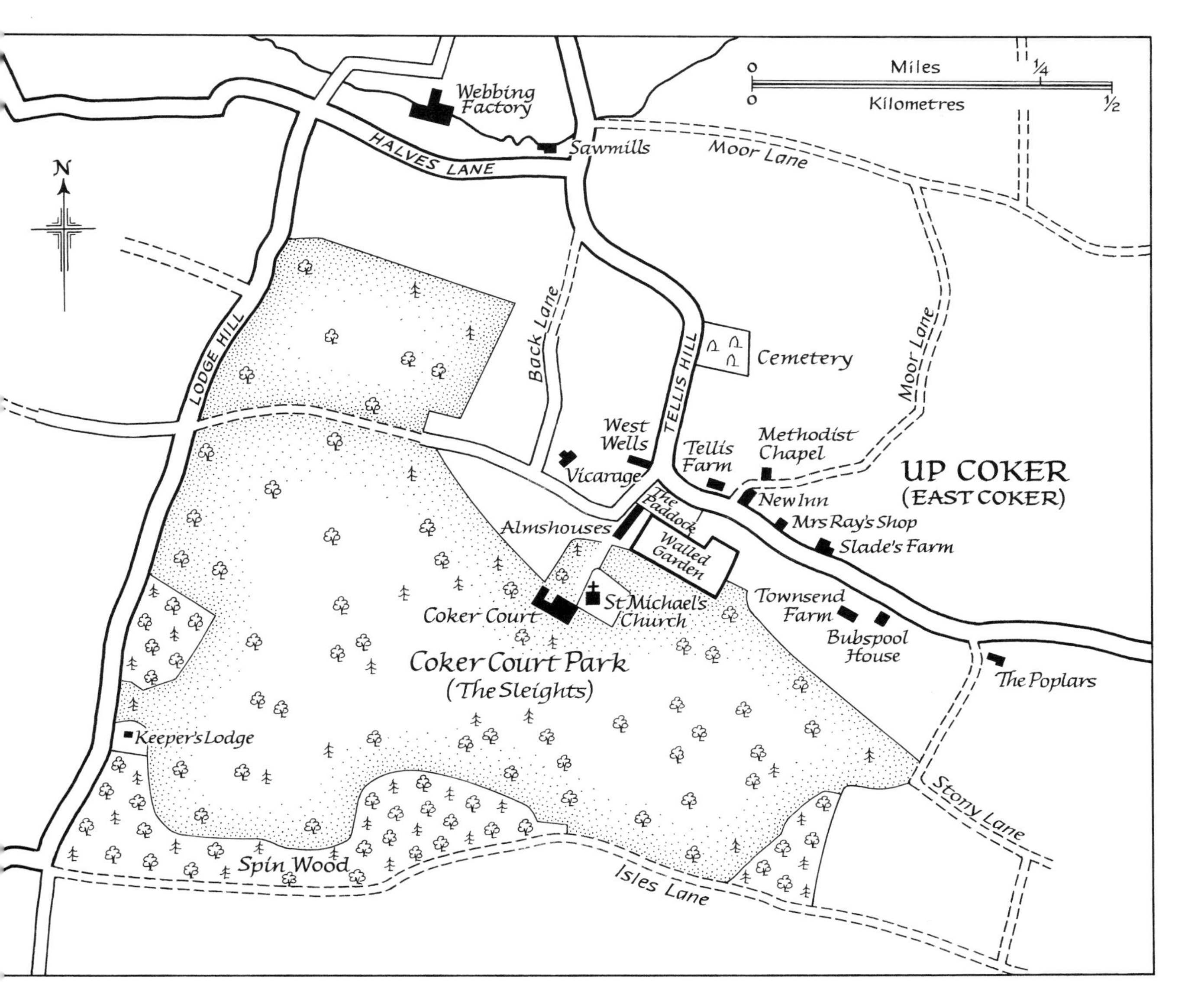

In the 19th century the area of the village closest to the parish church was called Up Coker, a place-name that still survives, although East Coker is more commonly used nowadays.

Sources

Sources include: taped interviews; family photographs and papers; the *Western Gazette* (held on microfilm at Yeovil Library) and other newspapers; *Kelly's Directories* (in the Charles Tite Collection, Yeovil Library); odd copies of the *Parish News*; Parish Council and Women's Institute minutes; British Legion records; school log books; sale catalogues; parish registers and church records; gravestones and war memorial; Ordnance Survey maps (modern maps at Yeovil Library, earlier maps at Somerset Record Office, Taunton).

A starting point for me when planning interviews:

Caroline Osborn, *A Practical Guide to Reminiscence Work* (Age Exchange, 1990)

When we Were Young, Memories of Growing up in South Somerset – A Record of a Rural Reminiscence Project, compiled and edited by Pam Schweitzer, Sarah Clevely and Paul Swatridge (Age Exchange, 1990)

Both the above from:
Age Exchange Reminiscence Centre,
11 Blackheath Village, London SE3 9LA

Some books and booklets I have come across in making this compilation:

Bill Andrews, *The Hand That Bowled Bradman* (Macdonald, 1973)

John S. Creasey and Sadie B. Ward, *The Countryside Between the Wars 1918–1940* (B.T. Batsford, 1984) p.89: buttermaking at Longlands Farm

Nora E. Davies, *In My End is My Beginning* (Five Arches Press, Tenby, Dyfed, 1976)

C. Day Lewis, poem 'At East Coker' from *The Whispering Roots* (Jonathan Cape, 1970)

T.S. Eliot, 'East Coker' in *Collected Poems 1909–1962* (Faber and Faber, 1975)

David Foot, *A Country Reporter* (David & Charles, 1990)

David Foot, *Beyond Bat & Ball* (Good Books, 1993)

Cecil C. Foulkes (in collaboration with the Revd David Hunt), *A Guide to St Michael's Church* (St Michael's church booklet, 1987)

Beatrice A. Hackwell, *The Story of Our Village* (October 1953, reprinted Swift Printing, East Coker 1979)

Margery Hall and Eileen Wilson (eds), *Our Village Then and Now 1918–1988* (East Coker Women's Institute, 1988)

Mac Hawkins, *Somerset at War 1939–1945* (Hawk Editions, 1996)

Dom. Ethelbert Horne, 'Somerset Holy Wells', *Somerset Folk Series* No.12 (Somerset Folk Press, 1923)

Somerset Federation of Women's Institutes, *Somerset Within Living Memory* (Countryside Books, 1992)

T.S. Eliot, poet 1888–1965, Foreword by the Revd George Mullard (St Michael's church booklet, 1967) includes address given by Sir Rupert Hart-Davis at memorial service for T.S. Eliot

H.V. Taylor, *The Apples of England* (Crosby Lockwood & Son Ltd, 1948) p.95: Coker Seedling

Violet Trefusis, *Don't Look Round* (Hamish Hamilton Ltd, 1989) includes a wonderful chapter covering her time living in East and West Coker during the Second World War

Bristol Evening Post
28/6/1949. East Coker: Village of Silent Questions – and Oddities (Life Around Somerset Churches, No.2)
16/11/1966. Cider making at Isles Farm
12/10/1970. Hereditary blacksmith hammers away

Bristol Evening World
7/9/1934. Dairy classes at East Coker school

Country Life
2nd January 1909. Article on Coker Court

The Farmer and Stockbreeder
13/4/1937. 'Jesse Crumpler, North Coker, Nr Yeovil, produces TT Milk and Farm Butter'

Somerset Archaeological and Natural History Society Proceedings
Vol.XVII. Engraving of Naish Priory

Somerset Countryman
October–December 1956, Vol.18, No.12, 'Portrait of East Coker' by David Foot

Western Gazette
An invaluable source of information, particularly in the Local and District News section

Radio: BBC West of England programme
Transcript of West Country Houses No.VI 'Coker Court'. Devised by Norah Richardson; production by W. Farquharson Small. Transmission: broadcast in the West of England programme from Bristol on Monday 21/11/1938, 8.25–9 pm.
Playback: Thursday 1/12/1938, 3.15–3.50 pm. (no recording survives)

British Library
Letters from T.S. Eliot to members of Tandy family 1936–7. Add.MS 71002

English Folk Dance and Song Society
Copies of songs, singing games and Ribbon Dance music collected by Cecil Sharp, from Vaughan Williams Memorial Library, English Folk Dance and Song Society, Cecil Sharp House, London. Original manuscripts at Clare College, Cambridge

Somerset Record Office, Taunton
Advert for Drake's Webbing Factory DD/X/LIV 26 G/194
East Coker Roll of Honour for the First World War D/PC/cok.e 6/3/1
Recipe book from Coker Court DD/WHh c/787. Addenda (not previously listed) 4

Correspondence or queries can be sent to: Abigail Shepherd, Coker Books, P.O. Box 2305, Bath BA1 5XY. I would be interested to hear about other old photographs of East Coker and its villagers, or pieces of historical information regarding the parish.
I hope to publish a history of East Coker: if you wish to be kept informed please send your details to the above address; for those living in the parish, any announcement will be made through the *East Coker Society Newsletter*.

COVER ILLUSTRATIONS

FRONT: A painting of East Coker post office in 1922 by Constantine R. Shand. Given to the Village Hall by Mrs Ivy Farnham.

BACK: East Coker School, *c.*1906. The school was built *c.*1850 by the Helyar family of Coker Court. The Helyar crest can be seen on the front of the building just below the school bell.